PRAISE FOR

PUREDESIRE

This is a most important book. Ted Roberts does a masterful job reminding us that the Church is filled with people who struggle with sexual addictions and pornography. He shows us it's possible to take a positive and hopeful approach to dealing with one of the most damaging addictions in the world.

JIM BURNS, PH.D.

PRESIDENT, NATIONAL INSTITUTE OF YOUTH MINISTRY
SAN JUAN CAPISTRANO, CALIFORNIA

Ted Roberts has demonstrated faithfulness, integrity, compassion and wisdom as a leading pastor in our region. His longstanding pursuit of purity for a culture set on impurity has been courageous. This book is honest, biblical and practical. *Pure Desire* is especially beneficial for the pastoral leader or counselor and those struggling with any level of impurity.

FRANK DAMAZIO

PASTOR, CITY BIBLE CHURCH
PORTLAND, OREGON

I've looked for this book for 10 years. *Pure Desire* is must-reading for every pastor who has experienced sexual temptation or works with men who are struggling with an addiction to sex or sexually explicit material. If you want to help strengthen marriages and families in your congregation, read this book and find practical help that will release the grace and power of Christ through you and healing to your people.

DR. JERRY R. KIRK

PRESIDENT, NATIONAL COALITION FOR THE PROTECTION OF CHILDREN AND FAMILIES
COCHAIRMAN, RELIGIOUS ALLIANCE AGAINST PORNOGRAPHY

Ted has an uncanny abililty to help anyone who has been broken at tender points through life's struggles or who has been blasted with hellfire and has crashed and burned. Count on discoveries in *Pure Desire* that will bring fruitfullness and fulfillment in one of today's most environmentally threatened areas—human sexuality.

JACK W. HAYFORD

PRESIDENT, INTERNATIONAL FOURSQUARE CHURCHES
CHANCELLOR, THE KING'S COLLEGE AND SEMINARY
FOUNDING PASTOR, THE CHURCH ON THE WAY

Every time I have heard Ted Roberts speak, I've been moved by his commitment to Christ and his love for people. In *Pure Desire*, he again demonstrates his amazing ability to crawl down into the trenches of life, put his arm around the hurting, broken and bound, and by the liberating love of God, bring healing to desperate hearts.

RON MEHL

PASTOR, BEAVERTON FOURSQUARE CHURCH
BEAVERTON, OREGON

I have prayed with multitudes of brokenhearted wives whose Christian husbands have sexual addictions. It is a very real problem within the Church today. This boldly written book will equip pastors to offer hope and healing to these men—and their wives. *Pure Desire* by Dr. Ted Roberts is a book I can recommend to those hurting families.

QUIN SHERRER

COAUTHOR OF *A WOMAN'S GUIDE TO GETTING THROUGH TOUGH TIMES*

Sexual addiction in the Church is more prevalent than most people have ever thought. Yet there are too few resources which adequately deal with this heartbreaking issue. Ted Roberts's uniquely biblical approach to healing and hope makes this book a great asset to both the struggler and the helper.

DR. JOHN TOWNSEND

AUTHOR OF *HIDING FROM LOVE* AND *WHO'S PUSHING YOUR BUTTONS?*
COAUTHOR OF *BOUNDARIES*
COFOUNDER, CLOUD-TOWNSEND COMMUNICATIONS

As a fighter pilot in Vietnam, Ted Roberts didn't shy away from battle. As a pastor and now an author, I am not surprised to find him on the front lines of a major spiritual battle. Sexual addiction isn't a minor skirmish being fought by a few in the Church; it is a life-or-death struggle faced by many. If you're serious about protecting yourself from falling, or ready to help God's people face this issue and finally find God's hope and healing, read this book!

JOHN TRENT, PH.D.

CHAIRMAN AND CEO, MINISTRY INSIGHTS INTERNATIONAL
PRESIDENT, ENCOURAGING WORDS AND STRONGFAMILIES.COM
PHOENIX, ARIZONA

Pure Desire is a must-read for those who need insight and practical tools that will help them lead others to sexual health and fulfillment. Dr. Ted Roberts has simplified complex clinical concepts about sexual addiction, offering sound advice through self-revealing and captivating stories, minus any platitudes. I have seen these principles in action within the church body, and they work! Every church leader needs a copy of this book. This message is timely. You'll want to absorb all you can—and then spread the word.

PAM VREDEVELT

AUTHOR AND LICENSED PROFESSIONAL COUNSELOR
GRESHEM, OREGON

I love Ted Roberts and East Hill Church. Ted's do-or-die commitment to honesty and the church's swallow-hard-here-we-go followers are changing people. Together, Ted and East Hill Church genuinely embody their motto of "being Christ's hands extended to a hurting world." *Pure Desire* is just one example. This book is an openhearted approach to freedom from the sexual addiction that is so destructively rampant among Christian men. Don't face this monster alone, guys! Here is hope and healing. As a pastor, I wish I'd had this book's ministry-wisdom many years ago.

STU WEBER

SENIOR PASTOR, GOOD SHEPHERD CHURCH
BORING, OREGON

PUREDESIRE

How one man's triumph can help others
break free from sexual temptation

TED ROBERTS

BETHANYHOUSE

a division of Baker Publishing Group
Minneapolis, Minnesota

© 1999 by Ted Roberts

Published by Bethany House Publishers
11400 Hampshire Avenue South
Bloomington, Minnesota 55438
www.bethanyhouse.com

Bethany House Publishers is a division of
Baker Publishing Group, Grand Rapids, Michigan

Bethany House edition published 2014
ISBN 978-0-7642-1566-7

First Edition, 1999
Second Edition, 2008

Previously published by Regal Books

Printed in the United States of America

The Library of Congress has cataloged the first edition as follows:
    Roberts, Ted.
     Pure desire / Ted Roberts.
       p. cm.
     ISBN 978-08307-4540-1 (trade paper)
     1. Sex addiction—Religious aspects—Christianity. I. Title
    BV4596.S42R635 1999
    241′.66—dc21
                                       99-11351

NOTE: The circumstances of certain events and names of individuals and locations have been changed to protect the privacy of the persons involved and to maintain confidentiality.

17   18   19   20   7   6   5   4

Contents

Section II: **A Place of Healing**

Foreword
By Stephen Arterburn

I don't know of any plague to ever reach into the homes and families all over the world and create as much damage or heartache than the struggle with lust, affair, pornography, perversion and sexual addiction. It seems that everywhere I look, it gets worse and worse. The Internet exploded the problem, and now cell phones transport pornography more portably than the computer and facilitates affairs with greater accessibility and secrecy.

Anyone who has not protected themselves from the temptations of the world has not done well in this new world of all-access, all-the-time, all-over-the-world.

When Hugh Hefner created *Playboy* magazine in 1953, he began a very successful campaign to convince the world that lust, sexual desire outside of marriage, and sex any way and all ways were not such bad things. He convinced people his magazine was harmless and simply full of beauty made by God. He successfully stripped the shame from a shameful industry that exploits men and women for profit. So it is no wonder that so many men and women have found themselves with a severe problem with no one to reach out to and no hope for change. At least that is how they feel.

Fred Stoeker and I wrote the *Every Man's Battle* series in 2001, and I was doubtful we would sell even 5,000 copies. Three million copies later, I am aware of just how desperate people are to find hope for their compartmentalized, shameful sexual lives. Millions live in shame and separation from God and their families and are even separated from the real person they were designed to be. If you have ever found yourself in this place, you know what it is like to not even know yourself anymore.

Fred and I wrote for those who had not quite crossed the line into sexual addiction. We wanted to reach those who were messing around but whose lives were not totally messed up. We were scratching the surface, and there were a lot of people who obviously needed to hear the message. I am glad I was part of that project, but it did not solve the problem for everyone who struggles.

I have been asked to look at numerous manuscripts, but I have never seen one as powerful for this particular problem as Ted's work. I think a lot of people are going to be reached and see the need to turn things around. I am so glad for Ted's attitude of comprehensive study and practical application. This book could change the lives of millions, but, more importantly, it could change your life. There are answers here. Are you ready to implement them into your life? I pray that you are.

Stephen Arterburn
Author and Host of *New Life Live*

Introduction

This is one introduction you definitely need to read!

There are myriad books about sexual addiction; this book is not just about that issue. There have been thousands of publications and manuals written about spiritual warfare and bondage; this book is not just about those issues.

Over the years, there has been a tidal wave of articles, books and tapes about the new millennium and the new battles that the Church will have to fight. *Pure Desire* is more than a description of a supposed battle to come. Instead, it is an open declaration that the battle has already begun, and the Church has not yet risen to the challenge.

In the same breath, I want to stress that this book is not for the spiritually elite, the super intercessor, or the fearless and tearless in the faith. It is for church leaders or pastors whose hearts are breaking over the sexual bondage they know is present in the Church, because people have trusted them enough to come for help. However, the leaders have a problem. They don't know exactly what to do. They give the standard answers, but in many cases the people they care for are still deeply embedded in the struggle.

There are excellent books calling Christians to holiness and purity, and I will refer to several. They are good books to read, yet they don't seem to be able to break the grip of what has hold of the person. The pastors or leaders know they need some additional practical firepower to help beleaguered individuals. This book is designed to give pragmatic, spiritual, heat-seeking missiles against hell; it can set a *church* free to begin hurting the adversary over this issue rather than being the victim.

This book isn't for the legalist who thinks the total answer to the soul's cry for purity is simply to try harder. They say, "If people were more committed to Christ, they wouldn't have sexual problems." Although this book works well with those who have recently come to Christ, it is primarily a book for those who have tried to build sexual holiness in their lives and failed . . . and failed . . . and failed. It is for inconsistent, shaky believers who have guts enough to admit that no matter how good they may look on the outside, their hearts are far from what they desire them to be with respect to sexual purity. Many of these people, despite growing up in the Church, have been trapped in the very pit of hell. *Pure Desire* will give these folks real hope and help. Within these pages are answers that have honestly worked for hundreds already.

The book's practical truths for healing didn't come from the hallowed halls of academia, but out of the grit and grime of attempting to follow Christ in the struggles of daily life. They are eternal, biblical and have been flight-tested in the severest conditions imaginable.

This book is also for shattered souls of mates who are puzzled, shamed and wounded by their husband's or wife's sexual bondage and secret life. Sexual sin and bondage is rarely about sex alone. It's about a family system, a way of seeing the world and dealing with pain. It's about how a person's inner "software" processes struggles within the soul. Therefore, sexual healing and health is often a family issue. These pages will give real understanding of a mate's inner battles. This book provides hope for establishing healthy personal boundaries. It will give the soul in Christ an anchor amid rough waters. It will give a new appreciation for Christ's healing power and presence.

The most challenging part of the reading will be learning how to think in new ways about old, explosive terms, especially if you've grown up in the Church. Christians frequently use language that draws false lines of distinction. I can understand how those lines were drawn, because we no longer live in a society based on a Judeo-Christian view of reality (in many ways the society has become hostile to a biblical perspective).

For example, some sections of the psychological/counseling community dismiss the reality of spiritual warfare and bondage, especially about sexual issues. This view makes it impossible for them to bring real freedom when spiritual bondage is present. Yet on the other side of the issue, some Christians automatically cast aside the terminology and concept of addiction as being just so much "psycho-babble." The difficulty with this stance is in ending up blind to the dynamics of addiction which the apostle Paul clearly delineated in Romans 7.

This book will challenge and provoke you to see the *full scope* of the swirling and vicious battle for sexual purity in our day. At times this battle is filled with demonic confrontation, yet ultimately it is about our inner brokenness. We must always remember: This is a spiritual *and* physical battle. For ours is a journey of faith where the glory of God fills us each day even though we are fragile earthen vessels with feet made of clay.

Ted Roberts
Senior Pastor, East Hill Church
Gresham, Oregon

Section I

A PLACE OF HOPE

CHAPTER 1

Dr. Ted Roberts: Sex Expert?

As I stood at the front of a room filled with Asian faces, I knew how "American" I looked to them. These men, who were mostly Christian businessmen, had gathered at a country club in Hong Kong to hear me speak.

The gentleman introducing me said some rather flattering things, which made me a bit uncomfortable. Then he dropped the bomb: "Gentlemen, I want you to know that Dr. Roberts is an expert on the issue of human sexuality, so feel free to ask him any question you might have on the subject."

My initial thought was, *Thank you, God, my wife isn't here to refute that claim!*

Before I began to speak, I took a moment to marvel at how radically my life had changed. My last visit to the Far East had been as a fighter pilot in the United States Marine Corps, trying to stay alive in the skies over Vietnam. After one particularly hellish day—during which I had "taken out" a few of the enemy firing on a forward air controller—I realized just how crazy my life had become.

I hadn't ever been much of a churchgoer, but my born-again Jewish wife hadn't given up on me. That evening as I sat, half drunk, reading her latest letter and browsing through a book she had sent me, I found myself praying. "Christ, I really don't know who You are, and I don't do this church stuff very well," I admitted, "but my life has become totally insane. So if You are there, sign me up!"

Nothing visibly miraculous happened. No lightning bolts or angels flew by, but somehow I knew my life had changed.

When I returned to the States, I still had a difficult time going to church. The people there didn't talk much about the hardships I wrestled with in the military. One day, however, my wife, Diane, convinced me to attend a Bible study with her. I figured that since I had made a commitment to Christ, at some point I would need to find out about the Bible.

You can imagine my consternation when I followed Diane into the room to find not one man in sight. Now don't get me wrong; they were nice ladies, but at the time I was a career Marine officer, and my idea of fun wasn't sitting around at a women's meeting, even if it was about the Bible.

The meeting seemed to go on forever, but eventually I sensed the leader was finally wrapping everything up. I was making plans for a quick getaway when she looked directly at me and said, "Sir, would you lead us in prayer as we close?"

Talk about being caught off guard; I had never prayed in public in my life! My entire prayer life had consisted of those moments in the air when the hours of boredom were punctuated by stark terror, and I would cry out, "Help me, God!"

Everyone in the room bowed their heads, and I sensed it must be time to pray. So, I gave it my best shot: "Lord, whatever the hell You want us to do, we're ready."

That was it—short and sweet. The reaction in the room was anything but sweet, however—more like stunned disbelief. But the study leader never missed a beat. She leaned over to me and commented, "That's the first time you've prayed in public, isn't it?" I wondered how she could be so perceptive. Then she added, "Would you like to know a prayer that God will always answer?"

"Sure," I responded.

"Then just ask God if there is anything in your life that He would like to change." I thought that sounded like a great prayer, especially since there was nothing I could think of that He would want to change in me right then and there. In fact, I thought I was doing pretty good.

That truly was my attitude at the time—I didn't have any major changes to make. However, during the next year, I discovered a number of disturbing things about myself. To begin with, I was an alcoholic. But that was just the struggle on the surface of my life. At a much deeper level, I was addicted to pornography.

In fact, my life was spinning out of control. Looking back on that time, I can see that control was a big issue with me—and precisely the reason why anger constantly simmered just below my surface.

HELL'S MASTER PLAN

Ironically, 20 years later, I found myself back in the Far East. This time I was speaking about God's grace. Now only God's goodness could pull off a transformation like that!

Yet, I didn't have long to think about God's abundant grace in my past, because I needed His grace right then. I had no idea what kind of questions would be coming my way in the next 30 to 45 minutes. These were Chinese businessmen, some of whom ran huge corporations. I wasn't familiar with their culture, and had no clue where they would be coming from. How could I respond to these men who were so different from the average American guys I had listened to for years? This was totally new terrain!

The questions came slowly at first, almost as if they were checking me out. And in a sense they were. Men don't easily talk about their sexuality, especially their struggles. After about 15 minutes, I was astounded. They asked the same questions I had answered for years in the States. They were fighting the same battles I had helped so many men deal with at home.

At that moment, a number of things came into focus. I realized what I had been seeing for the past several years. I felt like a man on a ridge line observing a gigantic ongoing spiritual battle which I had never *really seen* before. I had been so busy with the daily challenges of helping the men immediately around me in our flock, I had never seen the enormity of what was taking place.

The year before I went to Hong Kong, church leaders and pastors in Argentina asked me to speak to them about the Holy Spirit's ministry in dealing with sexual addiction. I tried with everything I had to get them to change the subject. I had been to Argentina, and I knew they had great families. Sure, sexual addiction would be an issue, but it wouldn't be nearly as severe as it was in the States, where families were experiencing disintegration.

To make a long story short, they wouldn't change the subject—and I am so glad they didn't. I ended up spending more than two hours talking and praying personally with the leaders, at times holding them in my arms as they wept and confessed incredible stories of addiction, bondage and incidents where hell was tearing apart huge ministries.

Our 10-member ministry team from my East Hill Church ministered to several Hong Kong churches throughout the week. In each church we spent hours and hours at the altar, praying and crying with individuals and families as they finally talked openly about what was destroying them. I don't know why I hadn't put the pieces together before. As I talked to those men in Hong Kong, I finally realized that over the last 10 years, in every country and in every region of the United States where I had spoken about the issue of sexual bondage, hell was tearing the Church apart.

As we progress through this century, there will be many people who will come up with all kinds of theories about the antichrist and the mark of the beast, warning us not to vote for certain kinds of legislation or not to move toward a cashless society, because we will end up with the mark of the beast on us. The mark is already on many in the Church!

In Revelation 17:5, the woman who sits on the beast is described in this way:

> This title was written on her forehead:
> MYSTERY
> BABYLON THE GREAT
> THE MOTHER OF PROSTITUTES
> AND OF THE ABOMINATIONS OF THE EARTH.

Sexual bondage in the Church and in our world is one of hell's master plans, especially in the last days. A spiritual battle rages over this issue. In the last decade, the Internet has become a stealth bomber from hell with pornography as its payload. I talk to more and more men who fight for their spiritual lives to get free from the electronic images that have taken their minds captive.

If we are honest and objective, we can't help but see the downward moral spiral of movies, TV and other forms of entertainment. Spiritually, we are in a total war, and, unfortunately, the Church has yet to join the battle. Oh, we launch campaigns to clean things up, but they are like solitary air strikes that sweep across the spiritual horizon, with little effect on the battle raging on the ground. A number of spiritual leaders have been hit by the ground fire of sexual addictions and have gone down in flames themselves. But it seems no one knows what to do, or how to counterattack the enemy's assault.

BELOW THE (BIBLE) BELT

I was speaking in the "Bible Belt" not too long ago. When I asked the gracious pastor what he wanted me to share about during the weekend service, he said, "Just tell them about the great work God is doing at your church."

I said, "I would love to do that, but I will end up talking about real life—about the bondage, addiction and trauma that so many people are struggling with today. And I will challenge them to open up these areas of their lives to God so He can heal them and set them free."

The expression on his face changed a bit and he commented, "Well, I don't think we have a lot of folks dealing with the depth of issues that you're talking about. This isn't just the Bible Belt part of the country. We call it the *buckle* of the Bible Belt."

But that pastor gave me the green light, so I didn't pull any punches. Then, at the end of the service, I gave an altar call for people struggling with sexual issues. No one moved at first. Then the dam broke, and they lined up three to four deep at the altar. It was obvious from the looks on their faces that they were reaching out to me, but I had to leave immediately or I would have missed my plane.

On the way to the airport, I was stunned when the pastor asked me, "Well, that was quite a service, but now what are we going to do with these people?"

He had perceived what had occurred as a negative. In a sense I can understand how he felt, because so many pastors I have met have no idea what to do with this issue other than preach against it. But what he was actually seeing was not negative; it was, instead, the true condition of the flock.

■ ■ ■ ■ ■ ■ ■ ■ ■ ■

The issue of sexual addiction and bondage is not simply a counseling issue for the Church; it is a matter of spiritual life and death.

■ ■ ■ ■ ■ ■ ■ ■ ■ ■

I have written this book for the express purpose of helping individuals just like that pastor, a man who loved God deeply, but had no "handles" on how to deal with this sort of problem. Here and now,

I must emphasize the most important point. *The issue of sexual addiction and bondage is not simply a counseling issue for the Church; it is a matter of our spiritual life and death.* We'll lose a lot of precious people to this attack if we don't develop an effective strategy, if we don't offer genuine hope for dealing with this issue in a world coming under the ever-increasing influence of a hellish spirit of sexual seduction.

I am not attempting to sound like some doomsday, end-time prophet. But the media is full of stories about violent crimes and addictions that were unthinkable 20 years ago. Churchgoers aren't immune to the attack.

TAKING THE OFFENSIVE

I remember when I first announced to our congregation that we were going to take on the issue of sexual addiction. I had a member of our staff give his testimony. He had been in church for most of his life, yet all the while he was getting more and more out of control. He was part of leadership, even entering the pastorate. Eventually, the lie he was living caught up with him. He lost everything: his marriage, family and ministry. In vivid detail he described the agony of being in such bondage. After he finished, I stood and outlined the groups we were going to offer for men, and eventually for women. I needed men who had come to some sort of healthy improvement in this area to volunteer to join the battle, to be trained to lead these groups. We'd had enough of hell destroying people's lives over this issue. I was stunned by the response to my announcement. In the services attended by the most unchurched (we have four weekend services), they responded by giving a thunderous standing ovation.

It was if they were saying, "Well, it's about time somebody did something about this; maybe the Church isn't so irrelevant after all." And the groups started forming even before we were ready. Several men approached me and asked if they could become part of a group as soon as possible. I told them I had to train the leaders before we could start the groups.

They were insistent. "We can't wait that long, Pastor Ted. Can we meet with you while you teach the leaders?"

I finally relented and picked a time we could start meeting. I will never forget our first get-together. They just sat there, mostly looking at the floor. Finally, one of them broke the silence.

"Pastor, this is the toughest thing I've ever done. In fact, I had to have a couple drinks before I could work up the courage to drive here."

Then another spoke up. "This is my last hope. I was headed down to 82nd Street to pick up a prostitute again. Then I remembered this meeting, so I came. But if I can't find real help, I don't know what I'll do."

The honesty and openness became contagious as others shared their struggles. A fellow with deep-seated fear in his eyes ventured out. "I'm struggling with homosexuality, and I know what Christians think of homosexuals—you hate us. I've heard you make gracious statements from up front, Pastor, but it could all be a façade you put on. I'm terrified to be sitting here." Another man started cussing a blue streak about nearly everything.

It is important to note that I had seen every one of these men frequently in weekend services. I looked at them with tears in my eyes—because they had touched my heart so deeply with their willingness to risk, with their desire for wholeness—and I said, "Welcome to church, guys . . . real church. Jesus is delighted you're here."

That day marked the beginning of a great adventure in healing that I have seen unfold over the last five years. Hundreds and hundreds of men have come to a place of hope and healing. Sadly, some of them strayed, but a surprising number stayed.

The married men in our For Men Only groups began getting so healthy that it became obvious that we needed something for their wives. We started For Women Only groups, because sexual addiction isn't just a sexual problem: *It is a family system or a way of dealing with life.* And finally, for couples who have gone through the FMO and FWO groups individually, we developed a For Couples Only group. Our call is not just to stop the addictive bondage, but to see our people come to the health and blessing God has designed for us in the marriage covenant.

This ministry has been a marvelous adventure in Christ's healing love. I have lost count of the number of times individuals and couples have come up to my wife or me and told us how the groups have saved their lives, spiritually and physically. I remember thinking several times, *What did we do before we started this ministry?* The answer is that people suffered in withering agony and silent shame.

Now here is the good news in all of this: Every church that wants to be a place of hope and healing can have such a ministry. It is not something reserved only for those with extensive counseling or academic backgrounds. Some of our most effective leaders have little, if any, academic or professional training, but they really know what they are talking about because they have fought with the dragon of sexual addiction themselves. They simply need leadership that will train them practically and provide a spiritual covering. Then they need to have the courage to take on the issue—and it is a major issue in every church I have ever seen, no matter where it is located. Sexual addiction is a principal tactic of hell aimed at the Body of Christ around the world.

SHARING THE TOOLS

This book will help you build such a ministry in your church. It is not a step-by-step plan, because we come to the task with different gifts, denominational backgrounds and histories. Instead, it is a strategy resource book. In this first section titled "A Place of Hope" is a detailed discussion of the addictive trap from a theological, pastoral perspective. There are all kinds of publications on the addictive process from a clinical perspective, but I have found this isn't very helpful for most pastors or church leaders. We need to see clearly the spiritual implications of the addictive process. Then we can understand why this has to be a vital part of the ministry of every church that truly wants to be Christ's hands extended to a hurting world.

In the section titled "A Place of Healing," we will get past the issue of just helping individuals stop their destructive sexual behavior. Instead, we will help them come to a healthy sexuality. In light of our understanding of the addictive process, we will deal with the root issues of the problem. Sexual addictions are not just about sex, but about how we process the hurts, hassles and hopes of our lives.

Finally, we will address practical "how-to" issues:

- How do you develop small groups that will deal with such a difficult area?
- How should a senior pastor support and develop such a ministry?
- What are some critical women's issues in this area of ministry?
- How do you help fallen leaders recover from such disastrous bondage?

We can't cover everything necessary in one book, but we will offer the necessary help to get started in dealing with this onslaught from hell.

In one form or another, one of the questions I hear most often sounds something like this: "Aren't sexual struggles, or what you call addiction, simply an indication that the person is unwilling to honestly turn his life over to God, that he just has never gotten serious about following Christ?" The question usually comes from well-meaning leaders and pastors who don't realize how desperately—and with futility—many people have struggled against this tenacious beast.

Every believer I have met or counseled who struggles with the issue of sexual bondage has done two things repeatedly. First, all of them have repented innumerable times and tried with everything they have to follow Christ in this area of their lives. By definition, addiction means *deciding not to do something and finding yourself not only doing it, but getting worse.*

Second, they have given their lives to Christ, completely—as best they could. They have tried diligently to do what their pastors or leaders told them to do, but still found their lives unmanageable. They have tried to remedy the situation by being more determined and spiritual, but it didn't work.

They are headed for heaven, but living in hell. Now please understand, these people aren't sex offenders who make the front page of the evening news. Sexual offenders make up only one percent or less of those who struggle with sexual addiction. Instead, they are the church counsel member or the pastor who constantly fights a battle with Internet pornography, the lady who serves in the choir who can't put down the romance novel and fantasizes about romantic relationships with men other than her husband, the teenager who is caught in a cycle of masturbation he just can't seem to break. Or it might be the single person who goes from one destructive relationship to another. None of these individuals is necessarily involved in actual intercourse with another, but they are as addicted as if they were. And this battle has become an epidemic in our churches.

Not too long ago I did a survey for a particular denomination concerning the issue of sexual addiction and discovered that between 21 to 29 percent (depending on the region of the country) of the pastors were sexual addicts. They weren't just struggling with the issue—they were *addicts!* This was a rapidly growing, Bible-believing, solid group of leaders, yet this was what was going on behind closed doors.

The bottom line is this: What the Church has been doing simply is not working for the people in the pews—or for those in the pulpit. It is time for a change. It is time for the Church to become a real place of hope and healing!

CHAPTER 2

Spirituality Is Sexy

Recently a friend gave me a description of the "rules of combat." He knew how I had come to Christ in Vietnam; he thought I would enjoy a humorous shot at the insanity of war. Two of the one-liners really brought back some memories: "Remember, if the enemy is in range, so are you," and, "Remember, your weapon was built by the lowest bidder."

I remember the first time I was involved in combat as if it were yesterday. Yes, I fired at the enemy, but it seemed just like bombing practice at the range. Then it dawned on me what those things flying past me were—antiaircraft shells! This wasn't pretend anymore. I was in range!

I will never forget the first time I landed on an aircraft carrier. The weather had been marginal on the way out to the ship, so I was low on fuel. While a tanker plane refueled my aircraft in flight, I had a bird's-eye view of the activity around me. Additional planes also were being refueled, while others circled, waiting for clearance to land.

In my mind I saw again the piece of metal fall off the plane that had just landed. I thought, *These things we flew were built by the lowest bidder!* But above all, I was struck by the violence of a carrier landing. It truly is a "controlled crash."

After years of counseling people trapped in sexual bondage, I am impressed with the violence of the battle they face. I think a lot of times we have only a vague comprehension of this creature's tenacity, of the viciousness and the shame faced by those who battle this beast of bondage. This clash is so severe for two reasons.

First, when we deal with our sexuality, we are addressing one of the most important battlegrounds in our fallen world. Scripture is clear: Christ came to destroy the works of hell (see 1 John 3:8). One of the most powerful nooses hell places around a person's soul is the snare of sexual bondage. Scripture underlines the importance of the battle by delineating very strong boundaries regarding sexual sin. God gives us those boundaries not because He is a prude, but because we are at war.

God isn't uptight about sex. After all, He came up with the idea, and He wants us to celebrate our sexuality within the covenant of marriage. Our sexuality is a gift from God, but hell's desire is to turn it into a dagger to plunge into human hearts.

In Genesis 1:26-27 God said, "Let us make man in our image, in our likeness.... So God created man in his own image, in the image of God he created him; *male and female he created them"* (emphasis added).

God's image is seen not just in man or in woman. God's image is uniquely displayed on planet Earth as husband and wife are intimately joined. I live in a beautiful part of the United States, with a view of Mount Hood's snow-capped peak directly behind my home. Within a short drive, I can hike into a magnificent wilderness full of skyscraper-tall evergreens, or stand and look out over the rugged Oregon coast. But none of these breathtaking sights comes close to revealing God's image to me. They display His handiwork, but not His image.

I taught astronomy at the undergraduate level, and I reveled in the times I would get a few moments to look through a research telescope. I was able to view brilliant images of distant galaxies or clusters of stars, yet I saw only the reflection of God's handiwork, not His image. God's image is revealed on planet Earth when a husband and wife come together in the covenant relationship of marriage. That is precisely why hell will do anything it can to destroy the marriage relationship. And one of its most effective weapons in that warfare is sexual bondage.

This truth in no way makes singles second-class citizens in God's kingdom, because there is one other place God's image can be seen on earth: in the Church. The Church is called the Body of Christ (see Rom. 12:5). This explains why we find such grit and glory in the Church as well as in marriages. The potential is so incredible that Satan will use every scheme, tactic and strategy at his disposal to attack God's image. And his master strategy, the one that hits both of his targets at the same time, is the noose of sexual addiction. That is precisely why it is so hard for people to talk about the subject within the Church, or, if they are unchurched, to realize they have a problem. Hell will do everything in its power to shame people into silence, or to convince them that God's guidelines are a collection of old rules that limit their "autonomy," rather than the road to true freedom.

THE MOST IMPORTANT ORGAN

"Pastor Ted, I want my freedom. These biblical directions you say will protect my soul don't make a bit of sense to me." I wish I had a dollar for every time I have heard people express some variation of that theme in my counseling office. The thing they don't realize is that God isn't just protecting their souls; He also is protecting their most important sexual organs—their brains!

The key to sexual fulfillment is not found in our glands but in our heads. Therefore, the roots of sexual bondage are found in the way we think.

I don't know if you have ever thought about it, but isn't it amazing how we are able to remember certain events in our lives and totally forget others? For example, can you remember what you ate for lunch on this date five years ago? I can't. Yet we are able to remember nearly every detail of an incident in which someone deeply embarrassed us five years ago. One of the differences between those two events is their depth of sensory impact. How many of our senses where involved, and how deeply? The embarrassment involved all of our senses, and was also underlined with a strong adrenaline flow. We wanted either to fight or to run in response to the disgrace.

When I am into a good book, I always read with a highlighter pen in hand so I can find the critical information quickly in the future. Similarly, our brains chemically highlight certain events for instant referral, separating the significant from the insignificant.

A major aspect of sexual activity is a strong release of adrenaline and endorphins, which is why sexual events become imprinted in the brain. These events are memorable because we rehearse them again and again in our minds, even affecting our very perceptions of life and how we deal with the present. This is the second reason why the battle over sexual issues can be so severe for some people.

So many times in the counseling office I have heard statements like, "Pastor, I am not alone in bed with my wife." These men are caught in the mental reruns. The videos of past sexual activity intrude into the present, a classic symptom of someone in sexual bondage.

■ ■ ■ ■ ■ ■ ■ ■ ■ ■

*Sexual addiction is not just a struggle over
a mental perspective; it touches God's very image,
as well as the depths of a man's soul.*

■ ■ ■ ■ ■ ■ ■ ■ ■ ■

The crazy thing about this whole process is how subtly hell goes about ensnaring people. In our society, where pornography has become a way of life, the dragon plies his trade with impunity. I use the term "dragon" very purposefully. First, it is a biblical description of our spiritual adversary, but I also discovered a parable a number of years ago that has been very effective in helping men understand why they find themselves in such a mess, and how they can get out. Sexual addiction is not just a struggle over a mental perspective; it touches God's very image, as well as the depths of a man's soul. It is not just a left-brained problem; right-brained imagery is involved as well. That's why the following parable has had such a powerful impact on the men I have ministered to:

There was once a great and noble king whose land was terrorized by a crafty dragon. Like a massive bird of prey, the scaly beast delighted in ravaging villages with his fiery breath. Hapless victims ran from their burning homes, only to be snatched into the dragon's jaws or talons. Those devoured instantly were deemed more fortunate than those carried back to the dragon's lair to be devoured at his leisure. The king led his sons and knights in many valiant battles against the serpent.

Riding alone in the forest, one of the king's sons heard his name purred low and soft. In the shadows of the ferns and trees, curled among the boulders, lay the dragon. The creature's heavy-lidded eyes fastened on the prince, and the reptilian mouth stretched into a friendly smile.

"Don't be alarmed," said the dragon, as gray wisps of smoke rose lazily from his nostrils. "I am not what your father thinks."

"What are you, then?" asked the prince, warily drawing his sword as he pulled in the reins to keep his fearful horse from bolting.

"I am pleasure," said the dragon. "Ride on my back and you will experience more than you ever imagined. Come now. I have no harmful intentions. I seek a friend, someone to share flights with me. Have you never dreamed of flying? Never longed to soar in the clouds?"

Visions of soaring high above the forested hills drew the prince hesitantly from his horse. The dragon unfurled one great webbed wing to serve as a ramp to his ridged back. Between the spiny projections, the prince found a secure seat. Then the creature snapped his powerful wings twice and launched them into the sky. The prince's apprehension melted into awe and exhilaration.

From then on, he met the dragon often, but secretly, for how could he tell his father, brothers or the knights that he had befriended the enemy? The prince felt separate from them all. Their concerns were no longer his concerns. Even when he wasn't with the dragon, he spent less time with those he loved and more time alone.

Over time, the skin on the prince's legs became calloused from gripping the ridged back of the dragon, and his hands grew rough and hardened. He began wearing gloves to hide the malady. After many nights of riding, he discovered scales growing on the backs of his hands as well. With dread he realized his fate were he to continue, and so he resolved to return no more to the dragon.

But, after a fortnight, he again sought out the dragon, having been tortured with desire. And so it transpired many times over. No matter what his determination, the prince eventually found himself pulled back, as if by the cords of an invisible web. Silently, patiently, the dragon always waited.

One cold, moonless night their excursion became a foray against a sleeping village. Torching the thatched roofs with fiery blasts from his nostrils, the dragon roared with delight when the terrified victims fled from their burning homes. Swooping in, the serpent belched again and flames engulfed a cluster of screaming villagers. The prince closed his eyes tightly in an attempt to shut out the carnage.

In the predawn hours, when the prince crept back from his dragon trysts, the road outside his father's castle usually remained empty. But not tonight. Terrified refugees streamed into the protective walls of the castle. The prince attempted to slip through the crowd to close himself in his chambers, but some of the survivors stared and pointed toward him.

"He was there," one woman cried out, "I saw him on the back of the dragon." Others nodded their heads in angry agreement. Horrified, the prince saw that his father, the king, was in the courtyard holding a bleeding child in his arms. The king's face mirrored the agony of his people as his eyes found the prince's. The son fled, hoping to escape into the night, but the guards apprehended him as if he were a common thief. They brought him to the great hall where his father sat solemnly on the throne. The people on every side railed against the prince.

"Banish him!" he heard one of his own brothers angrily cry out.

"Burn him alive!" other voices shouted.

As the king rose from his throne, bloodstains from the wounded shone darkly on his royal robes. The crowd fell silent in expectation of his decree. The prince, who could not bear to look into his father's face, stared at the flag-stones of the floor.

"Take off your gloves and your tunic," the king commanded. The prince obeyed slowly, dreading to have his metamorphosis uncovered before the kingdom. Was his shame not already great enough? He had hoped for a quick death without further humiliation.

Sounds of revulsion rippled through the crowd at the sight of the prince's thick, scaled skin and the ridge growing along his spine.

The king strode toward his son, and the prince steeled himself, fully expecting a back-handed blow, even though he had never been struck so by his father.

Instead, his father embraced him and wept as he held him tightly. In shocked disbelief, the prince buried his face against his father's shoulder.

"Do you wish to be freed from the dragon, my son?"

The prince answered in despair, "I wished it many times, but there is no hope for me."

"Not alone," said the king. "You cannot win against the serpent alone."

"Father," sobbed the prince, "I am no longer your son. I am half beast."

But his father replied, "My blood runs in your veins. My nobility has always been stamped deep within your soul."

With his face still hidden tearfully in his father's embrace, the prince heard the king instruct the crowd, "The dragon is crafty. Some fall victim to his wiles and some to his violence. There will be mercy for all who wish to be freed. Who else among you has ridden the dragon?"

The prince lifted his head to see someone emerge from the crowd. To his amazement, he recognized an older brother, one who had been lauded throughout the kingdom for his onslaughts against the dragon in battle and for his many good deeds. Others came, some weeping, others hanging their heads in shame. The king embraced them all.

"This is our most powerful weapon against the dragon," he announced. "Truth. No more hidden flights. Alone we cannot resist him."[1]

I have never been able to read all the way through that parable to a group of men struggling with sexual issues and not get teary eyed at some point. Every time, I see a vivid reminder of the battle I used to be involved in. As I look at the faces of the men I'm sharing with, many of them are wiping tears from their eyes. The scales of sexual bondage have grown on their souls, and the talons of spiritual bondage have gripped their hearts.

SPIRITUAL BONDAGE

What do I mean by the term "spiritual bondage"? Am I saying that sexual addiction is demonically energized? Or is it just a learned behavior that needs to be unlearned? Actually, I am saying it is both! It is not unusual for men to come to me following a service and ask me to pray for them and their sexual battles. "Pastor Ted, would you pray for me that this spirit of lust would be removed from my life, so I won't struggle with it anymore?" My response usually shocks them. "I'm sorry. I can't do that, because essentially what you are asking me to do is request that God pull out your brain and put a new one in its place. That's your job!"

For some reason, when it comes to sexual addiction issues, we seem to completely forget that Scripture admonishes us to renew our minds. After I explain to the men that a single prayer is not going to be the solution to their inner conflicts, I strongly encourage them to get involved in a For Men Only group in the church so they can be held accountable and start dealing with the way they think. No one can win this battle alone. Finally, I pray for them, because this is not just a battle of the mind; it is also a profound struggle with the demonic forces of hell. We can't defeat the dragon alone, and we can't defeat him simply by trying harder intellectually. It is, in the final analysis, a spiritual battle.

If a man is sincere about wanting to be free and not simply making another "I will never do this again" commitment, and if he is seeking prayer not because he has been caught or his wife or girlfriend finally put her foot down, then I try to help him understand how he was pulled into the dragon's process of deception. The dragon unfurls his webbed wings of deception with incredible subtlety.

In Luke 4:38-39, Jesus ministered to Simon's mother-in-law, who was afflicted with a high fever. The text says Jesus rebuked the fever. Interestingly, Luke used the exact same word in verse 35 to describe Christ's response to a man afflicted with an evil spirit. Luke, the observant physician, is not saying that every fever is caused by an evil spirit, but this one was. In our fallen world, the stuff of hell sometimes gets splattered on us. Simon's mother-in-law obviously was a godly woman, because as soon as she was released from the fever she got up at once and began to serve her houseguests. But in spite of her godliness, she was being affected by a demonic spirit, and Jesus dealt with the situation.

Later on, in Luke 13, Jesus had an encounter with a woman who wasn't just affected by a demonic spirit, she was afflicted. On a Sabbath, as Jesus was teaching in a synagogue, He noticed a woman who "had been crippled by a spirit for eighteen years" (v. 11). He called her out of the crowd and asked her to come forward. This was quite a risk for her because, in her culture, physical illness frequently was seen as a sign of God's punishment. Naturally, she would have struggled with a great deal of condemnation in her life. With the grace that only Christ could have displayed, He not only healed her, but also dealt with her condemnation as He called her a "daughter of Abraham" before the irate Pharisees. And Jesus left no doubt as to the cause of her malady: She had been bound by Satan for 18 years (see v. 16).

But hell's agenda is not only to bind us physically, but also to restrict our hearts' responses to God. That is why Paul tells us in 2 Corinthians 10:3-5 that we do not wage war as the world does. We don't just battle life on the physical plane. We realize that we are to demolish strongholds, things that would pin us down, things within our mental processes that would restrict us from becoming who Christ called us to be. Consequently, we must take every thought captive to Christ (see v. 5). The ultimate battle is always between our ears, not between our legs. The struggle with our sexuality is always a reflection of what is going on in our heads. Sexual bondage is not about sex. Bondage is about *how we see ourselves.*

But the dragon's strategy isn't complete until he has brought his dupe to the point of total domination. He isn't satisfied with swamping his victims with condemnation. His ultimate goal is to move us to the point of compulsion, where our behavior is so out of control that we destroy ourselves. He doesn't just want to destroy us himself; he wants the "joy" of seeing the King's sons and daughters destroy themselves.

Luke 8:27-31, the story of the demoniac of the Gerasenes, is a classic picture of this self-destruction. At times this man was driven into the wilderness by demonic forces. He lost control, appearing without clothes, living like a dead man among the tombs. We don't have to counsel people who are struggling with deep sexual bondage for very long before we run into modern-day examples of someone from the "Gerasenes." They may look great on the outside, but too many times they've ended up sneaking back home after being driven through the night by uncontrolled lusts and passions. This New Testament story is not some mythical tale. It is as current as yesterday's front page story of the child molester, or the well-respected community leader who has been disgraced because of the public exposure of his perverted sexual activity.

Hell's ultimate goal is to hurt the Father, and the only way he can do that is through His children. If there is one thing that God will be weak for, it's His kids. Therefore, the dragon will do everything in his power to seduce a son of the King. I have counseled many men who sincerely love the Lord, yet are totally overwhelmed with sexual bondage. They feel weak and ashamed because of their behavior. Like the son in the parable, they think they are worthy only of being backhanded by God.

One of the things I try to help these men see is that they can't be strong enough to win this war alone. They need God's help in their lives now more than ever. They need to fall into His arms as never before. And they need the help of men around them to fight the battle. Hell is treating them like pawns in order to tear at God's heart, and it is time they learned how to fight back with effectiveness.

After Jesus got through with the demoniac, the man ended up being the very first missionary to the Gentiles. And that's God's plan for today. Once I started the For Men Only group in our church, I started seeing men come alive who had been in the shadows for years. They finally came to a place of freedom in their lives. They no longer had to pretend during a weekend service that they were doing fine, and hide in the caves of their secret sins. I started seeing some warriors develop in the flock. No longer were they taking midnight rides on the dragon of destructive compulsions. Instead, they started soaring on God's wings of grace and power.

The other thing men need to understand is the specifics of hell's strategy in their lives. I usually sit them down and, in a graphic format, go through what I have just discussed. Then I ask them to identify where they are in the sequence. Using a high school math X-Y diagram, I lay out for them the steps the dragon takes as he attempts to lead someone down to the pit of spiritual bondage and compulsion.

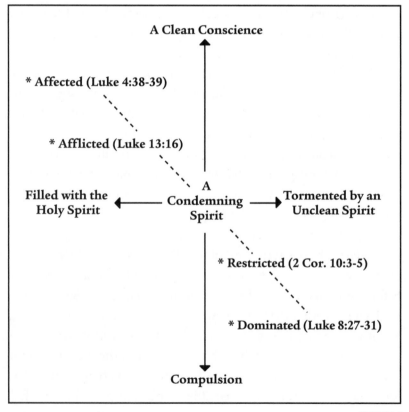

FIGURE 1

Then I ask them to mark where they are along this chart as shown in figure 1. This is not a description of the dynamics of the addictive process, which we will get to later. Instead, this exercise is an attempt to have the men honestly identify where they are spiritually. First, it helps them realize that this is ultimately about a spiritual battle they can win by God's grace. It also gives them something they can get hold of to understand how they ended up on the dragon's back, despite their love for the Lord. Above all, it helps them understand two critical factors in the battle:

1. There is a sequence of steps the adversary uses to take a person down. Therefore, if freedom is to "stick" in their lives, they need to move back up the graph. They will have to deal with the way they think about life, especially the way they cope with the difficult times. There is no instant fix for the problem, no magic wand we can wave over the enemy in order to win suddenly. We need God's truth as well as His power in our lives in order to bring us back to a clean conscience and a Holy Spirit-filled lifestyle.

2. Demonic forces of bondage are like buzzards; they feed on emotional wounds of the past. An addict uses the drug of choice to deal with the internal pain. In this case the drug is the high that comes from sexual addiction. The addict could be trying to cope with the pain of a dysfunctional home, trauma from his past or just the pain of experiences in which he was ensnared by a society awash in sexual bondage and brokenness. The pain of the past sets up a deadly cycle in the present as painful situations and problems batter a person's life. He deals with the pain of the present in the same manner he learned to deal with the pain of the past: medicate it with the addiction. But the dragon starts losing its grip once the addict comes to a fellowship of grace, led by men who understand the nature

of his struggle. Then he can sense the Father's embrace and start dealing with the stuff of the past the enemy has been feeding on. The buzzards don't hang around if there's nothing to feed on!

Therefore, the Church of the future, if it is to be effective, must become a place of practical grace. It must be a place where hope is the dominant theme, and denial, especially religious pretending, is nowhere in sight. That's a challenge for those in leadership, because personal vulnerability is the key issue. Leadership must be characterized by personal honesty that is open and forthright about their own struggles, yet at the same time able to speak from personal experience of the overwhelming victory available in Christ. In other words, servant-leadership will need to be New Testament to the core.

Paul declared that, because of his past, he was not worthy of the calling God had given him (see 1 Cor. 15:9-10). But by God's grace, we also can say, "I am what I am, and his grace to me was not without effect" (v. 10). A place of hope is created when the pastoral leadership of the Church is characterized by an unrelenting reliance and confidence in God's grace!

Note

1. Melinda Reinicke, *Parables for Personal Growth* (San Diego, CA: Recovery Publications, Inc., 1993), pp. 5-9. Used by permission.

CHAPTER 3

When Sex Gets Sick in the Heart

I had decided to do something my wife classified as stupid. She was right! We had been cave diving in Florida, which was exciting enough for most folks, but I decided to increase the challenge. During our time in the cave, I had noticed an air pocket near the ceiling. Because of all the divers in the cave during the holiday weekend, a substantial amount of air had collected in an alcove in the ceiling. I swam up to the air pocket, popped my head up into the collected air and enjoyed a break from having to breathe through the regulator. I thought, *You know, once we get to the surface, I bet I can free dive [without air tanks] back into the cave, find this air pocket again, get a breath of air and make it back to the surface.*

After we exited the cave and swam to the beach, I took off my tanks and headed back for the cave. My heart pounded as I dove toward the entrance. *No problem so far,* I thought. But I couldn't find the air pocket. It's amazing how intense things get when you are under water and running out of breath. I realized my lungs were too empty for me to make it back to the surface. I had to find that pocket! There it was, just ahead. I kicked rapidly toward it, only to bang my head against the cave's ceiling as I tried to find some air. Apparently there was a fissure in the rock that the captured air was leaking into. Fortunately, there was just enough room for me to inhale a partial breath. Feeling myself lose my composure, I had only one goal: Get back to the surface! Suddenly, I caught a glimpse of the cave's entrance. My lungs felt like they were going to burst.

I planned to explode from the cave and rocket to the surface, but I was yanked to an abrupt halt just outside the cave. The float that showed divers the place to descend was tied around a rock just outside the cave entrance. I knew it was there somewhere; I had followed it down earlier. But on my way back out, the rope that held the float somehow tangled around my leg and formed a noose that tightened its grip the more I pulled. Thank God, I had the presence of mind to pause and look down at the rope, even though everything within me screamed to rip through the rope and get to the surface before I blacked out. I would have died that day if I hadn't dealt with the noose.

RECOGNIZING THE NOOSE

I have talked with pastors and spiritual leaders who don't understand the noose of sexual struggles that traps so many people. The dragon of sexual addiction doesn't just take people for a ride. He also puts a noose around their souls so he can keep pulling them back. The result is that the harder they try to pull away, the worse it gets. They end up feeling like I did when I was tangled in that rope—literally dying. The enemy doesn't just lead people down the paths of condemnation, domination and compulsion; he slips a noose over their hearts to keep them there. Clinicians give the noose a technical name: the addictive cycle. I love what Paul calls it in 2 Corinthians 2:11: "After all, we don't want to unwittingly give Satan an opening for yet more mischief—we're not oblivious to his *sly ways!*" (*THE MESSAGE,* emphasis added).

The term translated "sly ways" is a fascinating word. The original Greek word is *noema,* and is found five different times in 2 Corinthians but only once in the rest of the New Testament. It has been translated into English words such as "mind," "scheme," "device." The root meaning of the word is mind or thought. But as authors

Arndt and Gingrich point out in *A Greek-English Lexicon of the New Testament*, in Hellenistic Greek it also meant a plot with an evil design, or a trap.[1] That is why "sly ways" is such a marvelous translation of the term. It brings into focus the sense of a mental trap, something that ensnares—a mental noose.

As I have spoken through the years to many groups on the topic of sexual struggles, again and again I encounter those who, unfortunately, have been given deadly advice. A spiritual leader has told them they simply need to read their Bibles more, pray more and try harder next time so they won't do it again.

In such instances, the counselor was oblivious to the spiritual noose around the person's soul, a noose that tightened and made things worse the more the person pulled. What that person really needed was to cut the rope! Telling someone to pull harder isn't going to work. In fact, it's counterproductive!

Now, as a pastor, I realize there are those who blame their problems on everyone and everything else. Such people need to get serious about God and decide to respond to the Lord's gracious discipline. Yet, almost without exception, by the time someone comes to me and openly admits he has a serious sexual problem, he has tried everything he can to stop. He is drowning and needs to have someone help him cut the noose from his heart and soul.

That's why this is not simply a book to describe an aspect of spiritual warfare, nor is it designed to analyze the clinical details of sexual addiction. Numerous authors have written several classic works on the subject already, many of which are listed in the bibliography of this book. Instead, it is to call the Church to step into the battle and truly become a place of hope and a place of healing. Only the Church of Jesus Christ has the message that can break the back of the dragon and cut the noose of addiction once and for all.

Although that statement may seem extreme, it is the truth. Later in the book I will demonstrate why it is true. Through the years, I have taken flack for making such a declaration—broadsides from fellow pastors and church leaders who declare that terms like "addiction" are merely "psycho-babble" and that people who repeat-edly battle with sexual problems or claim to be wrestling with a sexual addiction simply lack character and are unwilling to really repent and get serious with God.

On the other side, I have had clinical counselors openly scoff at the idea that the Church can be a place of hope and healing for peo-ple trapped in sexual addiction: "Do you know how many clients I have who say they're Christians and can't find any help in their churches? They say they would be openly shamed if they dared to mention they had such a problem. Do you know how many pastors I've had to deal with who only make their clients feel more guilty? They don't get any help from the Church; in fact, sometimes the Church is part of the problem."

■ ■ ■ ■ ■ ■ ■ ■ ■ ■

Our nation is getting trounced in this battle. Our moral fabric is unraveling, and the torn tapestry of people's lives is blowing in the winds of abuse, abandonment and personal trauma.

■ ■ ■ ■ ■ ■ ■ ■ ■ ■

I understand their concern. But they are dealing with a part of the Church that hasn't learned how to respond to the noose from hell known as sexual addiction. There is no greater prison than the one people find themselves in when they love Christ with all their hearts, but are slowly choking to death as the noose strangles the spiritual life out of them. All the counselors have said doesn't change the fact that Christ has commissioned and called His Church to be a place of hope and a place of healing. The gates of hell were never designed to be able to stand against God's grace.

In the midst of all this misunderstanding, there has never been a greater time for the Church to stand to her feet and start tearing apart the sly and deadly tactics of hell. Let me state the obvious: Our nation is getting trounced in this battle. Our moral fabric is unraveling, and the torn tapestry of people's lives is blowing in the winds of abuse, abandonment and personal trauma. Sadder still, the present-day Church does not stand as a bastion of purity and invincibility in this war. As Christian pollster and author George Barna recently pointed out, in certain situations, the divorce statistics for professed Christians are worse than for unbelievers.

Dr. J. D. Unwin unwittingly underlined the results of such a state of affairs in his book *Sex and Culture*. He studied 86 different societies throughout human history and made this amazing discovery:

> Sexual fidelity was the single most important predictor of a society's ascendancy. In human records there is no instance of a society retaining its energy after a complete new generation has inherited a tradition which does not insist on prenuptial and postnuptial continence.[2]

Now, because Dr. Unwin wasn't a Christian, he was puzzled by his findings and couldn't provide an explanation for such irrefutable data. But Scripture is clear: A society is doomed when it starts throwing marriage out the door and stops honoring sexual faithfulness. And when the Church is leading the way into infidelity, things are definitely desperate.

People are crying out for answers as never before. Upward of 88 million people in this nation are chemically dependent or are in a relationship with someone who's chemically dependent. One out of every four families in America suffers from alcohol- or drug-related problems. Thirty-seven million people are food addicts; 30 million are children of alcoholics; 4 million are compulsive gamblers;[3] and 25 to 35 percent of women in America suffer sexual abuse before they reach adulthood. Battering is one of the primary causes of physical injury to women in our land. Then throw in the incredible number of those who have gone through divorce or are addicted to work and materialism. What does that all add up to? If a church reaches out to the community at all, at least 60 to 75 percent of the visitors who walk in the door are battling with dysfunctional family problems, addictions or are simply out of control at some point in their lives.

No longer can we simply have people respond to Christ and then place them in some Christian discipling program, assuming that everything is going to be fine. We have an unusual number of folks respond to Christ during our weekend services, partly because we live in one of the most unchurched regions of our nation. We can shoot in almost any direction and hit the target! But we learned a long time ago that someone's initial commitment to Christ means the work has just begun. They need to have places were they can go to get healed and learn to deal with their wounds, traumas and addictions; otherwise, we will just train them to be religious. They will learn to pretend that now that they're Christians, their past is no longer an issue. They will develop skills in putting a Christian "veneer" over the problem that lies deep within. The result, down the road, is that they will either blow up, dry up or simply say this "Christian thing" doesn't work, and walk away.

Instead, they need help to realize that their minds must be renewed if they are ever going to experience real freedom from their past. Therefore, the Church is at a crossroads as we head into a new century. Are we going to become a place of healing and hope, or a place of tradition and theological debate about issues that have long since lost any sense of importance and meaning to the average person?

DEALING WITH THE NOOSE

If the Church doesn't become proficient in dealing with these issues of addiction and bondage, it will have little to say of relevance to our world. Martin Luther put it well:

If you preach the gospel in all aspects with the exception of the issues which deal specifically with your time—you are not preaching the gospel at all.[4]

So, from a pastoral perspective, what do we mean by the terms "sexual addiction" or "bondage"? The various clinical books published today on the subject list four decisive issues that always show up. These four elements are part of every accurate symptomatology of sexual addiction, because they constitute the core of the "noose." What are the four issues?

1. The addictive root
2. The addictive mindset
3. The addictive lifestyle
4. The addictive cloak

If the Church is to deal effectively with the problem, pastors and leaders need to understand what people actually are dealing with and how to help them. We need to understand the noose as found in figure 2.

Depicting the addictive cycle as a noose is not just for emotional impact. Once these four elements are in place, they operate much like a hangman's noose around the addict's soul. If he is given no other option than simply pulling against the bondage noose, he will end up spiritually drowning in the waters of his own guilt and shame. To deal with the noose of addiction, we have to cut the rope. We have to deal with the entire problem. We have to understand that the problem isn't just about the person's behavior or addictive lifestyle. It is about his past, the way he thinks and the defense mechanisms he has developed to keep from being exposed. Sexual addiction isn't ultimately about sex; it is about the way the person deals with life!

So let's begin at the beginning, which is a novel concept for most folks when you are dealing with the problem of sexual bondage. We

THE NOOSE OF SEXUAL ADDICTION

THE ADDICTIVE MINDSET

**Destructive
Core Concepts**
· Worthless
· Unlovable
· Alone
· Sexual High

THE ADDICTIVE ROOT

1. Family Dysfunction
2. Personal Trauma
3. An Addictive Society

THE ADDICTIVE LIFESTYLE

Fantasy

Further shame and guilt

Ritual

Keeping the lid on

THE ADDICTIVE CLOAK

· Denial
· Delusion
· Blame

FIGURE 2

instinctively tend to focus on someone's behavior. We think we have to help the person stop acting out unbiblical manners. At times that may be the case. If his behavior is extremely destructive to himself and others, we help him to establish points of accountability and boundaries. But if that's where we focus, our efforts ultimately are doomed to failure. It's like clipping weeds in the lawn. It looks good for a while, but it's only a matter of time until the problem resurfaces—usually in a much more malignant form.

It is crucial that we understand we are dealing with a type of behavior that has three interlocking elements. First, the problem has become *unmanageable*. The person repeatedly and unsuccessfully has attempted to stop the behavior in a number of ways. His behavior is not something that just recently erupted. In the initial counseling session, the man may suggest that it is a recent problem, but that is a manifestation of denial that has become part of the way he thinks. He is not so much purposefully lying; it is just the way he has learned to look at life.

Many, especially Christians, have developed a "binge" type of response to the problem. They will be out of control for a day, a week or a month. Then they tighten up the "willpower" screw a couple more notches and stay clean for a sustained period of time. But it's only a matter of time before they return to the old behavior.

Second, their behavior is *destructive* to them in some form. It is easy to understand the destructiveness of criminal sexual behavior or sexually transmitted diseases. But the first consequence of sexually addictive behavior is always emotional numbness. The person is attempting to use the addiction to medicate some painful emotional realities in his life. That's why, over a period of time, the numbness takes root in his soul. He begins to lose the capacity to honestly relate to those closest to him and to God.

This emotional numbness naturally leads to the third element: *increased intensity* of the activity over a period of time. Numbness becomes a way of life. Even the sexual high of past behavior isn't enough. The addict has to up the activity "dosage" to keep the same level of numbness. Sexual activity and fantasy, which produce the sense of pleasure, can actually alter a person's brain chemistry. This altered brain chemistry is a beautiful experience between a husband and wife. But for the addict, the "high," not the relationship, becomes the focus. That is why the other person becomes unimportant to him, no matter what he may say to the contrary. The other person becomes a way to get a "fix." And that is also why a sex addict can pursue seemingly irrational courses of action, such as repeated relationships with women other than his wife, or even prostitutes, despite the fact that he declares he is a deeply committed Christian. He gets a "buzz" from the danger of it.

In the secrecy, danger and excitement of a new sexual partner, he forgets for a moment his fears, loneliness, hurts and anger. The sexual acting out is usually just the tip of the iceberg. The ultimate issue is about what is within the man, not his outward sexual activity.

THE ADDICTIVE ROOT

We come now to the issue of the addictive root. This term refers to the root issues that drive behavior. The bibliography of this book contains a list of a number of outstanding secular, clinical books published on the research data supporting the fact that at least three issues lie at the root of most addictions:

1. Family dysfunction
2. Personal trauma
3. An addictive society

Family dysfunction is one of hell's major entry points into the lives of the vast majority of individuals I have counseled who struggle with sexual bondage. I use the word "individual" for a specific reason. Sexual addiction is no longer the exclusive domain of men. It is becoming an "equal opportunity noose." It used to be that we could draw a clear distinction between the two groups we had in the church dealing with sexual addiction. The For Men Only groups were for men, and dealt with sexual addiction. The For Women Only groups actually dealt with love addiction, which expressed itself sexually. But we soon discovered that many women were struggling with classic sexual addiction, not just a virulent form of love addiction. So we formed two For Women Only groups, one to deal with love addiction and the other with sexual addiction. My wife will deal with the specifics of women's issues in a later chapter.

■ ■ ■ ■ ■ ■ ■ ■ ■ ■

Family dysfunction is one of hell's major entry points into the lives of the vast majority of individuals. Sexual addiction is no longer the exclusive domain of men. It is becoming an "equal opportunity noose."

■ ■ ■ ■ ■ ■ ■ ■ ■ ■

For most pastors and leaders, the ultimate issue is God's Word, not clinical data. And that is as it should be. Scripture is our ultimate standard of truth. Human fads and ideas will come and go, but God's Word will still be standing, declaring the eternal truth. So is all this talk about family dysfunction and sexual struggles just so much psychological speculation, or does it have biblical validity? We don't have to search far in the Bible to find the answer to that question. There are innumerable examples. Probably one of the most unmistakable examples of sexual bondage and family dysfunction is found in the life of my Old Testament hero, King David, and his son Absalom.

Whenever anyone approached him to bow down before him, Absalom would reach out his hand, take hold of him and kiss him. Absalom behaved in this way toward all the Israelites who came to the king asking for justice, and so he stole the hearts of the men of Israel (2 Sam. 15:5-6).

Why would Absalom behave as such a rebel? I have heard sermons about the evil in his heart that would cause him to act in such a way against his father. But can we discover the reasons for Absalom's rebellion? Absalom's actions were part of a long and tortured sequence of events. It started with David's sexual sin with Bathsheba, the subsequent murder of Bathsheba's husband, and the cover-up of the whole sordid mess. And, if not for Nathan's obedience in confronting David, which could have cost Nathan his life, David would have continued to live in denial and delusion.

These events were followed by Amnon, David's oldest son, raping his half-sister, then covering it up. The son was acting just like his dad, sexually doing whatever he pleased. Even more revealing, David did nothing about it. He never confronted the problem of his oldest son being sexually out of control.

Absalom's response to his violated sister wasn't all that redemptive either: "Be quiet now, my sister; he is your brother. Don't take this thing to heart" (2 Sam. 13:20).

Once again, Absalom's response reveals the nature of the family's rules: *Don't feel; don't talk.* Classic dysfunctional family! Then, after seven years, the dormant seed first planted by David's sin erupted again. Absalom, in revenge, killed Amnon, which led to the insanity in 2 Samuel 15, where David was driven out of Jerusalem and lost his ability to rule.

So many times I have counseled men who, because of the destructive behavior of their children, have lost their ability to reign in life as Christ intended. But the ultimate tragedy occurred in 2 Samuel 18, as David convulsively wept over the death of Absalom, his son who was trying to kill him.

Why was Absalom such a rebel? There is a simple answer: He was part of a family system that deeply needed healing. Absalom was expressing the shame and pain of the family he grew up in. Now that's not to excuse his actions. But in order to help someone like Absalom embrace healing, we must be aware of the system he is tangled up in.

God created us to be in families, which become either the place of our connectedness or our bondage. I have counseled many who have struggled deeply with issues like anger or sexual addictions. They love the Lord, yet they have gone from one frustrating situation to another, never having been healed at the point of their family pain, as though they were spot-welded to their family's problems.

I clearly remember counseling a very respected church leader. He was a marvelous man with incredible abilities, but had one recurring problem—anger! When he lost his temper, he did destructive things. He had grown up in a family filled with rage and pain, but no one ever talked about it. Fifty years later, he was still expressing the family's rage and pain. And he had no idea what lay beneath all his anger. It had become so much a part of the "software" of his mind, he didn't even notice it anymore. He played a family role, and so did Absalom.

Now let me stress that these insights are not meant to blame David or anyone else's parent for a child's problems. It is instead to point to the fact that kids react to the needs of the family systems they grow up in. They follow a script, one they can easily take on for life. Some kids in a hurting home end up as entertainers. They have learned to keep the party going at all costs. They joke about everything so they don't have to face the pain. Others are the perfect kids in dysfunctional homes. They never create problems. No one ever hears a peep out of them. And that is the big problem—they can't be anything but perfect, no matter what the personal cost.

In homes with long-term dysfunction, we frequently find kids growing up as heroes. They feel like they're there to hold everything together. When someone grows up as I did, with an alcoholic mother and a parade of stepfathers passing through, it's easy to end up trying to be the adult instead of the kid. When Mom is passed out on the floor, it doesn't leave a lot of time to go out and play with friends. Or when Dad is using Mom for punching practice, the hero feels the need to fix things. Now the hero perspective, like the others I mentioned, can be really hard to detect, because the world can reward us for acting according to our family script.

The military applauded my hero mentality. In fact, they even gave medals for it. It wasn't until I began pastoring East Hill Church that I finally had to face myself. The church was in the final throes of a crushing financial indebtedness when I arrived. The previous pastor, who had been there for many years, was gone. When he left, many in the congregation did the same. I was asked by our denomination to take on the challenge of turning things around. To make a long and extremely painful story short, I had a nervous breakdown after about a year.

I found myself sitting at my desk, unable to walk, talk or do anything except cry. I couldn't fix this one, and that was part of the reason God sent me there. I didn't realize that I had been running all my life. That was what my previous alcoholism and sex addiction had been about. I fell out of my chair to my knees and ended up flat on my face.

And then the Lord asked me some very simple, penetrating questions: "Do you ever wonder why your life has been filled with such stress? Why you have ended up so many times near the breaking point? Why you couldn't just settle for a college degree—you had to get graduate degrees even though you were the only one in your family even to go to college? You couldn't be just a pilot—you had to be a Marine Corps pilot. And when someone in the squadron flew under a bridge, you had to go out the next day and fly under it upside down. Did you ever wonder why?"

I could only respond, "No, Lord, I've never thought about it."

That encounter with the Lord started the painful process of my getting rid of a lot of denial. I discovered that I had taken my family dysfunction, as well as the military, and tried to drag them into God's kingdom. They wouldn't fit.

THE MAGNITUDE OF THE PROBLEM

But I am not alone in my struggle. Not too long ago, I spoke about freedom in Christ to the leaders of a denomination. When I asked them how many had come from healthy homes, with few exceptions, I received the predictable response, "We all came from great homes!" But when I gave them an analysis to find out the facts about their families of origin, we found that 79.8 percent of them came from dysfunctional homes. The vast majority grew up in rigid or disengaged homes. There is no way we can truly walk in the freedom Christ has for us if we don't understand our own weaknesses, limitations and hurts from the past. And, because rigid or disengaged homes communicate a sense of abandonment, they also produce hidden wounds in children's hearts. Time and again, the issue of emotional abandonment, especially by a father, will surface in the life of someone who is having sexual struggles.

As leaders and pastors, we need to realize that most of the folks we are working with today did not come from healthy homes. Most of us didn't either. And it's going to be worse in the next generation. Therefore, three things need to be at the forefront of our efforts to help our churches become places of hope and healing.

KNOW OUR OWN WEAKNESSES

First, we need to know our own weaknesses very clearly. We all have weaknesses, because there are no perfect families. Here is where the Christian perspective differs radically from much of the popular perspective of today. Understanding the points of weaknesses that may have been passed on to us from our family backgrounds is not an investigation to fix blame. It is, instead, a discovery of the points where God's power can be released in our lives where we are weak, where we have to work at listening to God carefully, because our ingrained habit patterns can lead us astray. That is exactly where God can do His greatest work. It was only after I finally got a handle on just how much I had been ignoring in my life that God's power broke through in a unique healing ministry. It was then that my ability to communicate much more effectively really took off.

Am I saying we have to be messed up to communicate effectively? No, not at all. I am simply stating that we are all already messed up at some point; otherwise, we wouldn't need a Savior. It is when we forget that fact that we end up being religious and ineffective in a hurting world.

BE OPEN ABOUT OUR WEAKNESSES

We need to be open about our weaknesses and struggles. I'm not saying that if we're senior pastors we should stand up and bleed in front of our people each weekend. But I am saying that we need to be honest about our struggles and bold about our victories. Victories without struggles put us on a ridiculous religious pedestal. Struggles without victories make us communicators of heaviness instead of hope. We need to be open with our folks. We need to be honest and never hide behind the pulpit. The next generation is not going to be touched by fine logic or a well-reasoned argument. We are in a postmodern world where only 28 percent of Americans believe in absolute truth.[5] The statement that "there is no absolute truth" has become the absolute truth in our society. That obviously doesn't mean that we should stop speaking of God's absolute truth. It means that, more and more, we need to become living witnesses of that truth.

Recently, a young man came up to me after a service and said, "You understand, don't you?" I asked him what he meant. It turned out that he hadn't been in church since he was a kid. He was struggling with alcoholism. I hadn't mentioned a word about the fact that I used to battle alcoholism, yet he picked up on the fact that I understood what it meant to struggle. He committed his life to Christ that day and started to walk out of the hell he had lived in for years.

TEACH HEALTHY PRACTICALITIES

We need to teach frequently about family in a realistic way, and have as many groups as possible to help couples learn the practicalities necessary to have a healthy marriage and family. I can't emphasize this point strongly enough. Preaching is crucial, but folks need practical help in ways they never have before. They need mentors and models of how to live. And they need to see them at close range, because the models they had at home have frequently wounded, limited or confused them.

To do this effectively, we need a large team to help communicate in small-group settings the reality of God's healing grace in families. Preaching plants the truth, but in small groups the truth begins to take root. The Church, as never before, has to become a healthy family for so many who have experienced unhealthy families and don't even realize it.

Notes

1. W. F. Arndt and F. W. Gingrich, *A Greek-English Lexicon of the New Testament* (Chicago: The University of Chicago Press, 1957), p. 542.
2. Phillip Yancey, *Finding God in Unexpected Places* (Nashville, TN: Moorings, 1995), p. 16.
3. Barbara Yoder, *The Recovery Resource Book* (New York: Simon and Schuster, 1990), p. 2.
4. Charles R. Swindoll, *The Finishing Touch* (Dallas, TX: Word Publishing, 1994), p. 146.
5. Charles MacKenzie, "Facing the Challenge of Postmodernism," *RTS Ministry (Reformed Theological Seminary)*, spring 1995, p. 9.

CHAPTER 4

Clueless in the Midst of the Battle

I sat at rigid attention. I had finally made it. I had been looking forward to this since I was five years old. It's amazing how some things seem to stay forever burned into the depths of your memory bank. I'm told that when I was five, I went nuts when I first saw a fighter aircraft take off. I chattered about it for days, and from then on, I had one goal in life—to be a fighter pilot.

Now I was finally there, waiting for my instructor to brief me on my first ACM hop. ACM is one of those acronyms the military loves to use. It stands for Air Combat Maneuvering—better known as "dogfighting." The instructor read me like a book. As he scanned through my file prior to the mission briefing, he looked up at me and said, "Think you're a pretty hot stick, don't you?"

I replied in the typical testosterone-loaded response that characterized my life at that time: "Yes, *sir!*" I shudder now to think of how foolish I was.

"Well, I tell you what we'll do, hotshot," he replied. "I'll be out in the area. You come get me." He referred to the area designated as a training air space for dogfighting. Not surprisingly, airlines get upset if you end up dogfighting in their airways; thus the need for a designated area.

We took off five minutes apart as planned, and I could hardly wait to get airborne. This instructor was something else; he wasn't messing around with all the initially boring stages of ACM training. We were getting to the good stuff right away. And I had been practicing in my previous solo flights. I had figured out already, on my own, how this dogfighting stuff worked. And besides that, I was one awesome pilot. If you didn't believe it, all you had to do was ask me!

It didn't take me long to find the instructor's aircraft. He flew along—fat, dumb and happy. And it was obvious he hadn't even seen me sneak into the area. I climbed to altitude first and entered the dogfighting area. Rather than the standard procedure of climbing up through the area, I had planned it perfectly. I made sure the sun was to my back. He was a sitting duck. I swooped down on him like a hungry hawk.

As I rapidly closed the distance between us, he took no evasive action. My ambush was working perfectly. Then, suddenly, his aircraft shot upward in a maneuver I had never seen before. I flashed beneath him in a microsecond. And, without warning, the tables were turned. He was tracking me now. No matter what I did, his gunsight never left the back of my neck. I could almost hear him chuckling as I struggled, entangled in a noose of my own making. The engagement lasted 45 seconds at the most, and then I was toast. The instructor gave the command to disengage, because I was obviously dead. We faced off once again, and this time I lasted maybe 30 seconds—and that's giving me 29 seconds of grace. The rest of the flight went downhill from there!

We returned to base in formation and landed together. As I climbed out of my aircraft, I was a mess. I was so sweaty my flight suit looked like I had been under water. The oxygen mask had dug deep lines into my face, and I was weak-kneed from the heavy "G" loads I had been pulling trying to get away from the instructor's relentless gun sight. I must have looked pathetic. It was quite a transformation from that cocky kid who had climbed into the cockpit just an hour before.

As the instructor walked toward me, I came to attention, trying to look somewhat together. The guy was amazing. He looked like he had been out for a Sunday drive. His flight suit didn't even have a wrinkle in it. Hair in place. Not a drop of sweat. But his face didn't look serene. He stopped in front of me, leaned forward and said, "You will last about 10 seconds in combat. You know how to fly, but you don't know how to fight!"

That man gave me a great gift that day. He saw my arrogance, and he cared enough about me to get my attention. From then on, I was all ears for anything he had to say. In some sense, his declaration of reality to me is part of the reason I made it home alive. I never ended up in a classic canopy-to-canopy dogfight in combat. The vast majority of the time I flew close air support missions trying to keep my fellow marines alive on the ground. But his words kept my head up, my brain engaged and my pride at manageable levels whether I was in the air or on the ground serving as a platoon commander.

DOGFIGHT FROM HELL

Unfortunately, in their sexual battles, many men are caught in the same position I was in that day as a student. No matter which way they turn, the enemy just pulls the noose tighter. His gunsight constantly locks onto them, and the harder they try, the worse off they end up. They know how to fly in Christ. They have tasted His goodness and grace. But they don't have a clue about how to fight with hell.

When I returned from Vietnam I had been significantly changed in two ways. First, there was the positive change that began when I accepted Christ as my Lord and Savior. My wife had sent me a package. It arrived on a night I was half drunk and deeply troubled. I had taken out some of the enemy at close range and couldn't erase the picture from my mind. It was no longer a remote, impersonal air war, similar to a huge computer game. This was real, and we were splattering real blood. But above all, the whole war didn't make a bit of sense. Guerrilla wars seldom do at the foxhole level.

As I looked through the package Diane had sent, I found—along with some cookies that had turned moldy by the time they arrived—a little book that explained how to make a commitment to Christ. I didn't comprehend a lot that night, but I knelt and simply said, "Lord, I don't really grasp all that You are to me, but sign me up. I want to do things Your way."

I finished my tour of duty and came back as hard as a rock on the outside. I never got connected with a Bible study or a military chapel service. I tried going once, but it didn't make a bit of sense to me. I truly had been born again, but I was essentially clueless about the battle I fought deep within. And now I had some additional baggage to carry—trauma.

That is why my war with sexual issues only increased. I had three strikes against me at that point. My family of origin had given me a good dose of dysfunctional software. Vietnam gave me a huge load of trauma and reinforced my survivor mentality. And to top it off, I returned to a society that had gone topless—literally! As I stepped to the plate trying to be a man of God, I heard, "Strike three. You're out!" I didn't even know how the game was played. I didn't have the slightest idea how to fight this war.

As I mentioned in the previous chapter, the addictive root that lies at the core of someone's losing battle with sexual bondages usually is built around three issues:

1. Family dysfunction
2. Personal trauma
3. An addictive society

The first issue has become sort of a buzzword in much of the popular writing and self-help books of the day, so most of us are familiar with it. The second issue is seldom understood, and the third is ignored because what previous generations identified as perversion and flagrant sin, we have relabeled as personal preference and fun. We have learned to wear our nooses as party neckties.

So what do we actually mean by the term "trauma"? A fairly clear definition would be *severe stress that leaves deep emotional scars requiring special coping techniques.*[1] The last part of the definition can sound remote and clinical, but it can become very real if we find ourselves responding to life with special coping techniques.

For example, when I returned to the States I had a hard time relaxing, and loud noises startled me. If my wife came up behind me and touched me unannounced, I reacted violently. Those reactions and many others were conditioned survival responses I had developed to cope with the trauma of daily life in a war zone. The problem with the war zone is that it easily becomes a trauma zone we carry inside. And I wasn't alone in my struggles. The divorce rate for all Vietnam vets is in the ninetieth percentile. From 40 upwards to 60 percent of all Vietnam vets have persistent problems with emotional adjustment. Drug and alcohol abuse problems range between 50 and 75 percent. Forty percent are unemployed, and 25 percent earn less than $7,000 a year.[2]

■ ■ ■ ■ ■ ■ ■ ■ ■ ■

The vast majority of men I have counseled who struggle with sexual issues have father wounds in their souls.

■ ■ ■ ■ ■ ■ ■ ■ ■ ■

It's easy to see why veterans struggle, no matter what war they may have been part of. But there is another kind of war that is much harder to understand, and they don't give out medals for surviving this one. It's the war that comes from painful interpersonal relationships, especially when families are sick. Dysfunctional families don't just give us defective software for dealing with life; they can traumatize and scar our souls. I have lost count of the number of times I have come to realize in prayer that what I'm really distressed over in a particular conflict is not what is actually occurring. Instead, I am reacting to a "father wound" (emotional and spiritual damage stemming from a father's neglect or abuse of his son during the boy's formative years) deep within my soul, which caused me to misread what was going on. The vast majority of men I have counseled who struggle with sexual issues have father wounds in their souls.

But can family problems have the same traumatic impact the experiences of war can bring? The graph below will help us understand the various ways trauma can enter our lives. Simply stated, stress in our lives can move into the trauma zone, not just because of the sudden intensity of an event, such as an exploding bomb. It can also take root because of the frequency of a painful event, such as a childhood with a father who explodes at the drop of a hat.

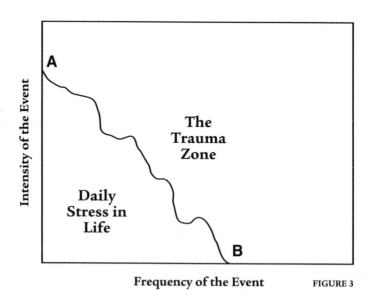

FIGURE 3

In figure 3, the vertical axis has to do with the intensity of the event. In a war, the frequency of the event may be relatively low (point A). As one man put it, "Flying fighter aircraft in a war zone is an experience of hours and hours of routine, punctuated by moments of stark terror."

The horizontal axis has to do with the frequency of the event. The intensity in an alcoholic home may not frequently reach the level of a war zone, but the battle is constant (point B). It becomes part of the very air we breathe. The transition area between the daily stress of life and the trauma zone is not a uniform curve, because each individual is unique. We all have our own emotional fingerprints. What's crushing to one person isn't for another. But if we keep pushing, at some point every human being will cross into a trauma reaction that leaves a scar on the soul.

Then the person begins to respond to life out of the context of special coping mechanisms. These can range from the knee-jerk reaction I developed to loud noises while I was in Vietnam to the anger that erupted out of my soul when I couldn't control things, which was the reaction to life I had developed in an alcoholic home. Both of these points of "trauma bonding" (having deep hurts inside and developing coping behavior) in my life only made me more vulnerable to the noose of sexual addiction that hell desired to put around my soul.

Through years in the counseling office, I discovered again and again that I was not alone in my battle. Person after person I counseled who was out of control sexually had a painful family of origin. Dr. Patrick J. Carnes and his associates provided clear clinical evidence of this phenomenon in their four-year study of more than a thousand recovering sex addicts and their partners. They reached a startling conclusion: All addictions and codependencies in the group were, in part, coping mechanisms for the trauma and stress of child abuse. They discovered that 81 percent of the men and women had been sexually abused as children, 72 percent had been physically abused, and 97 percent had been emotionally abused.[3]

What was particularly sad was how infrequently people even realized that what they had experienced was abuse. At least in a physical war the trauma is obvious. Yet, in our families of origin, we have no standard of comparison. We all leave home with a built-in standard of measurement or software of perception. But when that standard of measurement is an emotional pretzel instead of a golden rule, we end up crazy and frequently don't even realize it. One man in the Carnes report titled "Abused Kids, Addicted Adults" responded to the question of whether he had ever been sexually abused by saying, "I know many of us have, but I am one of the lucky ones. It never happened to me." When asked later about his earliest sexual memory, he said, "That was when my uncle started masturbating me. I was five."[4]

This trauma bonding explains why sexual addiction frequently joins with several other addictions. Recent research suggests that up to half of all alcoholics struggle with sexual behaviors, and many of them are sexual addicts. The percentages are higher for some other drugs. Two studies with inpatient cocaine addicts have shown that approximately 80 percent of them have sexual addictions.[5] There is obviously a strong correlation. The neurochemistry of cocaine affects the same centers in the brain that are involved in sexual pleasure, so it's not surprising that there are a lot of cross-addictions. Eating disorders are also very common among sex addicts.

The phenomenon of cross-addiction illustrates the critical truth that sexual addiction and sexual bondage are not so much about sex as about coping with the pain within. Just focusing on getting the individual to change his behavior on the outside, to become a "good Christian," can cause the problem to resurface somewhere else. Or, more commonly, it will go underground and eat away at the soul, until down the road there will be a sudden and catastrophic failure. We must deal with the addictive root or we end up playing religious games!

DESCENDING INTO HELL

Playing religious games is deadly in our addictive society. We have been trained by our consumer culture that we can get what we want, when we want it—immediately. We can get anything from fast food to phone sex almost as soon as the craving hits. And pornography is the ultimate "get it now, the way you want it and when you want it" fantasy. We are awash in a sea of pornography, and the waves are only getting higher. The average age of a first-time viewer of pornography is now down to 11. It will drop even lower in the future because of the flood of porn that is coming through the Internet.

Bondage to pornography is seldom something that develops later in life. Usually the seed is planted at a very early age, and by the time of young adulthood its tentacles have been deeply rooted into the person's mind. The Internet has greatly increased the stakes in the battle, because the "soft core" stage of pornography is rapidly being left behind for the hard core (showing penetration). It is estimated that 50 new adult sites appear on the Web every day! The last estimate concerning the porn industry is that it now generates more revenue than CBS, NBC and ABC combined.[6]

We often hear that pornography is harmless; it doesn't matter what someone does in the privacy of his own home. We know from Scripture that such comments are ridiculous, and nowadays even secular counselors are beginning to join the chorus of voices raised against the flood of pornography.

Dr. Victor Cline recently declared that more than 90 percent of his patients who were sexually compulsive or addictive had begun with viewing pornography. He also pointed out that others (including Jennings Bryant, Dolf Zillman, W. L. Marshall and S. Rachman), using laboratory and field study approaches, have found negative effects from pornography. With porno violence, the evidence is even more compelling. Cline also referred to another national study in which 254 psychotherapists indicated they had come across cases in their clinical practices in which pornography was found to be an instigator or contributor to a sex crime or another antisocial act. Another 324 therapists reported cases where they suspected such a relationship. I love his final comment in the article: "It would seem to me irresponsible to ignore such data."[7]

So many men I have counseled through the years have quietly picked up the world's view of pornography: There is nothing wrong with it; everybody does it. But that is exactly why so many Christian men are in such trouble spiritually. I estimate that 50 percent of the men in every congregation I have ever had an opportunity to minister to are struggling with this issue. And the sequence of events in a man's life is very predictable once pornography takes hold of his soul:

- *The emotional high; the fantasy.* They get hooked on the chemical and sexual high it gives them.

- *The escalation process kicks in.* The past level of excitement can be maintained only with increased stimulation. They move from mild to explicit, from sensual to violent, to more deviant material, and many eventually act out their fantasies. And the Internet provides for that need with just a keystroke and a MasterCard. From masturbating to sexually deviant imagery comes the downward road of a soul in ever deeper bondage.

- *Numbness of the soul sets in, which hardens denial.* A lack of remorse develops because they go deeper into disassociation. It is not that they don't care anymore, but their shame level has reached staggering proportions. If they were totally and honestly to face what they are doing and what they have done to hurt others, they would go nuts.

- *Now there are few barriers to acting out.* They may cycle into times of intense self-disdain and renewed commitments to "never do it again," but it is only a matter or time and they once more are out of control. Not infrequently at this stage, they will throw out all moral restraints and even declare that there is nothing wrong with what they are doing. They have found freedom from all the old restrictive religious rules—which is exactly what our whole society is doing.

The deadly part of that sequence of events is shame. Shame moves the person from struggling with an addictive root issue to battling with an addictive mind-set. Shame, because it is so addictive, easily becomes a part of life in our world. Today you can hear all kinds of declarations about being free as an American, or being free in Christ, or being free to find ourselves, but the truth behind the declaration frequently is quiet despair. The misery comes from the idea or belief that *something is wrong with me.* Shame is an inner sense of being diminished or insufficient as a person at some point.

■ ■ ■ ■ ■ ■ ■ ■ ■ ■

The majority of people I have counseled could give a long list of things they are good at. They also could state their character strengths and gifts. Most of them deeply love the Lord, but they didn't understand that we are as sick as the secrets we hold.

■ ■ ■ ■ ■ ■ ■ ■ ■ ■

Many people consider themselves very effective on the job, or as parents, friends, or whatever. Yet deep within their souls, they have an area they have carefully guarded for fear of being exposed, an area where they wrestle with shame. A sense of being defective as a person means they are haunted by a sense of emptiness. They don't just *feel* shame; their identity at some point has *become* shame.

Now let me emphasize that the majority of people I have counseled could give a long list of things they are good at. They also could state their character strengths and gifts. Most of them deeply loved the Lord, but they didn't understand that we are as sick as the secrets we hold. There was an area of shame within that they never shared with anyone, or an incident of shame they failed to fully understand. A script was penned in shame and handed to them at some moment in their lives, usually through their family, and they have responded to it.

I will always remember a dear friend—I'll call him John—who shared with me about his struggle. In his character and in his business sense, he was one of the sharpest men I knew. He was strong and had an engaging personality. The guy had everything going for him. Yet he sat in my office in a puddle of tears. He had been hit by corporate downsizing, and at the age of 45 he was ready to throw in the towel. I was amazed that John was affected like this. I had seen him take on seemingly impossible tasks in the past without so much as a moment of hesitation.

I have counseled long enough to realize that when a seemingly healthy person reacts in a manner that is way out of line with the stated cause, he may be dealing with a shame issue. I asked John, in the midst of his tears and confession, to tell me about his strongest memory in high school. I wasn't just fishing; I was responding to the Holy Spirit's leading.

John's face lit up a little, because he had been a superb athlete. He told me of the joy of winning a state championship. He earned a full scholarship to college because of his skills. After the championship game was over, he was voted the Most Valuable Player. He went forward and received the MVP trophy, with his father standing beside him. It should have been a red-letter day. I asked John what his father said to him afterward. The joy dropped off his face and tears streamed down his cheeks. He could barely say the words: "He told me someone else should have received it. I wasn't that good."

His own father had handed him a script of shame: "You are not good enough. No matter what you do, you are not good enough."

That was why John was ready to call it quits. He had been running on the treadmill of achievement, trying to be acceptable. Shame within causes a person to look outside for reassurance that he is worthwhile, since he secretly views himself as defective. It had taken 45 years for John to get to this point because he was so strong and gifted. But, like so many others, shame eventually caused John to break down.

BATTLING WITH SHAME

My next point is not that we should indict our parents for our problems—for our battle with shame—because that only feeds the cycle with blame. Instead, we need to realize that, yes, our parents or someone important to us abandoned us, but the real problem is that we have abandoned ourselves. That is the viciousness of shame. We end up giving ourselves away; we do things that bring self-destruction. We end up with an addictive mindset—a mind bludgeoned with the perspective that we lack worth, that we are alone or unacceptable, no matter what we do.

Guilt is about what we have done, but shame is about who we are. With guilt we can always get a fresh start. With shame we are caught in a noose, because the problem stays with us. We are the problem.

Shame can enter our lives from surprising sources. I had just returned from Vietnam, having done, to the best of my ability, what my country had asked me to do. Several of my friends didn't make it back, but I was alive and looking forward to going home. As I waited in the San Francisco airport for a connecting flight, two men walking by noticed my uniform and cursed and spat at me. It felt like I was back listening to one of my stepfathers berate me again. I was filled with anger, and I still don't know what kept me from reacting to them. Granted, it may seem senseless, but when the issues of shame are triggered within a person's soul, the associations aren't built on logical connections; the associations are all about the pain.

I had anticipated a "thank you" when I got home, but what I got was cursing war protesters. Suddenly, I was faced with the view that because I had served in Vietnam there was something wrong with me. I learned that Vietnam was a taboo subject, so it became a secret time in my life. It wasn't until 20 years later that someone finally said "thank you" to me for serving my country. A believer, under the anointing of the Holy Spirit, sensed and responded to the hurt I had within.

The critical issue to remember about shame is that it causes incredible pain. I used the two previous life examples to show the sense of pain apart from the issue of sex. Now, take a solid believer who has somehow fallen into the grip of pornography, continual masturbation, or sexual fantasies he seems unable to control—and our world today provides numerous opportunities for that to happen. (When was the last time a G-rated movie won an Oscar?) Then, to add to the depth of the pain, let's say the person was raised in a rigid Christian home, a home that tended to put a negative spin on the issue of sexuality with comments such as, "Now, son [or daughter], sex is dirty, so save it for the one you love."

Let that person slide into sexual bondage and the shame factor goes through the roof! He has nowhere to go. He has no one to talk to about his secret. He should be victorious in Christ; after all, Christ has freed us from bondage. The message comes through loud and clear: Shame on you for having such a problem!

But guess what he *can* count on? That's right—the sexual high he gets when he acts out. Which does what? Exactly; it increases his shame. I have met so many believers living in just such a hell on earth. The way they tend to handle it is to make ever stronger promises that they will not do it again. But that is always a frustrating effort, because they are just trying to screw the lid down tighter on their shame. At some point, someone has to help them in their war with the shame within.

These addicts must address their sense of worthlessness at the point of their shame. They have to find a safe place where they can finally let all the secrets out—with nothing held back. Small-group ministry is a critical key in this process. Without it we can never come to the place of confessing our sins to one another in order to be healed (see Jas. 5:16).

Obviously, confidentiality and careful structuring of the groups are essential. This process of breaking the addictive mind-set is never a quick-fix process. Time after time, I have told men who have finally gotten honest and faced the fact that they are out of control sexually, "I am so proud of you. Getting honest and dropping the denial is never easy. But let me warn you—our goal is getting healthy, not just stopping destructive behavior. And that will probably take three to five years, with the Holy Spirit doing miracles all along the way, as you cooperate."

That is shocking news to many Christians, because they expect Christ to deal with the problem miraculously. He does, but it involves renewing the mind, and that never happens overnight. We have to cooperate every step of the way. The sense of being unlovable that lies within an addictive mindset can only be dealt with through healthy relationships at close range. And that takes time. The sense of aloneness that sexual bondage brings to the human soul doesn't disappear quickly or easily. Those in the healing process have to give up their old friend, the sexual high, when they are feeling alone or worthless; and they have to learn to trust in who Christ says they are.

In the next chapter, we will look at the one and only thing that ultimately deals with shame in the human heart. But first, in closing this chapter, let me give several practical suggestions about dealing with shame in the Church.

1. *Use personal testimonies as a preaching tool.* Obviously, testimonies about such issues need to be handled very carefully, but I have always been deeply touched by the receptiveness of the flock when someone speaks of his struggle from a perspective of honesty and hope. At East Hill, I have the person write out his testimony so we can carefully incorporate it into the service. Several such testimonies, which we have actually used in our services, are placed throughout this book. The testimonies are especially good for giving hope to struggling folks. The testimonies help them realize that they are not the only ones dealing with these kinds of issues and that their church is a place where they can find help.

2. *Address the issue of the person's position and identity in Christ in as many ways as possible.* This is one subject we can't speak about too often. From every possible perspective, we need to make a bold declaration concerning the believer's position in Christ. We must underline repeatedly that the individual is accepted in Christ, secure in Christ and significant in Christ. Shame is like a charge from hell that violently attacks those truths, so these facts must be rebuilt constantly in the believer's life, especially if he has been entangled in sexual bondage. I have found two resources by Dr. Neil Anderson that are very helpful at this point: *The Bondage Breaker,* published by Harvest House Publishers, and a pamphlet called *The Steps to Freedom in Christ,* published by Regal.

3. *Deal with sexual issues very openly in a teaching series at least once a year.* Various surveys point out that the average American male thinks about sex approximately once every 30 minutes. Why not openly discuss what they're already thinking about? It's amazing how much interest it generates and what a great attention holder it is. Fortunately, Scripture has a lot to say about sex. For starters, there's the Song of Songs, the only R-rated book in the Bible. But the R is for romantic, not raunchy. When sex and sexual relationships are presented with a positive and godly perspective, it can go a long way in breaking the grip of shame in Christians' lives.

Notes

1. Irwin A. Horowitz and Kenneth S. Bordens, *Social Psychology* (Mountain View, CA: Mayfield Publishing Company, 1994), p. 662.
2. Chuck Dean, *Nam Vet* (Portland, OR: Multnomah Press, 1992), p. 37.
3. Patrick J. Carnes, "Abused Children Addicted Adults," *Changes,* June 1993, p. 81.
4. Ibid.

5. Mark Laaser, "Sexual Addiction," *Steps,* Vol. 8, No. 2, summer 1997, p. 7.

6. "Pornography Statistics," Family Safe Media, 2006. http://www.familysafe media.com/pornography_statistics.html (accessed November 2007).

7. Patrick J. Carnes, "Pornography: It's Not Harmless," *The Carnes Update,* spring 1995, p. 3.

CHAPTER **5**

The Answer to a Wounded Heart

The student sat before me at attention, chafing at the bit, just as I had years before. He couldn't wait to get airborne and test his skills against this ultimate challenge. He didn't look quite as impulsive as I had been, but that just meant he had a little bit more common sense than I had when I was a student.

Isn't it amazing how life can come full circle at times? I found myself back at the same naval air base where I had initially trained, only this time as an instructor. Now I was the one giving the preflight briefing. I was the one lecturing on the intricacies and demands of aerial combat.

Near the end of the briefing, another instructor joined us so we could cram two training flights into one. Initially, we were to practice some carrier landings, and on the way back we would throw in an introduction to dogfighting. The other instructor was an old friend who had just joined the training squadron. We hadn't flown together for quite a while, so I knew things would get interesting. Without saying a word, we knew that as soon as we finished with the carrier landing practice and left the airfield we would end up nose to nose. I told the student to hang on, because he was going to get a real introduction to dogfighting.

Sure enough, as soon as we finished our carrier practice, I pulled the aircraft nose up sharply and clawed for altitude. I tried to maintain my airspeed, since I knew my friend would be lying in wait. He was overhead, and in a few seconds we locked into a heated dogfight. As I threw my aircraft into a shuddering nose-high turn, with the student smashed down in the front cockpit because of the G-load,[1] my G-suit malfunctioned.

I felt instant, excruciating pain. A G-suit serves one primary function—to prevent all the blood from draining out of your head and into your legs in high-G maneuvers. If that happens, you pass out and lose—big time. The G-suit keeps the blood from pooling in your legs simply by increasing pressure around your legs in proportion to the increasing G-load. The G-suit is really nothing more than a glorified girdle that inflates around your legs and stomach as you pull into a severe turn. My problem was that my G-suit immediately went to the maximum pressure setting and beyond. The pressure exploded around my legs with such force that I felt as if my legs were being squeezed right into my helmet!

At that moment, my friend lost me in the sun and hesitated for a moment in the fight. I was dying from the crushing pressure on my legs, but I wasn't about to let him know. Besides, if I could just roll inverted and drop my plane's nose, I would have him in my sights.

Once I got inverted, I immediately tried to stomp the bottom rudder, but a searing pain shot through my right leg. I disconnected the G-suit, called off the fight and limped home.

THE BATTLE PLAN REVEALED

Earlier that week I had been sitting in church, giving it another try, but I still didn't understand a lot of what was going on. For example, I couldn't comprehend what excited everyone when they sang about the blood of Christ. It sounded like slaughterhouse religion to me—kind of a moribund memory. Yet they all seemed inspired by it, so I asked the Lord to help me understand what they were so joyous about. And, as only the Lord can do, He spoke to me in terms I could comprehend.

Scripture clearly states that we are involved in something much more intense than a practice aerial dogfight. We're not contending for the bragging rights my friend and I dueled for in the south Texas skies. This war is even more acute than the terror of a fight to the death in combat. It's about eternity. Fortunately, the Lord has given us a clear battle plan to win this ultimate contest, and it is clearly outlined for us in the book of Revelation.

In Revelation 12, the surface of life is peeled back to reveal the spiritual battle that lies at the core. But if there is ever a place where the historical and grammatical context are needed in order to understand their meaning, it is this passage. So, if you don't mind, I will avoid all the arguments about end-time prophecies and stick with two central facts concerning the text.

First, the apostle John, "the Beloved," wrote this letter during his "chain gang" experience, courtesy of Roman authority. Persecution had swept across Asia Minor, and John no longer led many of the churches he had built and nurtured over the years.

Second, John wrote truth that applies to all believers for all time, not just a specific group of believers at the end of time. There are obvious end-time implications to his words and, more specifically, to the entire book, but let's stick with the basics that apply to all those who have said yes to Christ.

> Then I heard a loud voice in heaven say: "Now have come the salvation and the power and the kingdom of our God, and the authority of his Christ. For the accuser of our brothers, who accuses them before our God day and night, has been hurled down. *They overcame him by the blood of the Lamb and by the word of their testimony; they did not love their lives so much as to shrink from death.*
>
> Therefore rejoice, you heavens and you who dwell in them! But woe to the earth and the sea, because the devil has

gone down to you! He is filled with fury, because he knows that his time is short" (Rev. 12:10-12, emphasis added).

In a few short phrases John wrote of Satan's savage evil, which is motivated not only by his treacherous nature, but also by the fact that he knows his days are numbered. Even more important, John clearly reveals hell's central strategy, and the believer's necessary response, which can break Satan's grip every time. In just a few masterful strokes, John outlined the ultimate spiritual dogfight that lies behind the daily struggles of our lives.

The historical context of this passage reveals the intensity of John's conflict. He is an aged man. He had walked Palestine's dusty roads with the Master. He had seen the blind receive sight, the sick healed and the dead raised. He had poured his life into the churches in Asia Minor for decades and he had watched his fellow apostles die as martyrs. Now he is in a chain gang breaking rocks on the tiny island of Patmos off Asia Minor's southwest coast.

■ ■ ■ ■ ■ ■ ■ ■ ■ ■

I have discovered that believers who are tied
up sexually are frequently mad at God.
They have prayed, and God apparently
hasn't answered.

■ ■ ■ ■ ■ ■ ■ ■ ■ ■

On a clear day, he might even be able to see the smoke rising from the burning homes of believers being crushed under Rome's crippling assault. For the next two centuries, the Church in Asia Minor would face repeated savage persecution.

There is little question in my mind that, right at that moment, John had to face the accusing, acrid words of hell: "It sure pays to serve God, doesn't it? Everything you've poured your life into is going up in smoke. God hasn't even kept His word to you."

The one who has accused believers since the beginning of time has been thrown down. Jesus Christ's shed blood has removed the accuser's ability to bring accusation against us before God. But he has never stopped making accusations about God before us.

What does this have to do with the issue of sexual bondage? Actually, a great deal, because I have discovered that believers who are tied up sexually are frequently mad at God. They have prayed, and God apparently hasn't answered. In fact, things have only gotten worse. Their reasoning runs something like this: *What good does it do to serve God? The guys on the job who don't care about God aren't breaking rocks on the emotional chain gang like I am. They're involved in all kinds of sexual sins, and everything is going their way. They're even enjoying themselves. Yet here I am, trying to do what's right, and all hell is breaking loose in my life.*

The apostle John was human, and at a deeper level, he must have faced the feeling of being deserted by God. This sense of abandonment is the kind of pressure hell uses to test a man's trust in God. When a man is deeply embedded in the wicked web of sexual bondage, he will, at some point, feel deserted by God. This is a classic strategy of hell, designed to increase the shame level in our lives, which only tightens the noose of sexual bondage around our souls. John masterfully outlined hell's vicious tactics. He knew them well. He had felt their brutal impact. Satan's methodology is one of accusation, always to increase our sense of shame, which increases his control over us. And the power of his methodology is found in his skill at interpreting events for us—if we let him.

John also tells us that Satan knows his time is short. He is filled with fury because his days are numbered. As a result, life will not always be fair. The good guys don't always win—this side of eternity. In fact, life isn't fair most of the time. We can start off in deeply dysfunctional families. There can be moments of intense trauma that we can't anticipate. We live in an aggressively addictive society that is driven by selfishness rather than a servant's attitude. A selfish perspective will always result in life being unfair for those around us and, eventually, for those who practice it.

So how do we deal with such an onslaught? John stated it simply: "They overcame him by the blood of the Lamb." The clear implication is that we can do the same thing. What did he mean by such a statement? The first thing we need to do is remember that Jesus didn't shed His blood for us in just one place, but in four:

1. At Gethsemane
2. With the crown of thorns
3. At the whipping post
4. At the Cross

"And being in anguish, he prayed more earnestly, and his sweat was like drops of blood falling to the ground" (Luke 22:44). Jesus was not surprised by the Cross. The battle at Calvary was preceded by the battle at Gethsemane. And the battle fought and won by Christ there was the first step in returning mankind to God's heart. It was a battle over the issue of will: "Father…not my will, but yours be done" (v. 42). Adam and Eve had declared in their sin, "Not *Your* will, but *mine* be done."

Christ was healing the breach between God and man. Luke's words tell us that the mental strain of the savage battle caused the capillaries in Jesus' forehead to break, bringing a mixture of sweat and blood to His brow.[2]

That battle of the will, fought and won by Christ in the garden, is one we all face many times in our lives. I was set free from alcohol's bondage in an instant. As I got out of my car to go to another Friday night happy hour at the officers' club, the Lord spoke to me—not in an audible voice, but a sense within—that alcohol's hold on my soul was over. I got back into my car and drove away, and never had another drink. It was a radical, incredible change for a fighter-pilot type who loved to get plowed with the guys as we shared flying stories. It was the supernatural touch of God's grace on my soul. Since then, every time I have a physical and it shows up that my liver was scarred from the depth of drinking I used to be involved in, I praise God for His deliverance from that addiction.

THE ONLY ANSWER TO SHAME

My battle with sexual bondage wasn't quite as simple. I went through nearly three and a half years of absolute war before I could see any daylight on the issue. And I went through all the standard failures. "Lord, I will never do that again," I promised repeatedly. But it seemed no matter how hard I prayed, cried, read the Bible, fasted and memorized Scripture, nothing worked. You name it, I tried it, but I kept ending up right back in the same pit of shame. The one thing that pulled me up was the knowledge that Christ's blood had been shed for me. It had been shed in the battle over my will. I just had to keep getting up and following the bloodstained path He had broken through for me. And, by God's grace, I was setting my will to do His will—no matter how many times I had to reset the heading.

> They stripped him and put a scarlet robe on him, and then twisted together a crown of thorns and set it on his head. They put a staff in his right hand and knelt in front of him and mocked him. "Hail, king of the Jews!" they said (Matt. 27:28-29).

Our Lord bled as the mockers shoved a crown of thorns onto His head. Christ knew what it felt like to be caught in the abusive games people play. So often, trauma becomes part of our lives because of others' sin and abusive behavior. Time and again, research has underlined the fact that addictive behavior frequently is triggered by past abuse. For example, the crazy interpersonal games our culture has developed, like living at such a frantic pace, has resulted in family isolation, which is at the core of much child abuse and addictive behavior. As a result, adolescent drug use in our culture is soaring.

Of the 26 most prosperous nations of the world, the United States has the highest rates of violence, murder and suicide among children. This tragedy is mostly the result of family stress.[3] And the trauma we experience in our families can become such a part of our mental software that we don't even realize it's there. It is a painful experience that was shoved into our lives and thinking processes like a crown of thorns.

I can remember my stepfather towering over me as I lay on the floor in my room. He had been beating my mother and, just for fun, tried to drown her in the bathtub. I stepped in to help her and, as a result, I received his unleashed anger. He followed me down the hall and cornered me in front of my room. He lashed out, knocking me back into my room and onto the floor. I was like a mouse being toyed with by a cat just before the kill. I was a freshman in high school, and he probably outweighed me by a hundred pounds. And, like the crowd of soldiers that surrounded Christ, he took delight in delivering pain to others. He stepped into the room and bellowed, "If you get up, I'll kill you!" I wasn't a fool. I didn't get up, but I vowed that day never to let another man treat me that way.

That vow became the source of a lot of the games I ended up playing as I grew up. I had to win. It wasn't really about the score. It was about never being humiliated by any man ever again. Consequently, the playing field became the arena of my self-vindication. Sports were not about the sport, but about the game I had been caught in years before. That's why, for years, I lived a love-hate relationship with other men: I needed their affirmation. If we are never fully accepted by our fathers, we seek the acceptance of other men. Yet we don't receive it because, at the same time, we compete against them.

I remember when I finally realized I had been living most of my young adult years in response to that vow I made from my bedroom floor. Once I realized Christ's blood had been shed so that I didn't have to be trapped in the games people play, I began to experience indescribable freedom. The gospel really became the good news to me.

"Then Pilate took Jesus and had him flogged" (John 19:1). Christ's blood was shed at the whipping post. His back and sides were ripped open with a whip before His hands and side were pierced. The prophet Isaiah, looking down the corridors of time, under the anointing of the Holy Spirit, declared:

> He was pierced for our transgressions, he was crushed for our iniquities; the punishment that brought us peace was upon him, and *by his wounds we are healed* (Isa. 53:5, emphasis added).

In case we may have missed the meaning of Isaiah's prophecy, Matthew, in watching Christ's healing ministry among the hurting and hopeless, points right back to the prophet's words and declares that they have been fulfilled (see Matt. 8:17). The Lord's healing ministry is a mystery in many ways, despite what many so-called experts may say. No formula for prayer or confession will force God to act the way we want Him to. With our limited understanding, we cannot dictate how and when He will act. But we can be sure of this one thing: Christ's blood was shed to free us from the hellish grip of sin and death in our lives. He is still setting folks free and healing supernaturally. He can heal the deepest hurts, traumas and bondages of our lives!

> God made you alive with Christ. He forgave us all our sins, having canceled the written code, with its regulations, that was against us and that stood opposed to us; he took it away, nailing it to the *cross* (Col. 2:13-14, emphasis added).

Every time we think we have fully comprehended what was accomplished on the cross at Calvary, we discover an aspect of our lives that was redeemed there that we never realized before. The Cross is infinite in its depth, because it is the total expression of God's grace to us in Christ. Paul declares a unique insight in this passage. The word that is used for "canceled" is a technical term of that day. It refers to the process of washing a piece of parchment clean for reuse.[4] Not only was the parchment clean enough to be written on again, it showed no evidence of ever having been written on in the first place.

Christ's blood washed away any record of previous sins and charges against us. That is why the cross of Jesus Christ is the *only* answer to the shame that lies at the very core of sexual bondage. Hebrews declares that Christ, "for the joy set before him endured the cross, scorning its shame" (Heb. 12:2). Christ hung stark naked on the cross. There was no loincloth to cover Him. He was ridiculed and shamed. All of our sin and shame were dumped on Him as hell unleashed its deepest fury. Therefore, we no longer need to live with any shame in our lives! The Cross is the only answer to the shame that can become so much a part of our lives in a fallen, addicted world.

Counseling is important. Small groups are essential. Understanding the noose of addiction is vital. But the cross of Christ is the only thing that can set us free. It has for all time declared our value. We truly matter to God. It's a tragedy when churches shame people who are wrestling with sexual bondage. When we do that, we become the priests of further condemnation instead of hope. We deepen the shame with the bony finger of a critical god, instead of revealing the open arms of the crucified Savior. We think we have to defend God's purity, even though Christ willingly took the pollution of our sins on Himself.

I'm not saying that the Church is called to be a harlot, casually accepting the world's standards of behavior. But in our efforts to keep the Church pure, we have battered the souls of hurting men and women who cry to be free from the shackles of their shame. We have become the modern-day version of the Pharisees, and we don't even realize it. God's most powerful weapon, grace, has been cast aside in our efforts to be spiritually pure. The modern-day Pharisee who focuses on avoiding sin is still focused on sin. In fact, he is little different from the person who is consumed by sin. Both are obsessed with sin—one to avoid it, the other to live in it.

. . . .

God's most powerful weapon, grace, has been cast aside in our efforts to be spiritually pure. The modern-day Pharisee who focuses on avoiding sin is still focused on sin. In fact, he is little different from the person who is consumed by sin. Both are obsessed with sin—one to avoid it, the other to live in it.

. . . .

UNDERSTANDING THE FATHER'S HEART

The day that my G-suit malfunctioned I stopped and talked to the flight surgeon about the excruciating pain I had experienced in my leg. That's when the lights finally came on for me about Christ's blood. The doctor's answer was simple and immediately made sense to me: "Well, Captain Roberts, you experienced a sustained period of extremely restricted blood flow in your legs. Prior to that you had been in a period of intense physical effort, which generated a lot of lactic acid and other waste products that needed to be removed from your muscles. Without the blood flow, you couldn't be cleansed, and you found yourself in a whole lot of pain." First John 1:7 came to mind:

If we walk in the light...the blood of Jesus, his Son, purifies us from *all sin* (emphasis added).

His shed blood is the answer to the deepest needs, pains and hurts in our lives. Ultimately, integrity is about the value we see in ourselves. And the Cross declares that God has placed an incomprehensible value on and in each of us. We really matter to God.

I will never forget when I finally realized that Christ had shed His blood at my deepest point of need—the bondage and hurt of my past. My performance as His son may not have been the greatest right then, but by His grace and blood, I was going to make it! Sure, I needed to understand why I medicated my pain by going for the high that pornography provided. Yes, I would have to face the craziness of the alcoholic, abusive home I grew up in. I would have to learn new ways of thinking and reacting, instead of seeking a quick fix. I would have to quit being such a driven, competitive man and become someone at peace with himself and with God, as well as becoming a servant to others. And I knew that wouldn't be easy. But I also knew this wasn't about performance, or about getting it right before God would accept me. I was already accepted in Christ. And that changes everything!

Understanding the power of Christ's blood, which is the ultimate answer to every wounded heart, has been an ongoing process for me. A few years ago our church had a huge summer picnic. We had managed to take up most of the county park, and friends had talked me into joining one of the many baseball games. As I stood there trying to pretend I knew what I was doing as a shortstop, a young man ran up to me on the field and yelled, "Pastor Ted, Bryan just got hit in the head with a baseball bat!"

I immediately turned and raced toward the other field where my son was. I felt as if my feet were mired in cement. Courtesy of hell, all my worst fears came roaring at me—thoughts like, *Your son is dead. All the promises God gave you about Bryan are gone. You've lost everything you hoped for.* The thoughts came at me like rounds from a machine gun. This clearly was more than just a little accident at a picnic. This was about a major spiritual battle. Little did I realize how profoundly God was going to speak to me through all this.

I had known and counseled a man whose son was hit in the head with a baseball bat. The young man lay in a coma for several weeks, his life ebbing away. That father had never told his son he loved him, and it tore him apart to watch his son die and not be able to communicate with him. I had not made that mistake. Long before, I had realized that any day in which I didn't tell God, my wife and my kids that I loved them was a wasted day. It doesn't matter how many sales or successes we have that day, how well the presentation may have gone or how well we did anything else. If we're not telling God and our family that we love them, we just wasted a day of our life.

I arrived on the scene, and my son looked terrible. Blood was everywhere. As I pushed through the gathered crowd, a little girl standing beside her mom asked, "Is he dead, Mom?" That was all I needed to hear. As I gathered my son into my arms, he slowly began to move. First one eye, then the other came into focus, despite the blood and pain. And then he mumbled to me, "I don't think I'm dead, Dad."

With tears streaming down my face, I pulled him close and then rushed to a waiting van. We sped toward the hospital. His blood was everywhere, all over both of us. I noticed he was trying not to cry and was in a lot of confusion trying to process the trauma. I simply said to him, "Hey, buddy, now is the time that strong men cry. Weak men can't cry because they're afraid of their emotions. As real men, now is the time we let the tears flow and start really praying in the Spirit." And that is exactly what we did together as I held him close. By then my face was drenched with tears. I had to let my tears express my inexpressible love for my son. I prayed with everything I had, telling Father God how much I loved my son, and asking for his life to be spared.

Then it hit me like a freight train: *I had my son's blood on my hands.* And, unlike my heavenly Father, I was taking my son to the hospital, not to the Cross! Without ever having a loving father figure in my life, I had struggled to understand God's heart. That day, I finally understood—*God loved me.*

Actually, "understood" may not be the right word, because I came to see that God's love for me is incomprehensible. And that day I grasped why Christ's blood was so powerful. In light of His love for me, there was no addiction, bondage, hurt from my past or threat in the future that could keep me down. His love lifted me that day. As I result, I have never been the same.

Some of us have to become fathers before we understand our heavenly Father.

Notes

1. One "G" equals the force of gravity on the body at rest; multiple G forces are generated when the person's body is subjected to severe acceleration as the aircraft makes sharp ascents, descents and turns.
2. Earle, Sanner and Childers, *Beacon Bible Commentary*, Vol. 6 (Kansas City, MO: Beacon Hill Press, 1964), p. 601.
3. "U.S. Leads in Child Homicides," *Arizona Republic* (February 7, 1997), n.p.
4. A. T. Robertson, *Word Pictures in the New Testament*, Vol. IV (Nashville, TN: Broadman Press, 1931), p. 494.

CHAPTER 6

When Sex Is Lord

In my final years in the military, I served as a safety officer and sometimes as an aircraft accident investigator. The wreckage from one accident proved easy to find; it was on the side of a mountain, just off the end of the runway, where it had crashed during takeoff in severe weather. We immediately concluded that the student, rather than the instructor, had attempted the takeoff—a questionable practice in marginal weather. Perhaps the student had been overwhelmed by the situation or he became confused. In either case, it seemed that the instructor had been unable to recover in time to correct the student's mistake. The result was a flaming hole in the side of the mountain. It appeared to be an open-and-shut case of pilot error. The instructor erred by letting the student try to handle such a difficult situation.

A closer examination, however, revealed that nothing could have been further from the truth. It wasn't a sudden event. In fact, it had probably brewed for some time. The investigation showed that shortly after takeoff the oxygen system exploded into flames. The fire weakened the main structural support for the wing and, as a result, the plane became a flying inferno. The pilots had almost no time to react to the emergency, let alone to figure out what went wrong.

At some point, the oxygen system had been improperly serviced, resulting in a buildup of corrosion and the system's eventual failure. Ground crews had ignored clear warnings concerning the danger of not servicing the system properly, with the result that two pilots lost their lives.

THE WARNING SIGNS

That tragic accident is like a parable of so many individuals I have counseled and known through the years. Their lives suddenly crashed for no obvious reason. They just slammed into the side of an affair, or suffered the agony of being exposed as a leader who was sexually out of control. Their lives "just suddenly" fell apart. But the truth is always different from the public perception. No one suddenly falls into sexual sin—no one.

■ ■ ■ ■ ■ ■ ■ ■ ■

One of the enemy's favorite tactics is to let us acknowledge God's conviction, to allow us to acknowledge we have a problem. But nothing ever changes, because we think the conviction itself means we've changed. Instead, the acknowledgment is simply the warning indicators being set off on the instrument panel of our souls just prior to impact.

■ ■ ■ ■ ■ ■ ■ ■ ■

The crash always is preceded by a significant amount of time living an addictive lifestyle behind the scenes. They may not have realized it themselves, because they were caught in the "sexual sin-I am ashamed-I will try harder-I love God" mental merry-go-round. But a cycle of corrosion has set in. Quietly, unobtrusively, the corrosion builds up until it results in a raging fire of lust and personal destruction that cuts through the very support structure of their souls. And the more prominent the person in public ministry, the more fiery the crash will be and the bigger the blast zone impacting others' lives.

The sequence never changes. It starts with a quiet corrosion of the heart. It isn't that those struggling with sexual addiction don't try to prevent the crash—like the pilots in the aircraft that day. They frantically attempt to do everything they know to prevent the impact, but it's too late. One of the enemy's favorite tactics is to let us acknowledge God's conviction, to allow us to acknowledge we have a problem. But nothing ever changes, because we think the conviction itself means we've changed. Instead, the acknowledgment is simply the warning indicators being set off on the instrument panel of our souls just prior to impact.

As I previously pointed out, the corrosion starts at an early age. In our society, the average age of introduction to pornography is 11 years. With the explosion of pornography on the Internet, this corrosion process will be starting sooner and sooner in young men's lives.

The story of a man whom I'll call Kevin is like so many others. His home looked ideal. He grew up with two loving parents who made family a priority. What could be better? But Kevin's father disliked confrontation and conflict, and gladly relinquished discipline of the children to his wife. During Kevin's first seven years, his dad traveled as a salesman three weeks out of every four, and, when he was home, disappeared to the bedroom at the first sign of any trouble.

Forced to function almost like a single parent, Kevin's mother used the only tools she was familiar with to ensure Kevin's and his sister's obedience—shame and guilt, yelling and threatening. When Kevin was four, he wet his pants. He couldn't remember the events that led to his accident, but he will never forget how his mother handled the situation. She diapered him and forced him out the door while he screamed and cried. Kevin had to endure the jeering of the other children in their apartment complex, as they laughed to see a four-year-old in "baby diapers." That was the first day he felt shameful.

Kevin also had to endure the frequent "Why can't you be like Billy?" refrain from his mother. He loved Billy, his older cousin, who later became valedictorian of his graduating class, leader of his church youth group and a gifted college athlete; but Kevin couldn't measure up to his idol, so he felt defeated. He was sure his mother was ashamed of him and wanted him to be someone else. He tried harder to please her. Kevin's father urged him to be compliant in order to spare his mother, since she also was having to deal with his sister's rebellious attitude.

His mother's shaming techniques and his father's avoidance led Kevin to a place of painful self-isolation. He became adept at showing everyone his "good" side, and determined he would have to learn to solve his own problems in private. In his "secret life," like many kids, he tried alcohol and cigarettes; but at about seven or eight, he discovered masturbation. He would go to his bedroom or the bathroom and experiment—more and more frequently. Then, when he was ten, he discovered the "medication" that had drawn his father to retreat to his bedroom at the first sign of conflict—the stash of pornographic novels and magazines.

He found pleasure and gratification in the pornography and in the secret life of the sleuth. It became a challenge to borrow his dad's material and return it without being caught, all the while maintaining his "good little boy" status. His shame grew. He felt compelled to hide his attraction to girls when he became a teenager. He didn't go on a date until he was a senior, and then it was low-key.

During college, he felt free of his family issues, but guilt and shame drove him into an early marriage when his dating relationship with a high school friend quickly turned sexual. The marriage lasted two years, but Kevin's fidelity was even shorter. His pornographic desires did not diminish with marriage, and he began an affair with another woman, named Sandra. Kevin felt that they were more sexually compatible than he and his wife, even though they argued about God. Sandra talked a lot about God to Kevin, even in the midst of their affair. But he resisted her attempts to convince him of the reality of God because he knew that if he acknowledged God's existence, he was in big trouble. After Kevin confessed his affair to his wife, they divorced and he married Sandra. Even before Kevin and Sandra married, their connection grew more relational, with less emphasis on the sex.

With the shift in their relationship and the fact that they were now married and were no longer having an affair, Kevin was more open to what Sandra had to say about God. Eventually, due largely to Sandra's recommitment to her faith and her persistent loving witness, Kevin asked Christ into his life. He and Sandra were working at building a good marriage, and he quickly grew to love Sandra's young son from her previous marriage. He thought he had the family of his dreams. The pornography battles were rare, coming up only when he went to his parents' house. He thought his war was won. He eventually got a ministerial license and became a pastor five years after he and Sandra married.

In spite of Kevin's embrace of Christian teachings and his desire for a deeper relationship with Christ, something was still wrong. The shame never left. He had no self-value and couldn't see how God or anyone else could love him. He was afraid to trust God, and was still positive he would have to solve his own problems.

When Kevin first embarked on his secret life, he had bought into a lie. The fantasy of pornography corrodes the soul with the lie that sexual pleasure is immediately and easily available. We don't have to deal with the challenge of relating to another human being. As we reach adulthood, we don't have to pay the price of mature love— putting someone's needs before our own. And we don't have to deal with the pain within; we can just medicate it with the endorphins and adrenaline generated from a sexual high. To put it bluntly, we don't have to grow up, emotionally or spiritually.

A DEADLY FANTASY

It's a deadly fantasy, because pornography provides no true satisfaction. A 1992 survey titled "Sex in America: A Definitive Survey" found that, of the 3,432 people interviewed, married couples had the highest rates of sexual satisfaction (88 percent). The study also found that married women had a significantly higher rate of orgasm than single women. "The marriage effect is so dramatic that it swamps all other data," said State University of New York sociology professor John H. Gagnon, one of the study's authors.[1]

The truth is, pornography makes great sex impossible. And the myth that sexual fulfillment can be found in the arms of a panting, always available, hot-blooded nymphomaniac is so silly it should be laughable. Sadly, however, the myth has become a part of the American male culture, resulting in the smoking wreckage of many men's (and their families') lives.

Actually, the word "men" is the wrong term. Chronologically they may be men, but emotionally and spiritually they are still boys. Through the years, I have counseled hundreds of boys who are 30, 40, even 60 years old.

One of the major differences between a man and a boy is that a man is willing to live a life of delayed gratification, because he has committed himself to a higher calling. That's why the enemy tries so hard to plant the seeds of sexual bondage while the victim is still young. If the devil can sow the myth of pornography or some other sexual bondage, he can prevent the development of a warrior in the faith. That seed of pornography will grow in the man's soul until it can block God's call to self-sacrifice. Satan will even let some of these men become prominent in the Christian community so he can infiltrate the Church. But eventually the hook in the leader's soul pulls him over the edge. That's why the man usually fights with all his might to retain his position, yet at the same time is inwardly relieved when his secret is exposed. Finally, he can get rid of the hook that hell planted in the depths of his soul. Kevin's experience was no different.

On the outside, things were going well. The little church he pastored was growing, and so was his family. He and Sandra had added two more sons. However, in time, his compulsive addiction resurfaced and grew, and he took great pains to hide his feelings of shame and worthlessness.

Once an addictive lifestyle is established, the act itself (masturbation, pornography, prostitution, homosexuality, etc.) is not the critical issue. When an addictive perspective is firmly in control, the addict often switches specific expressions of his bondage to add a greater high, or to avoid detection. We all have the foundational elements of an addictive perspective. We want to make it through life with the least amount of pain and highest amount of pleasure possible.

God doesn't call us to seek pain in our life; but in a fallen world, constantly seeking to avoid difficulty only leads to further pain, because it makes us into masters of the quick fix. And this quick-fix attitude often leads us to respond to life's challenges through fantasy or obsessive thoughts. As the obsessive thoughts increase in intensity, the hook is set and the corrosion builds. The addict has then learned that if he doesn't like the way he's feeling, just thinking about sexually acting out generates a subtle mood change. Each time the scenario replays in his head, he falls into deeper sexual bondage.

The illusion of control and power over the pain is tempting, because we don't want to accept the truth of the bondage and the increasing pressure of the shame. That's why the person thinks the problem exists outside of himself, or that the bondage is simply too big to overcome. Therefore, the destruction continues, and the sense of shame deepens as he heads for the inevitable crash.

To the outside observer, it's obvious that the person is destroying himself. However, for the man caught in the web of bondage, his actions make sense. The pressure of shame and denial is so deep he no longer has a sense of integrity or value in this area of his life. And remember, he can be doing very well in other areas of his life. He can be a great preacher, a great coach, a great businessman—you name it. But the hook has so torn apart his inner life that the only thing that counts is medicating the pain.

We may cry out to him, "Can't you see what you are doing to yourself, to your wife and kids, how your testimony for Christ has become twisted?" But integrity and relationships with others have become unimportant. The hook is imbedded deeper.

When the man responds by saying, "I'm not hurting anyone but myself," he is not just mouthing our culture's slogan; he's expressing what he has come to understand from his perspective.

Over a period of time, the addictive perspective and lifestyle develops into a delusion that directs the man's life. This perspective gains such strength that a wall of secrecy forms around him. He barricades himself. His bondage feels "safe," and no one else can enter, especially those who might expose his duplicity. A man caught in sexual bondage lives in a lonely world, because his primary energies are directed inward. He can spend enormous amounts of personal energy resisting the bondage and keeping it secret, all the while planning his next sexual high. It is a crazy—and sad—way to live! Paul may have expressed it best when he wrote the following in Romans 7:17-19:

> Yes. I'm full of myself—after all, I've spent a long time in sin's prison. What I don't understand about myself is that I decide one way, but then I act another, doing things I absolutely despise.... I can will it, but I can't do it. I decide to do good, but I don't really do it; I decide not to do bad, but then I do it anyway. My decisions, such as they are, don't result in actions. Something has gone wrong deep within me and gets the better of me every time (*THE MESSAGE*).

I remember when I first read that passage of Scripture. I was stunned. I had never heard anyone describe the way I felt as I struggled with sexual addiction. It was as though Paul were literally reading my mail!

Yet, as you may know, that is not the end of what Paul had to say about an addictive lifestyle. Romans 8—the very next chapter—is a symphony of praise about the freedom we can experience in Christ. But that turnaround usually comes through a time of crisis, a time of hopelessness and loss of control. I call them "pigpen times." In the incredible parable of the human condition known as the parable of the prodigal son (see Luke 15:11-31), a critical phrase describes the prodigal's decision to change—"when he came to his senses." The pigpen brought about a crack in his delusional perspective. In the midst of the increasing pain, a man can either reinforce the denial and delusion cycle or admit his powerlessness, cry out for help and find someone to help him face the pain. I love what John Climacus had to say in A.D. 640 about getting help with this issue:

> Do not imagine that you will overwhelm the demon of fornication by entering into an argument with him. Nature is on his side and he has the best argument. So the man who decides to struggle with his flesh and to overcome it by his own efforts is fighting in vain....Offer up to the Lord the weakness of your nature. Admit your incapacity and, without your knowing it, you will win for yourself the gift of chastity.[2]

Now Climacus was not saying that it is going to be an easy battle. When he said that "without your knowing it" you will be free, he was talking about breaking a vicious self-focus—not an easy effort. That's why his words are so insightful.

THE ADDICTIVE LIFESTYLE

When I explain to a group of men the addictive lifestyle as shown on the Noose of Sexual Addiction graphic, I can see the lights go on. All of a sudden they begin to understand what they're pulling against—and why trying to overcome it by their own efforts is an exercise in futility. This recognition is usually the first step to getting out of the pigpen of sexual bondage. Let's look at what we mean by the addictive lifestyle.

FANTASY

The cycle begins as a preoccupation or fantasy. I prefer the word "fantasy" because we are battling with a cleverly crafted lie from hell. The addict's thoughts have become focused on a sexual lie, created through pornography, memories of the past, adultery or just mental images. The mental focus is not the casual, fleeting intense sexual thoughts all of us have at times, but a prolonged intense focus that brings a mood-altering high, without actually acting out. It becomes a mental state of arousal that can blot out the current demands of real life. It is a buzz the individual cultivates as a coping mechanism. Even when he was young, Kevin spent more and more time in sexual fantasy.

With this obsessive fantasy in place, control rapidly ebbs away. And once a certain level of preoccupation dominates the thinking, it's nearly impossible to shut down the process. This mental phase of the cycle can consume enormous amounts of time. In fact, most of the person's time in the addictive cycle is spent in this phase. He truly is living in a fantasy world.

RITUAL

Eventually, the preoccupation will move to the stage of becoming a ritual. Rituals are an important part of all of our lives. We frequently use them to bring comfort at times of crisis or conflict. The person caught in a sexual bondage will do the same thing when he faces stressful situations. He will seek the comfort of his rituals—rituals that might include any of the following:

- driving by an adult bookstore
- cruising the street looking for prostitutes
- going to the singles or gay bar

- turning on the X-rated channel
- looking at someone in the office whom he finds sexually stimulating

A large part of the anguish with sexual bondage comes from the tension and struggle with the compulsive desire. The addictive ritual eases that tension, but once the person is involved in a ritual, the choice has already been made—it's only a matter of time. That's why he is, essentially, working at "keeping the lid on."

■ ■ ■ ■ ■ ■ ■ ■ ■

One of the most common rituals practiced by Christians who are in sexual bondage is to live constantly in crisis mode. They're always "fighting the devil," going from one stress situation to another—constantly living in overload. I need a high if I am going to make it, *they say to themselves.* In fact, I deserve this [sexual] release.

■ ■ ■ ■ ■ ■ ■ ■ ■

Rituals come in all shapes and sizes, even reactive ones. For example, a husband may pick a fight with his wife and then act out sexually out of supposed self-righteous anger. I know it sounds crazy, but we are talking about sexual bondage, not about a balanced life or thought process. One of the most common rituals practiced by Christians who are in sexual bondage is to live constantly in crisis mode. They're always "fighting the devil," going from one stress situation to another—constantly living in overload. The sense of impending disaster fuels the sense of being out of control. *I need a high if I am going to make it,* they say to themselves. *In fact, I deserve this release.* This is a frequent thought in the back of a sexually out of control pastor's mind. He has given so much to others all day, or week or year, he deserves this sexual release. The thought is so crazy he may not even voice it, but the myth still triggers the destructive response.

FURTHER SHAME AND GUILT

The final step in the cycle is obvious: an even greater sense of shame. After several laps around this track of insanity, there is no way out. It takes a pigpen to bring us to our senses. But even then, we will not move if we have a distorted view of our Father. The prodigal left the pigpen with loads of shame. He told himself he wasn't even worthy to be called a son. He would go back as a hired hand. But he knew his father was gracious, so he went back, despite the shame. The addiction may have corroded his soul, but in his heart he still knew he could go home to his father.

I have never counseled a man deeply mired in sexual bondage who didn't have a distorted view of Father God. One might exist, but I've never run into him. Kevin was convinced that God could not possibly love him. While his head understood God's goodness, hidden areas of his heart remained untouched by God's grace. So let's get several things straight before we look at some "how to" steps in the next chapter.

PRINCIPLES FOR THE PRODIGAL

The parable of the prodigal son in Luke 15 is a prophetic pattern for understanding our broken world and knowing how to minister to it. I want to underline several crucial points in that parable.

ALWAYS WELCOME

Many times I have treated God the Father like the prodigal did, and so have you. I have cried out for the quick fix, which is always the slogan of a person in bondage. I have demanded that God bail me out, fix me up and move with power on my behalf. "Lord, just solve this problem; I don't want to wait. I need help now!" What I'm really saying is, "I don't want the pain of having Your character worked into me."

But here is the beautiful part: No matter how many personal pigpens I have created by my own choices, He has always welcomed me home.

A PATIENT FATHER

In the parable, the father did not go drag the son out of the pigpen. And God the Father will not do that for us, either. Because He loves us so deeply, He will give us the dignity of choice. The one thing the prodigal son had left was his freedom of choice, and his father would not take that away from him. So many folks in the midst of sexual bondage ask God to come and bail them out. They want the Holy Spirit to come and "zap" them and change everything. He won't do that, because God's purpose in our lives is to heal us, not enable us. Through the years, I've learned that we can't help people until they want help.

SACRIFICIAL RESPONSE

I have always enjoyed picturing the scene in Luke 15, of the father running to the prodigal son. But not long ago, standing outside a village in Israel, I realized as never before the power of that scene. Previously, I had pictured the son walking up a long roadway to the father's huge farmhouse, like a plantation in the Old South. Then I realized the story was set in the cultural context of Palestine. The father's house was a part of a village, and as the son came through the surrounding farmers' fields, the word spread. The whole village knew of the son's return. The father could allow the son to make the long shame-filled walk to him, or he could sacrificially run to his son—he chose the latter. When the father met the young man, he hugged and kissed his son.

Our heavenly Father never asks us to come groveling to Him because of what we have done. He never exposes us to public shame.

But He does ask us to make an effort to step out of the pigpen and head home, admitting we need help.

God's Son was nailed to the cross so that we would not have to be impaled on the agony of our addictions. He was publicly humiliated and shamed so that we could be free from shame. That's the core of Christianity and the answer to every addiction that buffets men's souls.

RESPONSIBILITIES OF LEADERSHIP

The leadership within the Church must do two key things if people are going to get free from sexual bondage. First, they must be willing to *pay the price*. It is messy business trying to care for folks with corroded souls. People caught in an addictive lifestyle, which has become a common occurrence, eventually end up in the pigpen. They're a mess; therefore, we have to get our spiritual hip boots on. We're going to be "prancing in the poop." I don't know how else to describe it. Every time I've used that term in a discussion with leaders who are confronting such a situation for the first time, they immediately understand what I'm talking about—they're experiencing it!

But we shouldn't be surprised; that was the standard for the New Testament Church. If we honestly read through Paul's epistles, we'll find everything we're facing in the Church today, and more. It runs the full spectrum, from open resistance to God's standards of morality, to religious game playing while living like the world, to, as Paul put it, "sexual immorality among you...that does not occur even among pagans" (1 Cor. 5:1). Things haven't changed much, and the only way healing comes to situations of that corrosive depth is by following Paul's lead:

> Now I rejoice in what was suffered for you, and I fill up in my flesh what is still lacking in regard to Christ's afflictions, for the sake of his body, which is the church (Col. 1:24).

Paul paid the price to confront wayward people and churches so they might be healed. Ministry is an expensive proposition in a sex-soaked society. But if somebody doesn't care enough to confront in wisdom and love, people just keep crashing and nothing changes.

That obviously brings us to our second challenge: *caring confrontation*. I want to emphasize the word "caring." Sexual sin produces such emotional damage that it's easy just to let the person "have it." But we must remember, that is totally counterproductive, because the person in bondage is driven by shame. Yet on the other side of the scale, we mustn't forget that the person usually remains in sexual bondage for one of three reasons.

REMAINING IN SEXUAL BONDAGE

The first reason people remain in sexual bondage is that they *refuse to follow directions*. Most of us understand that change is an inside job. But we can make the false assumption that we can never change our actions until we first experience a change of feeling. We see the sequence of transformation in this way:

changed feelings = changed thinking = changed behavior

But the practical truth for someone caught in an addictive mindset is just the reverse:

changed behavior = changed thinking = changed feelings

Release from bondage has to begin with actions. We can't change simply by trying harder. But that doesn't mean we can't work on changing our daily behavior. If we are open to receive help with our actions and stick with it, eventually the feelings will follow. Some may feel like hypocrites because they have lived by their emotions for so long. But hypocrites from a biblical perspective are people who act counter to their convictions, not to their emotions.

That brings us to the second reason people stay in sexual bondage. Those who act counter to their convictions remain in sexual bondage if they *maintain a high-risk lifestyle* regarding their addiction. When a person finally decides to start dealing honestly with his sexual bondage, he usually makes a startling discovery: His previous lifestyle has developed a life of its own. The details of his life actually have been arranged to support and fit the very behavior he wants to be free from. If he doesn't change his environment, which can be filled with triggers and cues that remind him of the way things used to be, he can easily slip right back into the old behavior.

Most people do not understand just how incredibly complex and deep the web of sexual addiction can be. Figure 4 is a simple summary of the many factors that can hold a person in bondage.

- *Biological systems:* Refers to the dependence the person has developed to the high of the sexual addiction.

- *Relational networks:* Points to the friends and those close to him who actually enable the points of bondage in his life. As I previously mentioned, once our church started a group to help the men caught in sexual addiction, we rapidly realized we needed a group for the wives also. Sexual addiction is about a family system.

- *Family systems:* Refers to the person's present family as well as the family of origin issues he struggles with.

- *Concurrent addictions:* It is not unusual for a person to battle with several issues of bondage at the same time. For me, it was a threefold chain: alcohol, pornography and workaholism.

- *Cultural addictions:* In our pleasure-focused society, sexual addiction has become a way of life. In many cases, it has become big business. What Scripture calls sexual addiction is viewed by many as normal. Coming to sexual health is definitely an uphill battle in our culture.

THE WEB OF SEXUAL ADDICTION

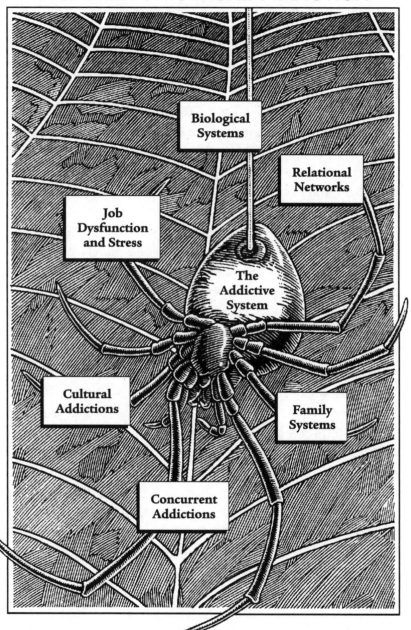

FIGURE 4

• *Job dysfunction and stress.* Eventually, the addict's job becomes structured around the bondage as well. I have encouraged people to change jobs when it is appropriate, even if it means adjusting to a lower living standard. It is better to live in a smaller house with a clean heart than to sit in a huge home with a big car while going down in flames.

Relapse is the third and main reason people remain in sexual bondage. No other issue demands more of us as leaders attempting to help people out of deep sexual bondage. To help them effectively deal with the challenge of relapse, we have to be tough and tender at the same time. It's a subject we'll reserve for a fuller discussion in the next chapter.

The weight of all of this underlines the absolute necessity of developing effective small groups within the church to help men face this battle. They *cannot* deal with the issue alone. They ended up in the pigpen because they chose to do their own thing.

Look at King David. He would have been destroyed if Nathan hadn't intervened. And Nathan didn't just point out David's folly with Bathsheba. He saved David from starting a building program that wasn't from God (see 2 Sam. 7). At the end of his life, Nathan saved David's family from the king's lack of attention (see 1 Kings 1:11-13). At critical points in David's life, Nathan graciously confronted David with the truth. One of the major reasons David remained a man after God's own heart (see Acts 13:22) was because he had Nathan's counsel.

Every man needs a Nathan. Without Nathans, the Church doesn't stand a chance of breaking the sexual bondage that has become so much a part of men's lives in our culture. Nathans help men understand that the Lord will not give up on them. And, when these men realize the Lord will not give up on them, they will keep getting up no matter how many times they relapse—and they will deal with the spiritual and emotional corrosion in their lives.

Gene McConnell shared the greatest testimony of that fact that I have ever heard.[3] He had been a youth pastor who loved the Lord deeply. Yet, during his years as a pastor, he was out of control sexually, even to the point of being arrested for attempted murder and rape.

His world totally collapsed. He was, however, very fortunate because his wife and family stood beside him. One day, after years of working through the grief and shame of what he had done, he was on a business trip. After a hard day's work on the road, he came to his hotel room and turned on the TV. He had specifically asked for the porno channel to be blocked in his room, but it was on. He sat there that evening in his fatigued state and slipped right back into the old habits after having been sober for an extended period of time.

As a result, he became so filled with shame he scarcely could verbalize it. He told himself he would never get free and real change was a joke for him. Later that night, he had a vivid dream. He saw himself sitting in a courtroom once again. The prosecutor stood to present the case and began by pulling down a screen, showing a video of Gene's life—in every sordid detail. He concluded the case by saying, "This man said he was gong to stop his behavior, and he never did. Look at how often he promised to change—but he lied." Gene could only bow his head in total shame.

The defense attorney stood to present Gene's case. He declared, "Everything the prosecution has shown you is true. Every detail is correct. All except one. He left out a key ingredient. Everything Gene did was paid for." Then his attorney pulled off his shirt and showed the scars on his back and asked that they be entered as evidence. He showed his hands, feet and side and proclaimed, "I don't deny that Gene has done what he has done. But it has already been paid for."

Gene said that night he understood for the first time how he could have done all the things he had done and still be washed, cleansed and forgiven. Yes, there would be consequences for his actions; he had already experienced that. But he finally understood the Cross—the new beginning offered to him. And it changed him to the core of his being. The noose was finally cut from his soul.

Notes

1. Laurie Hall, "The Great Porn Sham," *New Man,* May 1997, pp. 36-37.
2. Gary Thomas, *Seeking the Face of God* (Nashville, TN: Thomas Nelson Publishers, 1997), p. 63.
3. "The Church as Sex Educators and Healers," The American Association of Christian Counselors National Convention, 1998.

CHAPTER 7

When Jesus Starts Becoming Lord

Near the end of my flying career I did something I'd wanted to do for years. The biggest risk wasn't that I might be shot down; it was that I might be identified. So I planned carefully before I flew out of the Alameda Naval Air Station and headed south. My flight plan would make it difficult for anyone else to figure out exactly what I was doing.

The Big Sur area flashed underneath as I hugged the coastline. When I saw Morro Rock in the distance, I turned inland. I had hiked this familiar country many times, dreaming of the day I'd scream down this valley in my jet. My target lay just ahead. I knew it well; I had strolled its manicured streets for more than four years; I had mowed some of those lawns as part of a summer job. I accelerated slightly and checked the sun's angle to make sure it would be in the eyes of anyone on the ground as I tore overheard. You have to consider such things, because little old grandmas who can barely see have been known to pick up the serial numbers of fighter aircraft buzzing their homes.

Everything was set—the conditions were perfect. As I rocketed between the third and fourth floors of the administration building, I caught the startled look on a secretary's face as I shot past her window. I'm sure she jumped 10 feet when the sound hit the building.

Then I pulled the aircraft straight up, executing rapid aileron rolls as I disappeared from sight. I had done it. I had buzzed my college!

It wasn't a wise idea—in fact, it was beyond stupid. But it was something I had always wanted to do.

The rest of the flight was by the book and without incident. I landed at home base and went about my business, though I do admit I wore a sly, satisfied smile.

Several weeks later, the operations officer called me aside. I thought he was going to compliment me on an excellent job. (The Lord would eventually build humility into me, but first He had to tear down my walls of pride and denial.)

I noticed that the officer wasn't smiling; he looked rather perturbed. "Captain Roberts," he said in measured tones, "I have a very important question to ask you. Now, think carefully before you answer. This is a serious matter." Sweat beaded on my forehead. Then, with focused intensity, he got to the point: "Did you buzz your school several weeks ago?"

I was stunned. There was no way anyone could have seen me or traced my flight. He had to be bluffing. The school probably complained, so Operations looked up the records to find alumni. I was in the area, and they were on a fishing expedition. There was absolutely no way my stunt could have been uncovered.

A myriad of thoughts raced through my mind at lightning speed: *I can't tell this guy. And I don't have to; they're just guessing. If I tell the truth, they'll let me have it. I'll end up as permanent shovel officer behind the elephants at the local carnival. This guy has my career in his hands.*

Then I realized the officer didn't just have my career in his hands—he held my life! I had made a commitment to Christ, and this was a moment when I would decide what kind of man I would become. Would I continue to live in denial, or would I come clean and face the music? What would my testimony be—a travesty or the truth? Would Jesus actually start becoming Lord in my life, and not just Savior?

The Word of Our Testimony

The apostle John said in Revelation 12:11 that there were three things that would overcome hell:

1. The blood of the Lamb
2. The word of our testimony
3. Love that defies death

We've already discussed the power of Christ's shed blood. Now let's look at our word of testimony. It's easy to understand the phrase within its original historical context. John called out to men and women he had poured his life into. They faced the extreme choice of confessing Caesar as lord and being allowed to live, or speaking the truth—Jesus is Lord—and being executed. John calls out to them to stand their ground and speak the truth. Don't deny your Lord and Savior. But how do those words apply to our lives?

■ ■ ■ ■ ■ ■ ■ ■ ■

Addiction, at its spiritual core, is about idolatry—about where we're going to find life and fulfillment.

■ ■ ■ ■ ■ ■ ■ ■ ■

Interestingly enough, with the same intensity. Many folks don't even realize they make the choice daily—or that the choice is so crucial. In many ways, the choice John's original readers faced is exactly the same choice I faced when the officer asked me what I'd done. Would I live in denial or begin to walk in the truth, even though the results could be painful?

Addiction, at its spiritual core, is about idolatry—about where we're going to find life and fulfillment. Will we find it in a porno magazine, an affair, a bottle, a drug-induced high or in a lie to make us look good? All addiction is about trying to get our needs met in the immediate instead of the eternal.

At that critical point, I could no longer deny what I'd done. And that's a turning point that doesn't come easily in any man's life, especially when he struggles with sexual bondage. It's totally different from the familiar refrain of, "I'm sorry, Lord; I'll never do it again." Instead, it's a realization that I *will* do it again and again, but at the same time with an awareness that this just can't go on any longer. It's a devastating, emotional bind, but it's the first step toward recovery.

I always warn the men who come to me struggling with sexual issues that things will probably get a lot worse before they get better. The pain level skyrockets when they reach the turning point and have to deal with denial. As I stood before the officer, everything within me wanted to deny what I had done. But at the same time, *I desperately wanted to speak the truth.* I emphasize this point because it can be difficult for those around the person in denial to realize just how difficult it is to break free.

Unfortunately, a man with the noose of sexual addiction around his neck usually ignores the turning point, and the consequences pile up. He ends up going through a series of marriages or affairs, or his children start showing signs of addictive behavior in their own lives, or his career crumbles. Any number of events can surround him like a school of piranhas. That's why, in my counseling office, I've so many times asked the question, "How bad does it have to get?" I point out to the addict that if he continues, he will eventually lose everything.

When we deal with something like alcoholism, usually we can detect the problem prior to total collapse and possibly set up an intervention. But when it comes to sexual bondage, the shame factor is so high and the denial so deep, especially with Christians, that it's difficult to break through. That's one of the reasons I've found Dr. Carnes's Sexual Addiction Screening Test (see appendix B) such an important tool in helping men break out of denial.

People with a heart for God who are entrapped in sexual bondage have learned to compartmentalize their minds. They have segregated part of their lives in a corner of nonrecognition. They deeply love the Lord, and yet can't stand what they sometimes do, so that part of their lives almost takes on a separate identity. They realize they can't beat the bondage, so they wall it in with denial, hoping against hope that somehow it will eventually subside or go away, but it doesn't. That's why, if we can punch a hole through the wall of denial before it's too late, their love for God will lead them to reach out for help.

Dr. Carnes's SAST analysis consists of 25 simple questions, some of which I've updated for today's spiritual battlefield. I've found that most men honestly want to know where they are in this battle, because nearly every man, at some point, has struggled with this issue. If they score more than 15 yes answers, I advise them to seek help in the For Men Only Seminar we provide at the church. It's amazing how many men are surprised that they have a problem with sexual addiction. They know they've struggled at times, but they have no idea it's a serious problem. Denial has blinded their eyes.

I estimate that about 50 percent of the men in a typical church are quietly—and sometimes desperately—struggling with sexual addiction. When they finally see from an objective analysis that they're in trouble, they'll reach out for help if it's available and effective.

Jesus starts becoming Lord in every area of a man's life when he finally has someone help him understand that he has a problem, and that denial must cease. That's why I believe that as many churches as possible need to provide an effective, biblically compassionate ministry to help men win this battle as soon as possible. The only other option is to wait until we have to pick up the pieces after they've crashed, a devastating option because we're talking about the wreckage of their families—their grieving and confused wives and their wounded children.

DISCOVERING THE DANGER SIGNS

For pastors, counselors and lay leaders, the first step in helping these addicts is to understand the nature of the noose that has been placed around their souls. Then we need to help them reach through the walls of denial they have built through the years. This is never a pleasant experience, because their pain level first goes through the roof when the walls start coming down. That's why this next stage in their healing process is so crucial. This stage involves training them in four specific areas:

1. UNDERSTAND THE STRESSORS

This accountability requires an understanding of the specific noose hell has fashioned. First, the man needs to understand his temptation habits. The bondage cycle follows a predictable, but usually unrecognized, pattern. That's why he needs to ask himself such specific questions about his temptation:

1. What day of the week am I most challenged?
    - Monday   - Tuesday   - Wednesday   - Thursday
    - Friday   - Saturday   - Sunday

2. What time of the day am I most challenged?
    - Morning   - Lunch   - Afternoon   - Dinner
    - Early evening   - Late evening

3. Where am I tempted the most?
    - At work   - At home   - In the community
    - Away from home   - Other

4. How do I feel when I am battling temptation?

5. What does the sexual sin give me that I feel I need?[1]

It's amazing, but I have never counseled anyone who realized that his battle with sexual bondage followed a predictable pattern. Initially, they think the questions are silly. Then, if they take their time and answer the questions carefully, the lights start turning on, and they recognize that their enemy uses a specific strategy.

Once they have answered the previous questions, they'll be able to understand the *triggers* and *rituals* that have developed. For the first time, they'll begin to notice that the details of their lives actually have become arranged to support and trigger the very bondage from which they want to get free. Freedom from the noose will never be possible until they clearly identify the triggers—the issues that start the sequence of preoccupation and fantasy within.

Stress frequently triggers the slide back into the old way of doing things. It's one thing to decide to change our lives when everything's going smoothly, and quite another to stick with the commitment when things are falling apart. If people don't develop new approaches to coping with stress and the feelings of loneliness and worthlessness, the pattern will continue to tear at their souls. Once again, they need to be aware of Satan's schemes (see 2 Cor. 2:11) in order to know just how vulnerable they are to falling back into the noose. Most men fail to notice the clear indicators of falling back, because they're focused outward, directed toward *doing,* rather than being in touch with where they are emotionally. That's why I have found the following analysis helpful to men for understanding how vulnerable they are:

Rate yourself on a scale of 1 to 10 in the following areas and total your score at the bottom:

1. Physically:
   Exhausted/Tired   1 2 3 4 5 6 7 8 9 10   Energetic/Strong

2. Emotionally:
   Discouraged/Down   1 2 3 4 5 6 7 8 9 10   Encouraged/Up

3. Mentally:
   Bored/Discontented 1 2 3 4 5 6 7 8 9 10   Challenged/Content

4. Spiritually:
   Depleted/Empty   1 2 3 4 5 6 7 8 9 10   Growing/Full

5. Vocationally:
   Frustrated/Failing   1 2 3 4 5 6 7 8 9 (10)   Succeeding/Attaining

6. Relationally:
   Alienated/Cold   1 2 3 4 5 6 7 (8) 9 10   Close/Warm

7. Internally:
   Hopeless/Sad   1 2 3 4 5 6 7 (8) 9 10   Hopeful/Happy

8. Personally:
   Insecure/Unsure   1 2 3 4 5 (6) 7 8 9 10   Secure/Confident

9. Inwardly:
   Bitter/Angry   1 2 3 4 5 (6) 7 8 9 10   Open/Accepting

10. Presently:
   Wounded/Hurt   1 2 3 4 5 6 (7) 8 9 10   Appreciated/Loved

Total Score: _75_   2

Scoring:
100-90 — You are in great shape internally.
 90-80 — Good.
 80-70 — You need to start being watchful.
 70-60 — You're in the danger zone. You're a lot weaker
         than you think.
 60-50 — You're in real danger, and you probably sense it
         in some way.

These kinds of tools help men realize that dealing with sexual bondage is not like taking a hike on a sunny day. If a man thinks, *All I need is a change of scenery; it'll soon be over and then I can relax,* he's dangerously wrong. Dealing with the noose of sexual bondage is a challenge, a mountain climb, sometimes a cliff-hanger—hanging on by nothing more than God's grace. Recovering addicts must learn the skill of pacing themselves and staying in touch with where they are emotionally. They frequently battle with overconfidence because the enemy will lie low and wait for emotional low times to strike again, shoving the man down the slippery slopes of relapse.

At some point, the person has to understand that coming to good health can mean abandoning key aspects of the lifestyle associated with the bondage. For some, that's the biggest sacrifice of all. Sexual bondage doesn't spring up overnight. As the bondage grows, it becomes the centerpiece of the person's attention—the pivotal point around which everything else revolves.

Normally, the man will attempt to justify himself when he's in slippery conditions: *The circumstances make it impossible for me to change. I can't cut off the relationship with the other woman; it would hurt her deeply. How can I avoid pornography when it's all over the place where I work? All my friends are at the singles' bar [or gay bar].* The list is endless, but the situation stays the same. He pits his strength against the sickness of the environment that won't support his decision to walk clean, especially when he's down physically, emotionally or spiritually.

Once the man is down, he's set up to miss the ongoing temptation by focusing on the problems he perceives around him, such as, *My wife's not very loving,* or, *I'm having trouble on the job.* As a result, he loses sight of the real life-and-death battle. Once again, the noose of bondage is tightening around his soul.

As the stress increases, he may try to rev up his willpower another notch to remain clean. But the results are predictable. Because of the stress within, he can't keep the lid on, and he falls from his mountaintop commitment to walk with the Lord and returns to the pit of bondage.

That's why it's absolutely necessary for him to identify the specific things that set him up—the triggers and addictive rituals he's developed to make him feel better when he's down:

- What specific stressor is likely to lead him into the bondage sequence once again?

- What mind games does he tend to play so he will feel entitled to act out sexually?

- What rationalizations has he used in the past to talk himself into putting the noose around his soul?

If he answers these questions honestly, he will begin to see that the sexual bondage isn't something that just hits him, something he can't understand. There are always clear indicators that reveal when he's headed for trouble—if he's watching. The battle is about the way he's learned to deal with stress.

Helping him understand this sequence is exactly why small groups are so essential. As he makes himself accountable at the points of his weaknesses—his triggers and rituals—he's much less vulnerable to rationalize destructive behavior. The other men in a small group can easily tell when one of them is making excuses for his behavior, because they have done the same thing themselves so many times. And, more important, they can hold one another accountable for getting up the mountain together. They become emotionally roped to each other and, for some men, it's the first time in their lives they've had a significant emotional connection with another man.

LEARN EMERGENCY PROCEDURES

Flying a high performance aircraft can be a lot of fun when everything goes as planned, but it's another ball game when emergencies occur. Tearing through the air at 30,000 feet is not the time to think through for the first time what to do in an emergency. That's why we spend hours and hours going over emergency procedures before we ever strap that aircraft on. We must know ahead of time what to do in any given situation. We practice so many times that responding correctly becomes second nature. I remember a number of times "watching myself" respond to an emergency. I had so conditioned myself that I spent no time thinking about how I should respond. I knew what I needed to do and did it almost instinctively.

It's sad that so few men take such an approach when it comes to breaking the noose of sexual bondage. They've never thought through what to do when the temptation returns full force. At the altar, or during some spiritually high moment, they make a commitment never again to be involved in this sexual behavior. Those are critical moments of commitment—they're Holy Spirit inspired, and that's why the enemy keeps his head down for a while. But we can count on the fact that hell is not going to lose gracefully. At some point, all hell will once again break loose against them. They'll find themselves facing a spiritual emergency. And, tragically, few men have ever practiced any emergency procedures to handle the situation. That's why they'll find themselves back at the altar, once again crying out to God after they've crashed. We don't have to do that very many times before we start to become religious, caught in a trap of playing a game with God.

Christ died to break the guilt and shame in our lives. He rose from the dead so we don't have to endure endless trips to the altar over the same issue, constantly rededicating our lives. He rose from the dead so that we can live in a newness of life—not a perfect life, but a life without nooses around our necks.

Therefore, addicts need to do two things: First, they need to develop a series of action steps that can serve as an escape route when they find themselves moving into a high-risk time.

No temptation has seized you except what is common to man. And God is faithful; he will not let you be tempted beyond what you can bear. But when you are tempted, he will also provide *a way out* so that you can stand up under it (1 Cor. 10:13, emphasis added).

Here's an important truth: The way out doesn't appear by magic. Instead, it's something we purpose to receive from God, a conscious decision. We must determine our way out before the heat of the emergency hits. Otherwise, our emotions will dominate, and we'll be blind to God's provision. Therefore, we must:

- **Identify** concrete signs that a relapse is possible, based on our understanding of our emotional state and an understanding of the triggers and rituals in our lives.

- **Establish** a secondary point of health in our lives, such as recognizing that we drink too much coffee or eat too much food when we're under stress. We must be sensitive to our secondary commitments to health, and when we see them weakening, realize that it's a warning that we're approaching an emergency situation.

- **Line out** the specific action steps we need to take to prevent a relapse, such as calling a member of our small group for prayer, or easing up on our frantic pace.

- **Practice** the relational aspects of our action steps, such as calling a member of the small group. This is critical because, under pressure, we'll tend to draw back into our old patterns and not reach out.

- **Learn** to nurture ourselves. The enemy takes note of the changes that have occurred in our lives, and he doesn't like them. And he'll do everything possible to push us once again into a depleted emotional state where we are vulnerable. We should schedule hobbies, family time and rest into our lives and stick with it. Developing our physical fitness also helps in our overall emotional strength.

- **Memorize** scriptures that really mean something to us and that deal with our specific vulnerabilities. This battle isn't just about emotional health and learning to take care of ourselves. At its core, it's a matter of spiritual life and death. I have seen too many potentially great men of God go down in flames over this issue. It isn't a casual conflict. Therefore, we need to get God's emergency procedures down in the recesses of our minds. We must allow His

Word to be hidden in our heart so that when everything in our flesh screams to do something stupid, we will have God's emergency procedures written on our hearts.

Sometimes, coming out of bondage is acting in response to God's Word, no matter what our feelings tell us. We can never pull that off if we don't have Scripture embedded in our souls prior to the heat of a spiritual and emotional emergency.

Recovering sexual addicts need to understand clearly what to do in case they relapse. Some might ask, "Didn't my prayer for release guarantee me against falling again?" I wish it were that easy, but it's not. God does His part in getting the noose off us, but we have to do our part, too. Christ will never let us down, but we can drop the ball on our side of the court. Remember that only God is perfect. Every now and then, we get hit by our imperfection.

We have to think through what we'll do if we relapse into our old behavior. A plan doesn't give us permission to relapse, but it does help us to know how we can turn a slip into a future victory. I've lost count of the number of times I've seen men thrown into a sense of despair over a slip. And frequently it occurs right after a major victory. Instead of despair, we need to face the facts. We need to remind ourselves, *This is war, and, whatever it takes, I'll hang in there. Although this battle is much tougher than I ever imagined, Jesus will not forsake me, and I mustn't forsake myself. I need to learn from this failure. I need to have the Holy Spirit open my eyes.*

The eye-opening experience frequently comes through a discussion and confession with our small group. If we allow despair and resignation to grip our hearts, isolation and secrecy will keep us down. If, however, we have an emergency procedure for relapse that calls us to honesty and accountability with our small group, we'll eventually be able to cut through the noose around our souls.

Our small group becomes our lifeline during such times. When we slip, the first folks who should know are those in our small group—secrecy only increases the pain. We need to confess to them and ask them to give us insights into what went wrong. The small group is also the place where we need to share our emergency procedures for escape or the challenge of facing a relapse. The group can be of tremendous help in the preparation process; they can help us see if we've missed any important elements. Above all, they can give us support and encouragement.

UNDERSTAND THAT HEALING IS A PROCESS

The fact that healing is a process doesn't mean we can count on failing an infinite number of times before we are free of the noose of sexual bondage, but it does mean it's an emotional process. In figure 5 is a simple illustration I've used to help men understand how they'll feel emotionally as they come to good sexual health:

The Healing Process

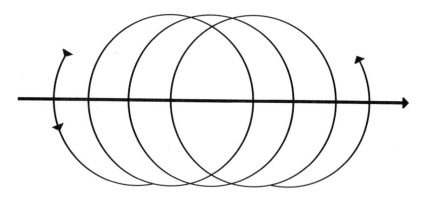

FIGURE 5

There will be emotional highs and lows. The highs are great. The recovering addict finally begins to see himself as Christ sees him. The lows are tough but necessary, because they're where we come face-to-face with the addictive thinking that has quietly controlled our minds for years. The lows are where we can reprogram our thinking to God's perspective so that the highs are built on the truth, not on our addictive thinking.

	FACE THE FACTS	TAKE A STAND	PUT ON NEW SELF	WALKING IN GRACE
CORE BELIEFS	Uncover the dysfunctional past or traumatic events	Challenge core beliefs with biblical truth	Receive and declare God's view of you	Integrate new core beliefs (Small Groups)
PAINFUL THINKING	Identify rationalization and distortion of reality	Confront distortions with biblical truth	Develop feedback system to keep reality in focus	Recognize ongoing need for feedback (SG)
RITUALS	Identify specific rituals	Confront rituals with consequences	Develop nurturing rituals	Develop deeper relationships (SG/home)
HOPELESS-NESS	Check for life-threatening depression	Seek help from coordinators and groups	Establish relapse strategies	Have no secret life (SG/home)
LOSS OF CONTROL	Face the consequences of your actions	Use consequences as a lever to honestly seek help	Establish back-up plan for relapse	Reach out to help others (SG)

FIGURE 6

The one thing that's so frequently missing from an addict's understanding of what's involved in obtaining freedom from the noose is the extent of internal change that is necessary. Sexual addicts have to face what they have been involved in and take an effective stand against it. They have to put on a new way of thinking and living. And the most challenging step of all is learning to walk in God's grace as a way of life. Figure 6 on the prior page shows how much is involved in this process.

This depth of change doesn't come in a moment. It usually takes three to five years to go through the process, with God working miracles every step of the way. The goal isn't just to get the noose off the soul, but to become someone who is experiencing all that God has for him.

FACE THE WOUND WITHIN

As I stood there that day, facing the operations officer's penetrating question, I was actually facing the issue of my wounds within, and I didn't even realize it. I swallowed hard and said, "Yes, sir. I buzzed my school." He paused for what seemed an eternity as I stood at rigid attention. By now the sweat beads had turned into a river on my forehead. I was just waiting for the hammer to fall. I knew I was a dead duck.

Then a twinkle came to his eye. He said, "Don't ever do it again," and walked away. I staggered over to the corner of the ready room and collapsed in a pile on a chair. At the time, I had little comprehension of the spiritual impact of what had just taken place. I was only concerned with my rapidly evaporating career as a fighter pilot. In retrospect, it was a profound step in my healing journey. For the first time since I had said yes to Christ, I trusted Him with my deepest wounds. For the first time in a very long, long time, I had made myself vulnerable to a male authority figure. Growing up in a profoundly dysfunctional home, I had concluded at an early age that trusting men in authority could be very painful. But the Holy Spirit will bring us back to face our worst fears and wounds so we can be healed and set free from our bondage.

That day started a journey that eventually resulted in the healing of the father wound that lay so deep in my heart. I realized that, despite what I might say to the contrary, I would give anything to have a father put his arms around me and say, "Great job, Ted." Just once! But eventually, I came to realize the painful truth. (Remember, I said that in the healing process things initially get worse before they get better.) I would never have a physical father do that. It was never going to happen, and I needed to grieve that fact. That was one of the reasons I reacted negatively at times to male authority figures; yet I was deeply drawn to them at the same time.

I remember when the issue came to a turning point in my office one day. The Holy Spirit gently began to challenge me as I was praying. I sensed Him say, "Give God praise for your father."

"Give God praise for my father?" I said. "I didn't even know the man." Then it hit me: God was once again helping me deal with my wounded heart. So I stood up in my office behind closed doors and uttered words that had never been part of my vocabulary. "Dad, I never got to meet you. I never knew who you were, but thanks for giving me life. Hopefully, I'll get to meet you at the other end." It was like a hidden dam broke. I wept convulsively for the next half hour. Those tears came from deep within.

> The Spirit helps us in our weakness. We do not know what we ought to pray for, but the Spirit himself intercedes for us with groans that words cannot express (Rom. 8:26).

I had been there before. In fact, it has been a constant pattern in my life. God the Father will not ignore our deep wounds. Years before, as a young believer, I had read through Romans 8. I had a night flight later that evening, so I had time to relax a little. At the beginning of the year I'd made a commitment to read through the New Testament, so I was giving it a try. It was strange territory for me, but I was plowing my way through Romans 8. I even had a *Living Bible*, but I still couldn't understand it. Then, I read verse 15:

"For you did not receive a spirit that makes you a slave again to fear, but you received the Spirit of sonship. And by him we cry 'Abba, *Father.'* The Spirit himself testifies with our spirit that we are God's children" (emphasis added).

Suddenly, the Holy Spirit went from speaking to the left side of my brain to the right side. I began to cry, and as I closed my eyes and leaned back against the wall, I saw a giant pant leg in front of me. (I guess I thought God was too big to get both legs in the house.) I saw myself as a little boy, instinctively running over and hugging that pant leg. Finally, I understood I had a Father who wouldn't flake out on me. He'd always be there, and His love for me wasn't conditioned on my performance. I finally had a Dad. The pain I'd carried in the inner recesses of my soul began to heal.

Eventually, that profound weakness became unique strength. I began to realize just how important a gift I'd been given in Christ, in being a dad myself. As I spent time with my kids, laughing, playing and having fun, I could be the kid I never had the chance to be. It was great; even at 30 or 40 years old I could go fly a kite, play in the mud, make silly sounds and giggle a lot. (They commit you to the funny farm if you do that without kids.) Now, I was better able to be the father I had always wanted to be—something I had struggled with before. I could love, protect, discipline and help my kids grow to their full potential.

The Father can make all things new. Sure, I was terrified. I didn't know how to do this parenting thing, and I was trying to learn how to be a godly husband at the same time. But my heavenly Father never let me down. He showed me how to do it, one step at a time.

One day, as I was driving with my son when he was young, I sat back and rested my left arm on the open window, with my right hand loosely gripping the wheel. Apparently my son thought that I was pretty impressive, because out of the corner of my eye I noticed that he was mimicking every move I made. It just blew me away that he was copying me so closely. I couldn't stop the tears.

(I know it sounds like all I do is cry. That's not quite true, but it happens when the Lord touches me, or when I see how good He is to me. So I guess I do cry a lot.)

I pulled the car over and began to tell my son how much I loved him, and how great it was that we had such a wonderful relationship. I told him I'd never had a dad, and it meant so much to me that we were so close. Bryan paused for a moment, then looked straight at me. I could tell his six-year-old brain was in high gear. Then he blurted, "Well then, Dad, how do you know how to raise me?"

For a second I was stunned by his penetrating question, but the Holy Spirit bailed me out. I said, "Son, I just look at how the Father is raising me, and I try to do the same with you."

In the book of Revelation, John the Beloved stated that there were three things that would break the back of hell:

1. the blood of the Lamb
2. the word of testimony *from a changed heart*
3. a love that defies death

That day, my son helped me to see even more clearly God the Father's love for me, which is revealed for all time in the death and resurrection of His Son. It's a love that defied the power of death and forever broke the power of hell's bondage in the human heart.

Notes

1. Adapted from Bruce H. Wilkinson, *Personal Holiness in Times of Temptation* (Atlanta: Walk Through the Bible Ministries, 1997), pp. 54-55. Used by permission.
2. Ibid., p. 55.

CHAPTER **8**

Fitting All the Pieces Together
By Pastor Harry Flanagan

We have covered an enormous amount of material in these first seven chapters. After sharing this information with literally thousands of pastors and leaders throughout the years, I have frequently heard questions such as, "Great information, but how does all this fit together? How does this practically work in a small group or in a church setting?" In response to these questions, I have asked Pastor Harry Flanagan, who oversees our For Men Only groups, to share with us how he applies these truths in the lives of hurting men.

Harry has come a long way. At an early age, he discovered his father's stash of pornography, which led to masturbation. He found this to be a "safe" way to medicate his problems in private. This was the beginning of his sexual addiction.

Harry finished college, got married and then became a Christian. He thought that if he became a pastor, he might get the validation he hungered for and stop masturbation. Yet nothing he did gave him the internal fulfillment that would numb his sense of inadequacy. Harry plunged back into masturbation, but soon he also started having encounters with women in his church. Eventually Harry's shame was exposed, and he ended up losing both his family and his church.

Nearly 14 years ago, Harry walked into East Hill Church a broken man—a fallen pastor who was convinced that God was through with him. But I saw in his eyes a hunger for wholeness and a heart for Christ despite his past bondage and tragic mistakes. I knew God was going to use him again. Harry came to learn through the men of his small group that God exposed his sin and secrecy not to reject and despise him, but rather exposed his sin so He could show him His outrageous love. God has restored Harry's life "exceedingly abundantly above all that he could ask or even think."

■ ■ ■ ■ ■ ■ ■ ■ ■ ■

I was in my office late one Friday afternoon when I received a call from Rob. I am usually glad to receive calls from Rob, as he's a member of East Hill Church and a fairly new member of For Men Only. He's become a friend of mine, and he has a witty sense of humor. It is not unusual for Rob and me to sit in Starbucks and shoot the breeze, as we men have the habit of doing, talking sports, religion or politics.

Rob works at a large company in the "Silicon Forest" in the greater Portland area. He is in management and has been very successful in his career. He has a wonderful wife, Shelly, and two daughters and one son. One daughter is attending college. Rob seems very devoted to his family.

But this phone call was different. Rob asked to meet with me in my office because he wanted to talk in private. As we spoke, I could hear the pain and anguish in his voice.

When Rob walked into my office with his head down and eyes averted from mine, it confirmed to me that something was very wrong. My friend was in trouble and hurting. Rob was quick and to the point. "Harry, I've really screwed up. Shelly found a pornographic video in my briefcase. I forgot it was there; I haven't looked at it in months, but Shelly doesn't care. She's now questioning whether or not anything in our relationship is real. I told her I was sorry. I really have repented, but she just doesn't trust me. What do I do?"

"We can't undo what's already been done, Rob," I said. "We can only move forward. You will need to rebuild trust with Shelly, but this really isn't about her. You can't control how Shelly responds to you, but you can make life choices that offer the opportunity to rebuild her ability to trust you again."

"What else can I do, Harry? I don't want to lose my wife and kids. It would kill me."

"It's your addiction that's killing you, Rob. In fact, because of your addiction, you've probably been slowly losing your family for a long time. You've been leading a life of isolation, hiding the truth of your addiction, right?"

"I do have secrets, but I spend time with my family. I love them."

"Right, but they don't know who you really are, because you've hidden your thoughts, feelings and behaviors. You've been wearing a mask. In fact, I'm not sure that you know yourself that well."

"Yeah, you're right. I don't think I've got any other choice. I feel so ashamed. I've just been afraid to own my problem. If people knew, they would run for the hills. I feel so empty."

"So," I said to Rob, "are you willing to face your issues, to dig into your problem?"

THE STEPS TO OVERCOMING ADDICTION

I can't tell you how often I have had conversations like this one as I counsel men or take them through their orientation to For Men Only. In reality, there are only two steps that Rob needs to take to radically move forward in his battle with addiction. Each of the steps is very doable, although I am not suggesting that they are easy or painless. In fact, I guarantee both pain and points of difficulty and struggle. Yet here at East Hill, we have seen scores of men gain victory over their addictions by following these two steps.

"What steps?" you may ask. Great question! First, Rob needs to become self-aware of the what, when, where, how and why of his addiction. In other words, he needs to determine why he does the things he doesn't want to do. Most people who battle with addiction not only avoid exposing their secrets to others, but they also avoid looking at those feelings, thoughts and beliefs that drive their addictive behavior. To take the first major step in healing, Rob needs to truly examine his addictive mindset and patterns.

The second step is for Rob to become truly accountable to himself, God and others. Accountability requires Rob to know himself (his feelings, thoughts, beliefs and patterns of behavior) as well as to share these new insights with the significant people in his life, such as Shelly, his family, his friends, his pastor and the men of his For Men Only group, where healing starts.

It is in his For Men Only group that he will learn the disciplines of vulnerable transparency. It is here that the transforming of his life begins. In this group, he will learn general information about the nature of addictions and discover the truth about his addictive patterns.

This happens in the context of Romans 12:15, where the apostle Paul says that "when one of us cries we all cry, and when one of us celebrates we all celebrate." That can only happen in the safe confines of a small group where grace is in place (receiving something good you don't deserve) and men learn to share their darkest secrets (face their pain) with the support of their new partners in healing.

Now let's get back to Rob's story. Our first job is to help Rob get an overview of what is driving his addictive patterns.

THE ADDICTIVE ROOT

"Rob, here's a copy of *Pure Desire*. Turn with me to chapter 3. Let's look at the Noose of Sexual Addiction. We're going to use the noose to discover what's going on with your addiction, and after that we will look at ways of preventing you from relapsing again.

"You will remember from the For Men Only orientation class that you've got to move through these two steps: (1) become self-aware to the internal and external patterns of your sexual addiction, and (2) take the practical steps of building accountability into your life.

"On the left side of the noose is the addictive root. It is here that we examine what's going on in your life and seek to discover both the present and past origins of your pain, anxiety, stress and fears."

Normally in a session such as this one with Rob, I would then ask several key questions to get an understanding of what's happening in a person's life. These key questions about the addictive root include some of the following:

- *Question 1:* Are you having issues at home that are causing you stress, anxiety, fear or emotional pain?

- *Question 2:* What was it like growing up in your family of origin? Tell me about your relationships with your father, mother and siblings.

- *Question 3:* Are you having issues at work that are causing you stress, anxiety, fear or emotional pain? Have you ever had painful experiences on this job? How about other jobs in your past?

- *Question 4:* Have you experienced personal trauma or significant loss recently or in your past?

Because Rob is a friend of mine and has shared some of his story with me, I already have an idea of some questions to ask.

"Rob, I know there have been some layoffs at your plant. Do you think your position is in jeopardy?"

Rob nodded. "You've got that right. We've lost more than 30 percent of our workforce, and we've been told that the next batch of layoffs will come from middle management, right where I live."

"So, emotionally, how are you handling the possibility of a layoff?"

"I'm terrified. With Sarah in college and the rest of the kids growing up so fast, I fear not being able to meet the needs of my family. Things are slowing down across the board in the microchip industry. I really don't know what I am going to do if I get laid off. We might have to sell the house and move into a rental—maybe even move away."

"That's some burden to carry. What does Shelly think of all of this?"

"Shelly doesn't know. She has enough going on with the kids and all that she doesn't need to fret over this. Now, with her finding the video of porn in my briefcase, I truly fear that she'll see me as a failure and leave me."

"So, does that mean you've been carrying these fears all by yourself? Is this new for you, or in the past have you ever felt like you had to carry the burdens of life on your shoulders—to be the strong, silent type?"

"Yeah, that's what I grew up with in my home. Dad was always busting his rear trying to make ends meet, while Mom tried to keep the five of us kids together. Truth is, though I'm sure they loved us, they were both caught up with their own problems, and if we brought up our problems and issues, we were shamed and ridiculed. Basically, from the time I was seven, I realized I was on my own."

"Is that true in your marriage? You and Shelly seem so connected when I see you at church."

"I love her dearly; she's my best friend. But between the long hours of work and the four kids, I feel like I'm repeating my parent's pattern. When I get home from work these days, I don't feel like I have much to give. I know that I'm not satisfied with our intimacy level, and I'm sure Shelly feels the same way. I'm sure the kids feel the tension that we're in now."

"Are you talking about not having much to give energy-wise, or are you saying that you as a person don't have much to give Shelly and the kids except to bring home the money?"

"Boy, you don't beat around the bush do you, Harry? But, you're right. I feel like a failure. Money, food and housing are about the best things that I can give my family. If they knew about my addiction . . . wow, life with my kids could get real ugly. It already is ugly with Shelly. I guess she's the best thing that ever happened to me, outside of me becoming a Christian. In fact, I wouldn't even have that if it hadn't been for Shelly helping me find my way to Christ. But I think God just tolerates me."

THE ADDICTIVE MINDSET

We can now begin to see the pattern with Rob. He is isolated and feeling anxiety and fears that are creating emotional pain and despair in his life. He may lose his job, and he's emotionally distant from his wife and kids. He's drifting all alone in the midst of a family that loves him. But he's just given us a big clue as to what's really going on: He doesn't find much value in himself.

My next set of questions will point to his addictive mindset. It is here that we discover why he thinks about himself the way he does and how it leads him into the addictive lifestyle. Below are the key questions I would ask Rob to discover the truth about his addictive mindset.

- *Question 1:* Have you been feeling worthless or feel a loss of value in your life?
- *Question 2:* Do you believe you are unlovable? Put another way, do you feel that if people knew what you've done or what you've been thinking, they would reject or abandon you?
- *Question 3:* Do you feel isolated or alone? Do you feel that there is a big difference between what people see on the outside and what you're thinking and feeling on the inside?

As I continue my discussion with Rob, I begin to incorporate some of these questions.

"Rob, it seems to me that you're feeling very isolated. Did you know that shame is defined as being exposed and feeling diminished by that exposure? If we assume that is a correct definition, then do you battle with shame and a diminished sense of value or worthlessness?"

"Yes, I just said that. I've been cheating on the wife I love by using pornography. I may lose my job, and my wife may leave me. Yes, I think I battle with shame or at least a sense of diminished value."

"Where did that come from? Who else made you feel that way?"

"That's easy—my parents. I don't think I ever heard my dad tell me that he loved me. When he did compliment me, there was always the implied, 'You could have done it better if . . .' My mom was also a perfectionist, and no matter how hard I tried, I failed. Now that I'm talking with you, I guess I've always felt alone at some level."

"So, Rob, do you feel unlovable? If so, who do you depend on to meet your needs?"

"Unlovable . . . yep, especially under these circumstances. I'm beginning to see that I've wanted to feel cared for but that I have always had to rely on myself. I guess I never related my isolation and loneliness with my self-reliance before. Knowing this makes a lot of sense."

THE ADDICTIVE LIFESTYLE

Once we have uncovered the source of Rob's addictive mindset, we can begin to ask some probing questions to determine when his addictive lifestyle began and what triggers in his life today set off particular behaviors.

"Rob, let's next talk about when your addictive behavior began. When you have a sexual high, you release drugs into your blood stream. These drugs temporarily make you feel better, right?"

"Right."

"So, when did you discover pornography and masturbation?"

"When I was 10 and found my father's stash of magazines. I was hooked right away. I don't know when I started to masturbate, but I know I wanted more. Because my parents were so wrapped up with life themselves, I almost always had access to pornography. Nobody seemed to care what I did until I met Shelly."

"Did you hide your behaviors?"

"Yes. I guess I realize they did care. I always feared I would get the snot beat out of me if I got caught. I felt guilty, maybe ashamed, so I did sneak and hide my activity. I thought I needed it."

"Rob, you've just walked through the mental reasoning for your addiction. Now let's look at how you've lived out your addictive lifestyle. To do this, I have a few of the key questions I want you to answer. First, do you have fantasies or daydreams that help you escape from your pain, fears or anxiety?"

"I do have a lot of fantasies. Many of these are about sports or music. But when I'm really tired and stressed, I play this mental DVD of past sexual experiences or of videos that aroused me. Eventually I need to act out, so I either head to the bathroom at work or I wait until everyone has gone to bed if I am at home."

"Rob, that's your ritual—the pattern of acting out that you usually repeat during a relapse. Okay, second question: What circumstances, activities and emotions lead up to your relapse? Do you do more than you have already described?"

"Well, I occasionally go to a porn shop, and I've purchased some videos like the one Shelly found."

"Here's the third question: Do you keep the lid on all of this by maintaining your secret?"

"Absolutely. I feel so very ashamed."

"Do you see what comes next in your addictive lifestyle?"

"Oh, I get it. I go back to fantasy. It's a spiral, isn't it?"

"Yes, Rob, it's a downward spiral. The addiction just sucks you in. Now the question is how you protect and justify your life. Let's look at the bottom of the noose. We have now come to the addictive cloak. It's here that we learn about how you hide from others."

THE ADDICTIVE CLOAK

In the next part of the discussion, I continue to ask questions to Rob to help him discover how he cloaks his addiction.

"Rob, here's the first question on the addictive cloak: How do you deny or minimize your addictive lifestyle to others?"

"I'm a pretty passive guy, except when I'm challenged. Then I rage, or at least get very angry. I chase people off. I come off with a 'how dare you' kind of attitude, as if I would never do what I actually do all the time. I guess I use anger, don't I?"

"This actually leads to my second question: How do you justify your addictive behaviors to yourself?"

"I have always thought that as long as nobody found out about what I was doing, I wasn't hurting anyone else. Now I see from Shelly's response that I lied to myself as well as to everyone else."

"The last key question is this: Who or what do you blame for these negative and painful circumstances in your life?"

"I never have thought of that, but I would guess that at one time or another I have blamed everyone else, including myself."

"Have you ever blamed God?"

"Yeah, I guess so. I never say it out loud . . . but yeah, I've blamed Him."

"Blaming God and others will send you back to the painful root of your addiction and tighten the noose ever tighter around your life. To break free of this noose, you must take the knowledge we've just gained and begin to move you into true accountability with your For Men Only group. My guess is that they don't really know what's going on, do they?"

"No, Harry, they don't."

"Next Saturday, you need to tell this entire story to them. Are you willing to do that?"

"I'm frightened, but yes, I will tell them my true story."

"Rob, I'm proud of you. It takes courage to do what you're about to do. Let's pray."

SAFETY PLANNING AND ACCOUNTABILITY

We covered much in this meeting with Rob as we helped him to begin the discovery of self-awareness. In future meetings, Rob will learn the details about being accountable to self as well as being accountable to others.

We each have our own dangerous scenarios in which we are most tempted to move into our addictive pattern. We must prepare and plan for those painful circumstances, because they will come to all of us. Often, people think that safety planning is about stopping destructive or poor behavior. Although it is true that this is part of what happens, we must also look to what we should be doing. Paul teaches us in Ephesians 4 that we are to take off the old man and to put on the new. We will all grow tired and fail if we just seek to resist. Instead, we need to move forward to our new life in Christ.

If we are truly moving toward Jesus becoming Lord in our lives, we need to focus on what we are called to live out in Christ. Developing a pattern of Bible study and journaling will be a great help. The Bible is alive and sharper than a two-edged sword and can certainly expose the issues that we face.

At East Hill, we use life journals to help people to discover the reality of God's Word and the truth concerning their own struggles and successes. There are many good Bible reading systems out there. We encourage people to find the one that works best for them. Such a system will give those who struggle a written and relational encounter with God that will go a long way in helping them become self-accountable in their internal thoughts, feelings and beliefs as well as in their external patterns of behavior.

One great tool that has benefited the Pure Desire/For Men Only Ministry is the FASTER Relapse Awareness Scale developed by Michael Dye for his Genesis Process for Change relapse prevention program (see www.genesisprocess.org). This tool provides a universal pattern for how individuals move toward relapse and offers tremendous insight into the addictive lifestyle. The FASTER scale can help individuals not only in the area of self-awareness but also in mutual accountability with others.

Here's how the FASTER scale works. At the top of the scale is *restoration*. Restoration is an attitude of accepting life on God's terms with trust, vulnerability and gratitude. Individuals at this stage have no secrets to conceal and are working to resolve problems. They identify their fears and feelings and keep their commitments to family, church, self and others. They strive to be open and honest, to reach out to others and to work for increase in relationships with God and others. People at this stage are also engaged in true accountability with others.

From this state, the person may progress through a process of relapse. Dyer identifies these stages as follows:

F: *Forgetting Priorities.* One of the first signs of a possible relapse is a shift in plans or priorities. At this stage, the individual begins to believe in his or her present circumstances and moves away from trusting God. He or she may begin to keep secrets, spend less time with God, avoid support and accountability people, engage in superficial conversations, break promises and recovery commitments, and neglect family. Forgetting priorities will lead to or cause:

A: *Anxiety.* At this stage, the person experiences a growing background noise of undefined fear and draws energy from his or her emotions. He or she may begin to worry and become increasingly fearful or resentful toward others. The person may also replay past negative thoughts in his or her mind, engage in fantasy, blame others for the way he or she feels, judge others' motives, engage in perfectionism, and make goals and lists that he or she can't possibly complete. Individuals at this stage may experience sleep problems; have trouble concentrating;

seek or create "drama"; or look for medications to control his or her pain, sleep or weight-control problems. Anxiety next leads to:

S: *Speeding up.* In this phase, the person experiencing a relapse attempts to "outrun" the anxiety he or she is feeling by consciously or subconsciously focusing on a variety of other priorities. The individual at this stage becomes overly busy and driven, and has a difficult time slowing down to relax. He or she may skip meals, work long hours, stay up late at night, consume increased amounts of caffeine and sugar, or over-exercise to keep up the pace. The person may find it difficult to turn off his or her thoughts (or identify what he or she is feeling), experience dramatic mood swings, have trouble being alone, and get easily distracted when attempting to listen to others. Speeding up leads to being:

T: *Ticked off.* A person at this stage begins to use anger as a way of numbing the pain that he or she is experiencing. The individual actually begins to get an adrenaline high from aggression and will react above and beyond what any given situation warrants. Traits of those at this stage include increased sarcasm, all-or-nothing thinking, irrational thinking, defensiveness, inability to forgive, sense of superiority, procrastination, and feelings of isolation and resentment. The individual will assume an "I don't need anyone" attitude and push others away. He or she may also experience physical side affects, such as headaches and digestive problems. Being ticked off then leads to being:

E: *Exhausted.* By this point, the individual's neurochemicals are nearly depleted, making the pain that the person has been seeking to avoid nearly unavoidable. As the individual comes off of the adrenaline high from aggression, he or she begins to experience a loss of physical and emotional energy. Depression soon follows, and the person may experience feelings of panic, confusion, hopelessness, helplessness and sheer exhaustion. He or she may sleep too much or too little, cry for "no reason," become forgetful, submit to pessimistic (even suicidal) thoughts, and crave old coping behaviors (such as sex, drugs or alcohol). Those at this stage often seek old unhealthy patterns of behavior, isolate themselves, miss work, become increasingly irritable, and experience a loss of appetite. This leads to the final stage:

R: *Relapse.* When a person relapses, he or she returns to a place that the individual swore he or she would never go to again. At this point, the person is out of control and is lost in his or her addiction. He or she has given up and given in, is lying to self and to others, and cannot manage without his or her coping behaviors (at least for now). The result is the reinforcement of shame, guilt and condemnation, and feelings of abandonment and isolation.

Most often, it takes an individual three to six weeks to progress through the stages to relapse. You can therefore determine where you are on the FASTER scale by answering the following questions:

1. What occurred the day of your relapse? (R)
2. What happened 2 to 3 days before your relapse? (E)
3. What happened 4 to 5 days before you relapsed? (T)
4. What happened 6 to 8 days before you relapsed? (S)
5. What happened 9 to 11 days before you relapsed? (A)
6. What happened 12 to 14 days before you relapsed? (F)

Based on the answers given, you should be able to determine what set up or triggered the relapse up to two weeks before the relapse actually occurred.

Where do you see yourself on the FASTER scale at this time? If you are not in restoration, then you have a choice: You can move toward relapse as you go down the scale, or you can choose to move back toward restoration by choosing to once again trust God. You can make the decision to move toward restoration by turning to God and once again adopting attitudes and behaviors necessary to keep you from relapsing.

MENTORS, PEERS AND FRIENDS

No healing can occur until you are able to take an honest and continual self-evaluation based on your relationship with Christ. But what do you do with the information? The answer is that you share it with those people who you believe will encourage and support you while you're walking God's path of healing. This is where groups such as Pure Desire/For Men Only come in. It is in these types of groups where you will find mentors, peers, friends and other men who you will eventually mentor. These types of groups become a sanctuary where you can learn to take off your mask and begin to walk the healing path.

To be successful in avoiding relapse, you need mentors who will lead you into healthy discipleship—people who are farther along in an area in which you recognize that you need to grow. Of course, to be effective, these mentors must commit to teaching and guiding you, and you must commit to following them. Here, as always, accountability must go both directions. This may be a long-term or short-term relationship, depending on the issue (for example, a person who mentors you on how to repair your plumbing is short-term, but someone who is leading you out of the addictive lifestyle will have a longer duration). Regardless, everyone needs people functioning in the mentoring role in their lives.

You also need to seek out peers and friendships. As with mentors, these types of relationships also need to be mutually accountable. However, unlike mentors, the reason for having accountability peers and friends is for their function to support—to admonish and encourage you. Peers and friends give you a second set of eyes to seek out problem areas in your life that might be easily overlooked. They love you enough to share what they see, but they also trust God enough to give you the dignity to make your own decision on what course to pursue.

The role of mentors and peers is to speak into your life and support you, but never to manipulate or control you. God will not seek to control you, either. Jesus didn't go chasing after the rich young ruler when he walked away from Him; nor did the prodigal's father run after his wayward son (see Luke 15). The father waited and looked for his son, but he did not pursue or nag him while the son made some incredibly poor choices. This is a great view of your heavenly Father. He waits for and anticipates your return, but He allows the painful consequences of your poor choices to move you to return your hope to Him instead of depending on yourself and/or others to overcome your pain-filled circumstances.

Finally, always remember that you—yes, *you*—are called to disciple others. Even in your brokenness, God will use you to help other people. In fact, your past life with all of its failures and struggles will become great fertilizer for your growth and your ability to identify and help others. A time will come—and probably sooner than you think—when people will turn to you and seek your guidance and input. Our experience here at East Hill has proven this. Our groups give men a safe place to learn how to live in open accountability. What a great gift these groups are, not only for their members, but also for their families! Men take the skills they learn and implement them in their relationships outside of the group.

In conclusion, to develop and maintain quality leadership, the men must know in their heart of hearts that you truly love them and that you are committed to their success as men and as leaders.

I seek to have regular contact with the men, and in my conversations I ask questions about their lives and families. The point I hope they receive is that I care about them and their families.[1]

Note

1. Pure Desire Ministry International (PDMI) is devoted to healing men and women who have become addicted to sexual behaviors that are harmful to their social, family and spiritual well being. By supporting local churches, PDMI is setting men and women free so that they can walk in the saving grace of the Lord. God has called PDMI to help local churches and their frequently overloaded pastors address the unspoken, undermining truth of sexual bondage that is invading our society today. That is not to say PDMI is limited to just the church environment; across the nation, small groups are using Pure Desire Ministry materials in corporate and community environments.

Section II

A PLACE OF HEALING

CHAPTER 9

The Cleansing Hope
of a Vision

I tried to be patient as I stood in an aircraft hanger waiting for several hundred sailors to get pointed in the same direction. But, being the typical Marine, I was convinced it would take these sailors an eternity—and it was beginning to appear that I was right. A new commanding officer was taking over the Navy training squadron I was assigned to. My task in the change-of-command ceremony was to march out in front of the assembled squadron, call everyone to attention and then go through the obligatory sword drill as each unit reported, "All present and accounted for."

I appreciated the opportunity because it gave me a chance to meet the new C.O. (commanding officer), and to be an important part of the ceremony recognizing his position and authority. It never hurts to have an "in" with the man who's going to be writing the fitness reports that determine your potential for promotion and advancement. In other words, I wanted to make a good impression.

But the sailors took forever, and I could feel the tension caused by the delay. In order to avoid getting uptight, I diverted my mind to other things. My thoughts wandered to my recent experience of going to a Bible study for the first time. As I mentioned in an earlier chapter, my wife had dragged me to the study, and it was a disaster. I was the only man present, which made me doubly nervous—part of the reason, I'm sure, why I blurted out my first public prayer the way I did. But the leader of the Bible study, a precious lady named Dorcas, did me a great favor when she leaned over to me after I stunned the group with my prayer, and said, "That was a good beginning. That's the first time you've ever prayed in public, isn't it?"

Then she asked me a question that would come to impact my life in a way I never knew possible: "Would you like to know a prayer God will always answer?"

When I responded that I would, she said, "Just ask God if there is anything He'd like to change in your life." Although I couldn't think of a single thing that God might want to change in me at that point in time, I deposited her statement in my memory bank for future reference.

Now, as I stood there waiting for the change-of-command ceremony to begin, that suggested prayer came to mind. I didn't have anything else to do, so I just blurted out the prayer: "Lord, if there is anything You'd like to change in my life, take Your best shot." (I have since come to realize that isn't always a wise prayer in a public place.)

The ceremony finally got under way. The adjutant's call sounded, and I strutted forth to call all the elements of the squadron to attention and receive their reports. But before I actually received their reports, I had to go through a sword drill. I was to pull my officer's sword from the scabbard, wave it in the prescribed pattern and return it to its original position. I was good at it—I would have told anyone who asked.

After the squadron reported in and was prepared for the rest of the ceremony, I positioned myself before the new commanding officer, a man I was trying to impress with my professionalism. He received my sword salute and I was finished. All I had to do was return my sword to its scabbard. Piece of cake—I'd done it hundreds of times before. It's a procedure you perform by feel, because you're standing at rigid attention and can't look down. However, a simple procedure can get dicey if things aren't lined up correctly.

A Marine officer's sword is an impressive piece of equipment, long and curved, giving it a touch of elegance. But that means the scabbard is also curved, so they must match up or there's a serious problem.

I responded to the commanding officer's salute by returning my sword to the scabbard; but, somehow, the scabbard had turned 180 degrees in the wrong direction. To this day, I don't know how it happened, but I suspect an angel quietly turned it while I strutted around up front. The sword wouldn't fit! The harder I tried, the worse things got. The commanding officer's face turned crimson; I was transforming his change-of-command ceremony into a comedy routine. Under his breath he growled, "It's stuck, you idiot!" My anxiety—and my frantic efforts—increased. Then my scabbard fell off its retainer clip and clattered loudly to the concrete hanger floor.

I picked up the scabbard and slunk back to where I had previously stood at attention. Only a few moments before, I'd been wondering when the Navy guys behind me would get their act together. Now they laughed at the antics of this arrogant Marine. I could almost feel them struggling to contain their urge to pump their fists in the air with a resounding "Yes-s-s!"

I stood there in disbelief. How could this happen to me? I'd done that sword drill for years without missing a beat. What was going on? Then I remembered what I had prayed before I went out to strut my stuff. God certainly had answered! In the devastating quietness of my humiliation in front of my peers, I heard the Lord speak to me for the first time: "Ted, see what an arrogant little man you are? But I would make you great. I would make you a lover."

I'll never forget that moment as long as I live—not the embarrassment, but the promise of God's grace and transformation in the middle of my blindness and personal agony. The enlisted members of the squadron frequently reminded me of my arrogance in the days ahead. I didn't have to be a rocket scientist to figure out their expressions as they saluted me. And every now and then, a fellow pilot said something like, "Hey, Captain Roberts, how's your sword drill coming?" It kept me humble. Denial isn't an option when your failures have had such a public exposure. But that promise to make me a lover was one of the most powerful God has ever spoken into my life.

Learning True Intimacy

In the first part of the book, we looked in depth at the noose of addiction. But it's critical that we understand that our ultimate goal isn't getting the noose off someone's soul. The total effort of a church cannot be focused on stopping the destructive behavior. Christ didn't die just so we might stop certain behaviors. He died and rose again to empower us to go way beyond that and really live—not that we might be just hopeful, but truly healthy. And that includes our sexuality.

After more than two decades of counseling people through some of the most difficult times in their lives that were caused by sexual bondage, I've discovered some foundational elements that must be part of a man's life if he is to experience healthy sexuality from a biblical perspective—and they're not rigid concepts or principles.

I've lost count of the number of men I have counseled who knew all kinds of biblical truth. They understood the pillars of the faith—the eternal truths of Scripture. But they were like someone who'd never gotten out of ground school. In fact, they'd essentially been in spiritual ground school for 10, 20 or even 30 years, but they had no concept of the sexual freedom available in the Spirit. They could tell all about the technical aspects of a particular biblical truth, just like someone who had spent his life in ground school could tell all about the technical and performance aspects of a certain aircraft. But they never knew what it was like to experience the freedom and challenge of actually flying. Real dynamic spiritual and sexual health was only an academic concept.

Sexual bondage is essentially an expression of immaturity or woundedness, because those who are trapped avoid intimacy. Instead of experiencing the incredible heights of a healthy sexual relationship, the addict is trapped in a cheap and deadly imitation of one of God's greatest gifts to mankind—and that's truly a tragedy.

■ ■ ■ ■ ■ ■ ■ ■ ■ ■

Our sexuality is a revelation of God's very nature.
But the revelation is destroyed when sex is "solo"——when it
isn't characterized by a responsible and caring relationship
between a husband and wife. Sexual bondage
is always a solo experience.

■ ■ ■ ■ ■ ■ ■ ■ ■ ■

Scripture makes it very clear that our sexuality is one of the greatest gifts God has given us. The very first pages of the Bible declare that fact:

> Then God said, "Let us make man in our image, in our likeness. . . . So God created man in his own image, in the image of God he created him; *male and female he created them*" (Gen. 1:26-27, emphasis added).

Our sexuality is a revelation of God's very nature. But the revelation is destroyed when sex is "solo"—when it isn't characterized by a responsible and caring relationship between a husband and wife. Sexual bondage is always a solo experience. Another person may be involved, but sexual addiction and bondage are self-focused; they are not about a healthy relationship.

That statement makes sense to most men who have said yes to Christ, yet they may still struggle with their relationships with their wives, because the relationship has subtly become a solo experience. They struggle because they instinctively read Genesis 1:27 this way: "In the image of God he created him, male he created them."

After sharing at men's seminars for more than 20 years, I have learned an important truth: I can increase a man's understanding of the woman in his life by 200 percent if I can help him understand two words: radically different. God's image is seen in the relationship between male and female—not in male alone. And if male and female are ever going to have a chance of coming together as God designed, the male has to understand that he is dealing with a creature radically different from himself.

Intimacy is impossible unless the male realizes the incredible challenge he faces. Not only is he challenged to relate to a fellow creature who is beyond his comprehension, but he also must deal with the fact that sin has entered the picture and driven a wedge between the two sexes.

Healthy sexuality isn't just about stopping certain destructive behaviors; ultimately it's about the incredible challenge of male and female becoming one—and that's no easy task.

For example, science has once again managed to catch up with biblical truth by discovering that men and women are totally different. Unisex is a myth. And the greatest difference is not just in exterior anatomy, but in our brains. Women have 40 percent more connectors to both sides of their brains than men.[1] They receive and can simultaneously process more information than men can. Women also tend to have better color perception, hearing and sense of taste and smell. In fact, 8 out of 100 men have color perception problems, whereas only 1 out of 200 women has such problems.[2] This fact explains the average man's appreciation for black, gray and brown.

This difference can make relating to my wife an experience in adversity at times, because I'm the typical male in every respect. I remember not too long ago when we were shopping, and Diane came to me all excited about a particular pillow that she had found. She wanted me to come and see if the pillow would match the shade of fuchsia we had in our living room. I didn't even know it *was* fuchsia! I thought it was red. She got all upset with me because

I wouldn't help her. I couldn't even see the difference!

At times, women's sense of smell can be 1,000 times more sensitive than men's.[3] My wife is a classic example of that fact. During breakfast at a conference where we were speaking, she complained that the water smelled funny. I thought, *That's it; she's gone too far this time. There's nothing wrong with the water; it smells fine!* But right after that thought, a couple sat down at our table. The wife leaned over to me and commented, "Have you noticed how funny the water around here smells?"

Probably the greatest difference, however, is simply the data-collecting experience. I come home after 10 to 12 hours of work and my wife always asks, "How'd it go at work today?" I give the standard husband response: "Fine." She looks at me with this puzzled expression on her face as if to say, "And that's all you have to say? I mean, come on, tell me what happened today."

I can recall times when we have worked all day in the same office, and she could come home and talk for hours about it. She had picked up so much more information through both sides of her brain than I had—it's simply amazing! And she wants to talk about it, while I want to rest. I'm goal oriented; I always cut to the bottom line. She's holistic, taking in much more information. Talking actually gives her energy—it's the way she deals with problems. Not me. When I'm under pressure, I withdraw, get quiet and try to figure things out, which results in my not giving her the very thing she needs when she's under pressure—me.

Being as one, displaying God's image in our fallen world, isn't easy. Intimacy as husband and wife is the most demanding ministry we can undertake, and that's why sexual bondage and addictions are so common. That's also why the average church is filled with marriages that aren't even close to experiencing the freedom and joy God planned for them in His great gift of sexuality. If the Church is to become a place of healing, its goal cannot be just to stop destructive sexual behavior. Our goal must be much higher than that.

A BIBLICAL PATTERN

Additionally, our sexuality is an illustration of how God wants to relate to us. Sin interrupted the intimacy between God and man and between man and woman. Genesis 3:7 tells us that when sin entered the picture, Adam and Eve became self-conscious and ashamed, so they covered themselves. That covering illustrated the separation between man and woman, as well as their separation from God.

But God wouldn't allow a division between Himself and mankind to continue. That's why the Bible uses the term "to know" as a euphemism for sexual intercourse, as well as the term for deeply relating to God. The Hebrew prophets—Isaiah, Ezekiel and especially Hosea—used the concept of sexual union between a husband and wife as a picture of God's relationship and desire for Israel. Time and again, sexual relationship between a couple in the covenant relationship of marriage is used as an illustration of the passion God has for His people.

Finally, the gift of our sexuality is a *mystery*. In the New Testament, the revelation with respect to our sexuality is taken much deeper.

> For this reason a man will leave his father and mother and be united to his wife, and the two will become one flesh. This is a profound mystery—but I am talking about Christ and the church (Eph. 5:31-32).

Paul reaches back to the very beginning as he quotes from Genesis, then points to the fact that godly sexual relationships between a husband and wife are a picture of the way Christ relates to the Church. Now, that's a staggering truth. I've never thought about Christ's ministry to the Church as I made love to my wife! But that's what Paul says is being patterned, and it's a mystery, folks! When we follow God's ordained pattern of sex within marriage, we're in the presence of holiness. Holiness and our sexuality—now there's a paradox for the normal church mindset. But that's part of the reason we have so many people struggling with sexual bondage in their lives. Satan knows what's being pictured in the spirit, and he hates it, which is why this battle over our sexuality has so much spiritual intensity involved in it.

■ ■ ■ ■ ■ ■ ■ ■ ■

Nearly every passage in the New Testament concerning the husband and wife sexual relationship calls for mutual submission. Not only are the two seen as equals, but they are also declared to have equal rights and responsibilities in the act of relating to one another sexually.

■ ■ ■ ■ ■ ■ ■ ■ ■

Nearly every passage in the New Testament concerning the husband and wife sexual relationship calls for mutual submission (see 1 Cor. 7:3-5; Eph. 5:25,28). Not only are the two seen as equals, but they are also declared to have equal rights and responsibilities in the act of relating to one another sexually. Sacrificial love is to characterize the sexual response of a husband to his wife and of a wife to her husband. The marriage bed is to depict the kind of *agape* love Christ pours out on His Church.

It's because this sacrificial pattern is so overlooked and misunderstood that bondage and sexual addictions are such a common part of our world. Healthy sexuality is a tall order. In fact, it's only possible through God's grace. Consequently, these issues in a man's life can never be viewed as fixed principles, because we're talking about a dynamic relational response. They can't be seen in a left-brained manner as simply pillars of truth that must be followed. For the obvious reason, they have to be lived out with a mate—or, for a single person, in close and appropriate friendships with members of the opposite sex in the community of faith.

Maybe I can use a flying analogy again. One of the most important tools for mastering a high-performance aircraft is the control stick. It moves in four basic directions: fore and aft, and left and right. But, as you may know, these options are in a dynamic relationship. The pilot can move in several directions at the same time—the possibilities are infinite within the operational limitations of the aircraft.

Each of the character traits necessary for healthy sexuality addresses a specific aspect of the addiction cycle, and each has to be in place for the noose to be broken; but they're more than preventive measures. Once these character traits reside in a man's life, he will have the capacity to fly in his marriage sexually. I'm not referring to just an adrenaline rush found in sexual addiction, which soon leaves the addict with an even deeper sense of guilt, shame and denial. Nor am I speaking primarily of the great physical highs we can experience as husband and wife when we respond to one another with sexual abandon. I'm talking about that mystery of God's gift of sexuality, where we come to know our mate and ourselves before the Lord. We don't experience it on a daily basis, but when it happens, we know it. Words can't describe the depth of that joy. Paul called it a divine mystery.

HOPE FROM A VISION

Simon stood before Jesus. Andrew, his brother, had dragged him there. And Simon heard those startling words from Jesus: "You will be called Cephas," which is Aramaic for the name Peter (John 1:42). In essence, Jesus was saying, "You're going to be a rock someday, Simon. There will be a stability and solidness about your life that will affect your world." But little did Simon then understand how difficult it would be to follow Christ—how much he would suffer and struggle before he would take on the character God had purposed for him from the foundation of the world. He looked like "Rocky" after the fifteenth round with Clubber Lang, but he made it. That vision that Christ spoke into his soul cleansed him after he had fallen. It gave him hope; it wouldn't let him go, because Christ wouldn't let him go. The vision cleansed him.

"Ted, I will make you a lover." That was a vision that Christ spoke to my soul, a vision that has repeatedly picked me up, given me new hope and cleansed me. It hasn't been pretty, nor has it been easy, but I am making it. I am becoming a man who is learning to walk in God's gift of sexuality. And if I can make it, so can anyone else.

"But how can I become someone who hears God's words of vision for my life?" This is a common question. I think Peter heard that cry from many men, and that's why he stated such an incredible promise:

> Therefore, my brothers, be all the more eager to make your calling and election sure. For if you do these things, you will never fall, and you will receive a rich welcome into the eternal kingdom of our Lord and Savior Jesus Christ (2 Pet. 1:10-11).

Do you want to make sure that you have a handle on God's vision for your life? Do you want to be a man who doesn't fall morally? (Peter was a pro at falling, so he knew what he was talking about.) Then learn (as you read the remainder of this book) and develop in your life the character traits that not only break the noose of addiction, but allow you to experience fully the gift of sexuality that God has given you.

Notes
1. Chris Evatt, *He and She* (Berkeley, CA: Conari Press, n.d.), p. 124.
2. Joe Tanenbaum, *Male and Female* (Incline Village, NV: Erdmann Publishing, n.d.), p. 36.
3. Ibid., p. 41.

CHAPTER 10

The Power of Vision

In the previous chapter I referred to Peter's incredible statement, "For if you do these things, *you will never fall*" (2 Pet. 1:10, emphasis added). At times, Peter was a master of exaggeration. He made such classic comments to Christ as, "Even if all fall away on account of you, I never will" (Matt. 26:33), and the incredible hyperbole, "Even if I have to die with you, I will never disown you" (Matt. 26:35). He grossly overestimated his ability not to buckle under pressure. But his comments in 2 Peter were the words of a seasoned warrior in the faith. He had come to see clearly his heart's stubborn nature.

Peter had tasted defeat in the worst possible areas of his personal life, which is why the statement about never falling seems so startling. Peter was the master of falling, the sultan of sinking to incredible depths of disaster, and saying dumb things. But somehow he had come to realize, through all his catastrophes, the key ingredients for never falling. That's why it's so important for us to study carefully what he meant by the phrase "these things." Doing "these things," Peter declared, was the key to not falling. And when we are battling sexual bondage, we need to find the key, not just to avoid falling again and again, but to live a victorious life.

A Primary Dimension of Wholeness

Fortunately, we do not have to guess what Peter was referring to. In verses 5 through 7 of that same chapter, he made it clear:

> So don't lose a minute in building on what you've been given, complementing your basic faith with good character, spiritual understanding, alert discipline, passionate patience, reverent wonder, warm friendliness, and generous love, each dimension fitting into and developing the others (2 Pet. 1:5-7, *THE MESSAGE*).

Peter points out several areas that need to be developed and fit together in a man's soul to make him failure proof. These integrated areas will enable him to come to wholeness in the very depths of his being—including his sexuality. They will give him the ability to stand against the schemes of hell—without a noose around his soul.

The primary dimension of wholeness in a man's life is vision. Good character and spiritual understanding aren't things we produce just by trying harder; yet Peter challenges us to complement our basic God-given faith with good character and spiritual understanding. Those issues lie at the very core of a man's vision. Our faith is a gift from God (see Eph. 2:8), but if we are to grow spiritually, God's graciousness doesn't exempt us from personal effort. "Faith is not only a commitment to the promises of Christ; it is also a commitment to his demands."[1]

Spiritual growth isn't an issue to be taken lightly—Peter sees it as a goal that calls for all we have every day. There's a delicate balance in spiritual growth dynamics. God gives the gift; then, in gratitude, we respond wholeheartedly. Our response must be wholehearted because our adversary fights us every step of the way as we get the noose of sexual bondage off our necks. Satan's primary goal is to keep us from maturity in Christ, and he's not above any tactic. Once the noose is off, we threaten him as we grow spiritually.

"Good character" is a much stronger term than the English translation would lead us to believe. It's been translated as virtue or goodness. The original Greek word *arete* is rare in the New Testament, but not so in the secular writings of the day.[2] And the emphases of courage and excellence show up again and again. The dual sense of this term underlines right from the start that Peter's understanding of spiritual maturity has a very practical focus.

This practical focus is even stronger in the word translated "spiritual understanding." The Greek word *gnosis* is about practical knowledge. It's the ability to apply God's wisdom to specific situations. It enables a man to decide rightly and act honorably and effectively in day-to-day circumstances.[3]

Both of these terms lie at the absolute center of a man's vision. Biblical courage is never possible without vision. And practical wisdom becomes a penetrating and transforming force once a man grasps God's purpose for him.

In John 1:42, it was no accident that the first words Simon heard from Jesus' lips were, "You will be called Cephas (which, when translated, is Peter)."

■ ■ ■ ■ ■ ■ ■ ■ ■ ■

When God is going to build a great man, time and again He starts with the man's vision. How powerful is the issue of vision in a man's life? In a fallen world we can't possibly have godly character without it.

■ ■ ■ ■ ■ ■ ■ ■ ■ ■

When God is going to build a great man, time and again He starts with the man's vision. He spoke to the teenage shepherd boy David by sending Samuel to anoint him as the next king of Israel. David had to face years of testing and training in the wilderness as he was chased by a crazed King Saul before he reached the goal. But it all started with a vision of what God was going to do in his life. Paul's turnaround happened on the Damascus road, while he was on his own agenda of murder and destruction. But Jesus hit him with such a powerful vision that it spun him around and sent him sprawling on his face in the dust. God begins with a vision when He's going to rebuild a man's life.

How powerful is the issue of vision in a man's life? In a fallen world we can't possibly have godly character without it. But with it, courage takes root so deeply that a man is able to live with real spiritual understanding.

When I get to heaven I want to see some scenes from Paul's life. One in particular is Paul's incredible confrontation with Felix in Acts 24. Paul was under arrest in Caesarea, a seaport Herod created from virtually nothing. There was no natural harbor in the area, so Herod created one—and its incredible surrounding city. Archaeologists have uncovered a magnificent amphitheater in that ancient city, which I have had the privilege of visiting. As I stood on the amphitheater's reconstructed marble floor, I caught a glimpse of the majesty the city must have had in Paul's time.

Acts 24 implies that Felix and his wife, Drusilla, a Jewess, were seated in an imposing setting, possibly even that same amphitheater. Paul was brought before them to present his case. Felix, the Roman governor, was surrounded with all his symbols of power. You know the scene: The limo pulls up and out jump Secret Service agents wearing dark glasses, scanning the crowd, ready to pull out weapons and deal with any sign of trouble at the twitch of a trigger finger. Meanwhile, the government official walks by the crowd, knowing full well that he has enough firepower backing him up to deal with anyone who wants to cause trouble. Now take that scene and amplify it a million times, because the Roman army didn't bother to read people their rights before they put a spear through them. My point? All Felix had to do was raise his little finger and Paul was shish kebab! Then an amazing thing happened.

As Paul discoursed on righteousness, self-control and the judgment to come, Felix was afraid and said, "That's enough for now! You may leave. When I find it convenient, I will send for you" (Acts 24:25).

This little guy Paul blew Felix out the back door. He terrified the guy! Felix knew about righteousness and the judgment to come; his wife, after all, was a Jewess. But once Paul started talking about self-control, which is what Peter's entire list in 2 Peter 1 is about, Felix shook in his sandals.

The power of self-discipline is amazing. Initially, that can sound rather strange because of all the negative stereotypes we tend to connect with the concept. The normal picture that comes to mind is long stretches of boring routine. You know the concept: "sucking a lemon for Jesus" in order to be spiritual. But if we stop and think for a moment, we realize that nothing could be further from the truth. Nothing of any significance in our world takes place apart from self-discipline:

- No gold medals at the Olympics
- No great teaching in the classroom
- No long-term effectiveness in the business world
- No great dads or moms
- And, definitely, no great marriages

Nothing of positive, lasting impact is possible without self-discipline. When Jesus was tempted in the wilderness, the issue wasn't merely about resisting hunger or personal power; it was about whether He would take a shortcut from the Father's plan for humanity's salvation. In the English translation, the enemy's address to Christ in the wilderness—"*If* you are the Son of God," (Matt. 4:6; Luke 4:3, emphasis added)—doesn't carry the full meaning in the original Greek text, which implies not only *if* but *since* you are the Son of God you have the power to turn these stones into bread.[4] Jesus was faced with an incredible temptation that can be distilled into one sentence: Jesus, why put up with all this suffering and inconvenience?

The question that was settled in the wilderness testing was one of self-discipline, or self-control. And Jesus didn't flinch. Unlike the first Adam, the last Adam (Jesus) responded to hell's challenge with courage and spiritual understanding. I think that's why Luke started the section noting that Jesus went *into* the wilderness "full of the Holy Spirit" (4:1), then sums it up by showing that He came *out* of the wilderness "in the power of the Spirit" (v. 14). We'll never have the power to withstand hell's assaults without self-discipline.

But, as we've previously discussed, we have a problem. The terms "self-control" or "self-discipline" have deeply negative connotations for many people. Trying harder, which is the only way these people understand the terms, doesn't work. And it doesn't work for two reasons.

The first reason is what I call the "polar bear problem." Several years ago researchers did an interesting experiment with some college students. They asked the students *not* to think of a white polar bear. Then they said, "If you happen to slip and think of a white polar bear, we've given you this little button to push as we talk during the next 30 minutes." Guess what happened? They nearly wore the button out![5] In fact, I challenge you not to think of a white polar the rest of the day. Under no circumstances are you to think of a white polar bear. Lots of luck! Suppressing a thought only reinforces it. It gives it energy. That's the first reason that trying harder to be self-controlled is a waste of energy. We can grit our teeth for only so long.

The second reason trying harder doesn't lead to self-control is the hardest one for us to recognize, and the most difficult to deal with once we do. You see, we all have a major failing—we're usually blind to our own problems. I think that's one of the main reasons God gives us a mate. They do everything in their power to help us recognize our problems for the simple reason that they have to live with them!

Breaking Down Doors of Blindness

It was early in the morning, and I was once again praying that familiar prayer: "Lord, if there is anything in my life You want to change, then take Your best shot." I'd learned not to voice that prayer in public, but I think I'd forgotten just how powerfully God will respond to a sincere request from the heart. It was one of those times in prayer when I was lost in Christ's love, not fully cognizant of what I was saying.

After praying, I returned to the frantic preparation for getting to the weekend church service on time. With four weekend services, things can get hectic. Normally, my wife and I drive to the services in different cars since we operate on two completely different schedules, but that day we needed to go together.

I looked at my watch. I had to be at the service in 20 minutes. My wife was nowhere in sight. No problem; I decided to pull the car out of the garage and wait for her.

Then it was 15 minutes before the service started. Then just 10 minutes before I had to be there to tell everyone how much Jesus loves them. I knew if I broke every speed limit between our home and the church, I'd just make it! At 8 minutes before the service started, I told myself, *That's it; I'm going to go upstairs and drag my wife to the car!*

So I jumped out of the car, only to see the car lurch backward and start down our driveway. It was in reverse! I'd been so anxious as I waited for my wife, I didn't even realize what I'd done. I'd had my foot on the brake with the car in reverse, ready to bolt out of the driveway as soon as my wife hopped in. Now the car was moving down the driveway—and I wasn't in it.

Fortunately, the old fighter pilot reactions didn't fail me. I managed to jump back into the car and reach for the gearshift lever just in time—just in time, that is, to see the open driver's side door wrap around the basketball pole next to the driveway. Glass exploded all over the driveway, all over me and all over the front seat of the car.

I managed to stop the car, with a lot of help from the basketball pole. The driver's door, now barely attached, looked like it had been hit by a speeding train. And in five minutes I was supposed to be at church to tell everyone about Jesus' love for us. At that moment, as if on cue, my wife stepped out of the garage. Her eyes widened, her mouth dropped open, and she said, "What happened?" I just sat there with the engine racing.

It's amazing how the Lord sometimes gets our attention. As I sat in the car with shattered glass all over me, the Lord gave me this thought: *Ted, you really have a problem with being impatient, and most of the time you don't even notice it.* Well, I couldn't ignore it that day. The evidence was all over me and the driveway. To be honest, I felt like replying to the Lord, "You could have just told me." But the truth is, He had been trying to tell me for months, but I wasn't listening. All of us, at some point in our lives, are truly blind to our own problems.

What's the solution? How can we become distinguished by good character and practical knowledge, which are the foundations of self-control or self-discipline—the very traits that were so obviously missing in my life that day? The answer may come as a surprise. In Philippians 3, Paul reveals something of his heart and soul. Paul refused to fail, no matter what was thrown at him. He had come out of the worst addiction of all: the religious addiction of self-righteousness. Yet, in Philippians 3, you hear the passionate words of a man freed from hell's deepest chains. And you not only hear the passion of a man set free, you see the reason for the freedom that has led to such self-discipline:

> But whatever was to my profit I now consider loss for the sake of Christ. What is more, I consider everything a loss compared to the surpassing greatness of knowing Christ Jesus my Lord, for whose sake I have lost all things. I consider them rubbish, that I may gain Christ and be found in him, not having a righteousness of my own that comes from

the law, but that which is through faith in Christ—the righteousness that comes from God and is by faith. I want to know Christ and the power of his resurrection and the fellowship of sharing in his sufferings, becoming like him in his death....Not that I have already obtained all this, or have already been made perfect, but I press on to take hold of that for which Christ Jesus took hold of me (Phil. 3:7-12).

Dr. Karl Pribram and others did a fascinating study a number of years ago.[6] They analyzed successful people in all lines of employment to see if there was a common factor in the lives of those who were successful, regardless of their specific field. The results were conclusive and somewhat startling. It didn't matter if the person was a brain surgeon, truck driver or housewife. One factor proved to be critical in determining whether or not people would succeed in their field. It wasn't their I. Q., technical skills or even their people skills. The one factor that stood out above all the rest was self-discipline.

This is where the research becomes very interesting. It turned out that self-discipline was a learned behavior, not a simple phenomenon. It wasn't just a fancy word for putting forth a lot of effort. It was a complex matrix of seven different issues, but one issue in particular. It was the focal point of all the other parameters that held the matrix together. This one aspect was so clearly displayed in Paul's life. That crucial aspect is a passionate vision: "I want to know Christ and the power of his resurrection and the fellowship of sharing in his sufferings."

Self-discipline is a little like trying to make harbor in a sailboat in the middle of the night in rough seas. We can see the lights ahead and fix our focus. Though the winds and waves may be counter to us at times, we've set our heading. We'll do whatever is necessary to make sure we get there. In the process of keeping our eyes fixed on the lights and reacting to the difficulties that may arise, we learn the skill of keeping on course.

But I want to underline a very important distinction about the biblical view of self-control. Since Dr. Pribram's research was from a secular perspective, it didn't take into consideration the unique vantage point of those who walk with Christ. By the world's standards, Paul was a very disciplined man prior to his encounter with Christ on the Damascus road; but as I have pointed out, it was a discipline driven by self-righteousness, not a relationship to Christ. He was driven by a cause; but at some point, causes always betray us. It doesn't matter how good or noble the cause may be, eventually it will end up in the flesh. That's why people kill others in God's name, as Paul did. That's how an evangelist, pastor or teacher can lead a crusade against pornography while at the same time be visiting adult book shops or prostitutes.

■ ■ ■ ■ ■ ■ ■ ■ ■

At some point, causes always betray us. It doesn't matter how good or noble the cause may be, eventually it will end up in the flesh. That's how an evangelist, pastor or teacher can lead a crusade against pornography while at the same time be visiting adult book shops or prostitutes.

■ ■ ■ ■ ■ ■ ■ ■ ■

We must remember that Christ didn't die for a cause. In the Garden of Gethsemane, He wasn't thinking about dying for a cause. In fact, He asked that the cup (the intense trial) be removed from Him. He didn't say, "All right, Father, I'll die for the cause of saving the world." He looked for another option. I'm not saying Jesus didn't love us deeply, but I am saying He wasn't going to die for a cause. When the Father said there was no other option, Jesus, out of His love for the Father and for us, laid down His life. He died because of His love relationship with the Father and His compassion for us.

Redemption was the result. That's an important truth to remember, because causes eventually make us vulnerable to anger and deep hurt, which only increases our vulnerability to addictions.

I think a lot of this midlife crisis stuff is about causes gone sour. A guy lays down his life for his career, his personal dream or his ambition, but he eventually ends up with a sense of shallowness and emptiness. So he leaves his wife and runs off with a younger woman. Or worse, he jumps off the proverbial cliff with the noose of sexual bondage around his soul. I don't think Paul ever had a midlife crisis. When we realize we're going to live forever, there is no such thing as a midlife crisis.

The whole issue of how deceiving causes can be came to a clear focus for me a number of years ago. The Public Broadcasting channel presented a series on Vietnam. I sat transfixed as the show documented the American government's many lies that helped trigger the war, as well as the lies that continued throughout its duration. After the show was over, I sat there, stunned. Enough time had passed since the events that the producers had been able to substantiate the actual deceptions. In fact, some of those who had done the lying and scheming openly admitted what had taken place. It didn't take long before my soul began to explode in rage and anger. They lied to me! I'd had friends who died for a lie. I went to serve my country, while some of our leaders had conducted themselves with less honor than the enemy we fought. My comrades and I had faced bullets so they could play political games.

As I sat there stewing, my wife called down to me from upstairs and asked if I was ready for bed. *"No!"* I shouted, as I burst out of the house. I had to walk off the anger. I ran more than walked, because my emotions were so stirred up. It was pouring down rain, but I didn't care. I must have gone more than a mile before I stopped. There I was, standing in the middle of the street, sopping wet, shouting to God. Even if people in the neighborhood looked out their windows and reached for their phones to dial 911, I didn't care. I was furious.

"God, they ripped me off! I'm not ashamed of fighting for my country, but I've frequently been ashamed of it since I returned. This is the last straw: I risked my life for the cause of defending our nation—and it's all about lies!"

"That's right, son," the Lord said to me. "You'll find yourself in situations like this when you fight for causes. But if you follow Me with all your heart, and focus your life on our relationship, you'll never find yourself standing out in the rain feeling ripped off."

Something changed in my soul that night. I hurried home with an indescribable joy in my heart. The sense of shame and trauma were gone. I truly began to understand just how awesome it was to serve the Lord God Almighty.

THAT I MAY KNOW HIM

Paul declared that one thing consumed him: "that I may know Him" (Phil. 3:10, *NASB*). Out of that kind of passion will come a love that directs us to a powerful purpose. I'm sure you're familiar with the scene where Peter breakfasted with the resurrected Christ on the shore of the Sea of Galilee. Jesus had to provide the food because Peter had fished all night and hadn't caught a thing.

After breakfast, Jesus asked Peter if he loved Him, and Peter responded by using the Greek words best translated "I like you." Don't make too much out of the fact that Jesus used one Greek word and Peter responded with a different term. But the dialogue goes through three different question and response cycles. Jesus was calling Peter back to the relationship between them, and Peter was stuck on his performance. Christ was calling Peter to quit looking at his performance ratings and look at his heart. Peter deeply loved Christ, despite his own incredible failure, and Jesus was helping him see that love is what really counts. Christ is the One who gets us to the finish line. That joy of serving Christ, however well I might or might not do, is what I came to realize out there in the rain that night.

Then Jesus gave Peter a surprising command: "Feed my sheep." He didn't ask Peter if he liked sheep; He told him to feed them. You can almost hear Peter protest, "Hey, wait a minute. I'm a fisherman, not a shepherd of sheep or people." There's a tone of that reluctance in his response to Christ as he questions what will happen to John. Jesus replied, "Follow me."

Peter, follow me. We can substitute our names in Peter's place if we've said yes to Christ, because it doesn't matter what our jobs are. The only question that really matters is, are we following Him?

One of the great things about being a pastor is how little children often respond to us. Not too long ago, one of them came up and hugged me. I knew the little guy had already faced some tough times in his life, being raised by a single mom. His dad had decided to leave one day. I understood what that felt like, so this boy was kind of special to me. After he hugged my leg, he looked up at me and asked, "Pastor Ted, if you love flying so much, why are you a pastor?" I thought, *Great question, because I've thought about quitting several times this week.* But I remembered the day Christ called me to follow Him—not just to accept His salvation.

It hadn't been easy to walk away from a flying career. I had set my sights on becoming a pilot when I was five years old. Yet, after I left the military and entered seminary, as I stood watching an air show one day, I determined to follow Christ wholeheartedly. As the Blue Angels performed, flying the very aircraft I had gone into combat with, I realized I really had only one option. Because of my love for Christ, I would never go back to flying, and not because I didn't want to. My soul yearned to go back, but I could no longer serve Christ solely by flying or by being in a cockpit. I was responding to a much more profound vision in my life than flying combat aircraft.

I looked down at my little friend still grasping my leg, and said, "I'm not flying anymore so I can be here for you." You should have seen his face. I had come to battle for something really worthwhile. I was responding to Christ's calling in my life, a much higher one than I'd chosen to call myself to.

What does this have to do with winning the battle against sexual bondage and addictions? To put it simply, everything. As Proverbs 29:18 declares, without a vision people "cast off restraint." Vision is at the very core of self-control. A God-inspired vision enables us to face three powerful fears: fear of boredom, fear of long-term commitments, and fear of limited options.

FEAR OF BOREDOM

In our addictive society, boredom is unacceptable. Through the years, I've counseled many young men who found themselves tangled in the vicious web of sexual bondage as the result of a decision to relieve boredom. They bought a magazine or rented a video. They decided to cruise the bars or visit a prostitute. Or, the most common of all, they masturbated because they were bored. These days it seems that the unpardonable sin is to be bored.

I remember after I had just committed my life to Christ, I ran into an old flying and drinking buddy. He said, "Hey, Ted, I heard you've really changed. What happened to you?" I tried to say it quickly because I'd never shared Christ with anyone before, and I was somewhat embarrassed.

"Well, I decided to give my life to Christ."

"Oh, so you've become one of those Jesus freaks," he shot back with a smile. "So, what does that mean—given your 'life to Christ'?"

"Well, I'm working at staying married, paying the bills and trying to learn how to be a dad," I nervously responded. "I guess you could say I'm just showing up each day and giving it my best shot."

I'll never forget his response: "How boring!" There was a smile on his face because of our friendship, but I could tell he wasn't kidding. I would have laughed if it hadn't been so sad. He'd gone through two marriages and was an alcoholic. I know because I used to drink with him.

Some people develop an addictive mindset simply through trying to relieve their boredom. Hell quietly places the noose of sexual bondage around their necks as they lean forward looking for a thrill.

That's not to say that following Christ is a call to a boring life. But a commitment of the heart eventually will bring us to a place where we have to deal with boredom, and at that point we have to increase our commitment.

FEAR OF LONG-TERM COMMITMENTS

In the midst of the challenge of boredom, we have to make a decision to risk again with God. We made a commitment to follow Christ, and now we're faced with the challenge of developing spiritual disciplines. The Holy Spirit confronts us with the fact that we have an anger problem, an impulsiveness with finances, or some other issue.

For example, a man may be married, but one day a young lady at the office starts putting some moves on him. She knows he's married, but she doesn't care; besides that, right now his wife isn't being very supportive. The arrival of their new child means he can forget getting that new boat or car or whatever "toy" he's been dreaming about. Being a dad is starting to wear him down, too. Marriage and fatherhood are long-term commitments, and long-term commitments have become a tremendous point of fear for many men today. One of the major reasons for this fear is the fact that many experienced the devastation of their parents' divorce.[7] Yet commitment is exactly what these men need. Long-term commitments are absolutely crucial if the dysfunctions of our past are ever going to be reprogrammed.

Long-term commitment to my church has helped me to understand the gift of extended family. My long-term commitment to my wife has allowed me to discover true sexual fulfillment and intimacy. Because of our dysfunctional families of origin, the destructive patterns of our past can be so strong that long-term commitments are like lifeboats in a raging sea. When we take the path of least resistance, avoiding long-term commitments because of our fears and hurts, the results are always tragic. The path of least resistance in a man's life has the same effect it has on a river—they both end up crooked.

FEAR OF LIMITED OPTIONS

I remember the first time I read the book of James and ran into the statement, "Consider it pure joy, my brothers, whenever you face trials of many kinds" (1:2). I don't mean to be rude, but I remember thinking, *That fellow's a whole lot of French fries short of a happy meal.*

James didn't make a bit of sense to me. But, through the years, I've changed my mind and come to see the wisdom of his words.

First, he didn't say "if," but "when." Problems are inevitable, and they present us with limited options. They're not an elective. James goes on to tell us that the purpose of the trials is to test our faith. A lot of folks seem to think God is into destructive testing, like taking a product off the assembly line and smashing it with a hammer to see if it can take the blow. But there's nothing like that in the Bible.

■ ■ ■ ■ ■ ■ ■ ■ ■ ■

God doesn't bring us into a time of testing in order for Him to see what's in our hearts. He already knows that better than we do! The trials are for us to discover what's in our hearts. God sets up the trial so we can discover that we can make it.

■ ■ ■ ■ ■ ■ ■ ■ ■ ■

And God doesn't bring us into a time of testing in order for Him to see what's in our hearts. He already knows that better than we do! The trials are for *us* to discover what's in our hearts. God sets up the trial so we can discover that we can make it. Time after time in Scripture we see God saying to someone in the midst of difficulty, "Do not fear. I am with you." He set the whole thing up for our healing and growth. This is especially true in our lives at the point of our past traumas, the places where we've been abused, battered, betrayed or shamed by our bondage.

In the midst of those stressful situations, we discover God's dream for us. The first time I ever shared with a congregation that

I had struggled with an addiction to pornography in the past, I thought I was going to die emotionally. It took me back to my fear of being discovered, and God was asking me to face that fear publicly. Since then, I've come to understand that God will use me most mightily at the point of my past weakness. That week after my sharing, many men wrote to tell me about how they too wanted to be set free. They were touched by my courage in addressing the problem. They were living in the limited options of secrecy, and God was calling them to face their fears.

HIGH-ALTITUDE FLYING

The first time I saw the SR-71 aircraft, it was under top security wraps. I was amazed at its capabilities. I'd just landed at an Air Force base and heard the pilot report that he was descending through 70,000 feet. I wondered how high the thing went. After a lot of hassles and red tape, I was finally able to talk my way past the security and see one of the birds for myself. It was incredible! I couldn't believe how big it was and how fast it looked. But on closer inspection, I felt disappointment. The thing was leaking all over the hanger. There were even drip pans under it. And this plane was being prepared for takeoff in a short while. I asked what was wrong with it.

"Nothing," I was told. It was designed to fly at high altitudes and airspeeds. Once the plane got up to speed it would expand, and the resultant heat would cause the dripping to stop. The SR-71 has another unique feature: A significant portion of it is constructed of titanium—a metal that actually gets stronger as it heats up.

I often think back to that encounter with the SR-71, because it's such a powerful picture of a man who has set his heart on Christ. He's a man who is designed to fly in the heat and at high altitude. There are only two types of dreams or visions: the self-centered ones and the God-given ones. Sometimes it's difficult to tell the difference. But God's dreams are designed for the heat. They're failure proof, and they won't leave us alone. Every time we say we're going to quit, they keep pulling at our souls. That's when self-control and self-discipline begin to set deep roots. If my focus is just to stop some destructive behavior, sexual or otherwise, that's a good beginning, but it's like settling for flying a Cessna when God designed me to operate at high speed and high altitude through the vision He put deep into my heart. Without a God-given vision, we live a low-level life; in that mode, the addictive mindset can never be broken.

How do we get such a vision or dream for God? It's a very straight-forward process. It isn't anything mystical or hyper-emotional. It's based on the fact that Christ wants to speak to us of His plan and purpose—even more than we want to hear it. The Cross has established that fact for all time.

Here is a test to help discover your spiritual altitude:

Rate yourself on a scale of 1 to 5 in the following areas:
1=rarely; 2=occasionally; 3=sometimes; 4=weekly; 5=daily
Total your score at the bottom.[8]

1. I read the Bible and apply it to my life: 1 2 3 4 (5)

2. I pray and praise the Lord personally: 1 2 3 (4) 5

3. I confess my shortcomings and sin: 1 2 3 (4) 5

4. I am accountable to a small group: 1 2 3 4 (5)

5. I put forth time and effort to serve the Lord: 1 2 (3) 4 5

6. I allow the Holy Spirit to flow through my life: 1 2 (3) 4 5

Total score: _24_

25+ — You're a high flyer, and God will give you amazing ability to handle the heat and see far over the horizon spiritually.

18 — You're losing altitude and may not realize it.

14 — The ground is coming up, and you may have a hard time sensing what God is trying to tell you about His purpose and plan. Your vision is getting blurred.

12 — You're headed for trouble spiritually, and are flying blind or just going on past experiences.

This evaluation won't precisely analyze every individual, but it can give us clear indications about where we're headed. It also gives us a fairly precise assessment of the potential for the Holy Spirit to speak significantly to us about what lies ahead—a critical issue in all our lives, because, without a vision, self-discipline is a losing battle. And that's precisely why so many perish.

Notes

1. William Barclay, *The Letters of James and Peter* (Philadelphia: Westminster Press, 1997), p. 330.
2. James H. Moulton and G. Milligan, *The Vocabulary of the Greek Testament* (Grand Rapids, MI: Eerdmans Publishing, 1974), p. 75.
3. Barclay, *The Letters of James and Peter*, p. 301.
4. A. T. Robertson, *Word Pictures in the New Testament* (Nashville, TN: Broadman Press, 1930), p. 31.
5. "Suppress Now, Obsess Later," *Journal of Personality and Social Psychology*, Vol. 53, n.d., pp. 5-13.
6. Karl Pribram, *The Neuropsychology of Self-Discipline* (Newark, CA: Sybervision, n.d.), p. 13f.
7. Archibald Hart, *Healing Adult Children of Divorce* (Ann Arbor, MI: Servant Publications, 1991), pp. 209-226.
8. Adapted from Bruce Wilkinson, *Personal Holiness in Times of Temptation* (Atlanta: Walk Through the Bible Ministries, 1997). Used by permission.

CHAPTER 11

The Bitter Waters of Healing

My wrapping the car door around the basketball pole illustrates how God loves us enough to, at times, lead us to bitter waters for our healing. What do I mean by that? In previous chapters we looked at three factors that can lead to an addictive mindset (an addictive society, family dysfunction and trauma), and how a God-given vision can bring healing and self-control into our lives. We can easily understand the impact of an addictive society, and we hear so much about how the dysfunctional patterns of our family of origin can affect us. For most folks, however, the impact of personal trauma is hard to get a handle on. Moreover, because we live in an increasingly violent society, personal trauma is becoming a growing issue.

DEALING WITH PERSONAL TRAUMA

I think personal trauma can be a mystery for most pastors and church leaders, too. They're at a loss to know how to respond to someone who's dealing with trauma. When I first tried going to church, I found they couldn't help me with my trauma from Vietnam. This internal trauma had intensified my struggle with sexual addiction and had left me in a sad state of affairs.

Trauma can so affect our perception of reality that it becomes nearly impossible for us to grasp God's dream or purpose for our lives. It's as if we're driving a car down life's highway, but instead of having an unobstructed view through the front window, we can scarcely see around the rearview mirror. That rearview mirror has become so large, due to our past trauma, that our vision automatically becomes focused on what's behind us. Instead of responding to what lies ahead, we constantly react to what has happened to us in the past, even in present situations. Eventually, we end up driving right off the road or into someone else. But what's truly amazing is how long we can live like that. The human capacity to cope can be nearly unbelievable. We can appear almost as if nothing's wrong, as long as there are no violent turns or twists in our journey. But the hairpin turns always come.

A mom recently wrote to me about the violent turn that had taken place in her life:

> I walked in on him when he was in bed with my daughter, violating her. He jumped out of bed and turned his back to me. I had no idea what was happening until I got my daughter away from him and she fell apart. I told her it wasn't her fault and held her until she stopped crying and fell asleep. I was in shock, but I went downstairs and confronted my dad. He told me I just had a seductive daughter, and that he didn't do anything.
>
> But my daughter was only eight years old! I kept saying over and over, "How could you do that to my baby?" I kept it a secret two years. I blamed myself and thought I must have done something wrong as a mother. Then I remembered that Dad had done the same thing to me.
>
> I almost didn't live through it. I ended up in the hospital for a month. It's a long painful story, but the bottom line is that *I know Jesus still wants me on this earth*. And just as you said in the service last night, it is in the crisis times that God proves His love for us.

I realize that there have been situations, induced by implanted thoughts during unethical counseling sessions, when people come up with false memories. But the Holy Spirit doesn't operate that way. Instead, He lifts our heads in the tough times and helps us see the event in our past that has been there all along. We don't have to dig that memory out of our subconscious. It's been there like a huge rearview mirror we've ignored and tried to look around. People in these situations usually ignore the trauma because they've been shamed and told *they* were the problem. That mother's letter illustrates the fact that sexual bondage not only affects the victim and the offender, but also the entire family. (My wife will address the problems women face in dealing with their sexual bondage and the bondage of their mates in a later chapter.)

God didn't cause that grandfather to violate his granddaughter, but the Holy Spirit brought that mom to the place where she had to deal with the bitter waters of her own past. Similarly, in Exodus 15 is one of the greatest contrasts in all of the Old Testament. At the beginning of the chapter, Moses and the people of Israel are singing to the Lord because of their deliverance from the bondage of Egypt:

> I will sing to the Lord, for he is highly exalted. The horse and its rider he has hurled into the sea. The Lord is my strength and my song (Exod. 15:1-2).

Yet by verse 24, the people are grumbling against Moses. Now, I know they did that a lot in the wilderness, but they're hardly on their way and already complaining about God and Moses. What was the problem? God had led them to bitter waters.

The region the Israelites found themselves in has changed little. Even today it's a bone-dry wilderness. Thus, when rain falls, the soil leaches significant amounts of chemicals into the flow. The place where Israel was looking for water in Exodus 15 was just such an area. The water sources there are frequently loaded with calcium and magnesium,[1] which are excellent chemicals to ingest in a very hot environment. They're used as mineral supplements by athletes when they have to perform in hot, scorching conditions. In high concentrations, this water becomes a very powerful laxative! Now do you understand the people's distress? Several million people were gulping down water that was closer to milk of magnesia than H_2O. And there wasn't a tree in sight! It must have been total chaos.

Why would the Lord lead them to such a water source? The people were certainly asking that question. But there's a very simple answer: The land of Goshen, where they had lived as slaves for more than 400 years, was filled with irrigation canals. By the time the Nile reached Goshen on its journey to the sea, its movement was very slow. Thus the canals were loaded with parasites. The canals were the general population's water source, as is true in some parts of Egypt even today. The point is, the Lord not only was getting them out of Egypt—He was also getting Egypt out of them!

■ ■ ■ ■ ■ ■ ■ ■ ■ ■

When people are deeply hurt as children,
especially if the trauma is sexual abuse, they'll abandon their
childlikeness as soon as possible. They quickly lose their
spontaneity and vulnerability. Their sense of childhood
wonder and trust is destroyed.

■ ■ ■ ■ ■ ■ ■ ■ ■ ■

As I've mentioned previously, our society has become filled with the parasites of trauma and deep hurts, which are at the core of so much of our struggles with addictions and dysfunctions. Violence begets violence. Again, there's a significant correlation between people who sexually abuse and those who have been abused. This factor underlies much of our nation's rising statistics of abuse, violence, alcoholism and sexual addiction.

These statistics don't just have social implications; they also have a profound spiritual impact. When people are deeply hurt as children, especially if the trauma is sexual abuse, they'll abandon their childlikeness as soon as possible. They quickly lose their spontaneity and vulnerability. Their sense of childhood wonder and trust is destroyed. Add to that the deeper sense of tragedy that comes with remembering Jesus' statement in Matthew 18:3: "Unless you change and become like little children, you will never enter the kingdom of heaven."

This question of childlikeness strikes at the very heart and foundation of spiritual maturity. Therefore, people fighting intense battles with internal trauma face a tremendous barrier to their spiritual development. Hell knows it, which is why so many Christians become what I call "ballistic believers." They accept Christ and take off like rockets, only to crash before too long. They can't escape the gravity of the trauma within. That's why some have said yes to Christ, but like the Israelites, grumble constantly. They're living with and battling emotional parasites they picked up in their past that suck the life from them.

The four biggest parasites in our world today are denial, minimizing, rationalization and disassociation.

DENIAL

Some denial is healthy. It allows us to function in a potentially stressful environment. When I flew in a combat situation, I never let it enter my mind for any length of time that I could be shot down or killed. After all, I was convinced I had the "right stuff." But these survival patterns can make us look foolish once we're out of the environment that gave rise to them.

I'll never forget my first couple of weeks at seminary. To me it seemed like everyone walked around speaking in Greek, Hebrew or theological terminology. I didn't have a clue what they were talking about. It also seemed that everybody had these *huge* black Bibles. All I had was my green, plastic-covered *Living Bible*. Their Bibles were filled with footnotes and references; mine had coffee stains from reading it in the ready room prior to a flight.

To add to the pressure, I knew I could handle aerodynamics, flight systems and emergency procedures, but I didn't know about this theology stuff. I might fail miserably; then what? That's when I started wearing my flight jacket to class. My excuse was that I rode a motorcycle to school, and the jacket would keep me warm. But the real reason was that I wanted everyone to see all the flight patches on my jacket. I was something else, and I didn't want them to miss it. I had the right stuff.

At the same time, I began to act so arrogantly that I embarrassed my wife in public. Fortunately, she chose to pray for me instead of trying to confront me. She made the right choice, because I was so deeply into denial that confrontation would have done no good. I was reverting back to an old trauma-filled pattern of behavior. Consequently, I was unaware that I was becoming so obnoxious. A person embedded in denial the way I was isn't aware of any other options. Finally the problem came to a head one day as I walked to class. I had my jacket on, of course—it was my flack vest against rejection and failure. Then the Lord just asked me a straightforward question in my heart: "Why are you wearing that jacket, Ted?"

"It gets cold when I ride my motorcycle," I responded. Of course, since it was more than 70 degrees that day, my response was ridiculous, and I knew it. So then I just told the truth. "Lord, I'm afraid of failing at seminary. I wear it so I'll feel like somebody."

Christ responded, "I died for you; that's what makes you somebody. Get rid of the flight jacket and trust Me."

Living in denial takes a lot of energy. I was sweating, wearing that thing when it got warm. But, at a deeper level, patterns of denial cause us to be at war with ourselves. We know what we should do, but our fears or hurts from the past paralyze us. We end up like a car driving around with its parking brake on. Living in denial can make us feel crazy. We can't clearly explain why we act the way we do. I couldn't have told you why—even though I was embarrassing my wife—I acted arrogantly in public. It just seemed to happen. Victims living in denial frequently hurt others. I was hurting others with my arrogant remarks; denial makes us crazy.

■ ■ ■ ■ ■ ■ ■ ■ ■ ■

Victims living in denial frequently hurt others. I was hurting others with my arrogant remarks; denial makes us crazy.

■ ■ ■ ■ ■ ■ ■ ■ ■ ■

The jacket and my behavior are easy to see, but most denial is more difficult to identify. When, to deal with the trauma in their lives, people develop patterns of denial at an early age, that denial can become an art form. I remember one young lady my wife and I ministered to. She was in trouble, but we couldn't quite put our finger on the problem—primarily because she wouldn't let us. Finally the situation came to a crisis. She was found drunk at a local restaurant with her kids. If she had managed to get into her car to drive home, the results could have been disastrous. We talked her into going to a detox facility. After she finished detox and went home, we had a counseling appointment with her. She revealed that her father had sexually abused her from the time she was eight years old until she was a teenager.

I said to her, "No wonder you've been battling the bottle most of your adult life. You've suffered some of the worst abuse possible. That kind of searing trauma can drive you to all kinds of addictions if you don't deal with it."

I'll always remember her response: "Oh no, that wasn't abuse. My dad loved me." This was an intelligent, highly educated woman who was very effective in her career. I was stunned, but I came to understand the incredible grip that denial of past traumatic events can have on our lives.

MINIMIZING

The Israelites repeatedly looked back at their years of slavery in Egypt and implied that it wasn't so bad. After all, they had onions and garlic to eat then, and now they were stuck with boring manna. But the truth is, we can't compare pain. We can't say, like in the old *Rocky* movies, "It didn't hurt so bad." In order to get better, we have to be truthful. (Did you see Rocky's face at the end of the fight?)

Because our culture tends to minimize emotional pain, we do too, which leads to some strange responses. If someone gets hit by a car and ends up in the emergency room, the flowers, cards and letters pour in. But let that person have an emotional breakdown or end up in the mental hospital, and the response is very different.

I served as a pastoral intern at a mental hospital for a short time, and the difference in responses to physical and emotional pain was amazing. I didn't see the parade of concerned relatives coming to a mental hospital that I would have seen at the typical hospital. And in some mental hospitals, pastors aren't allowed easy access to the patients. The restrictions were created because some pastors did more harm than good when they expressed such comments as, "OK, you've been emotionally down for a couple of weeks, but let's have some faith and snap out of it. After all, the Bible says the joy of the Lord is our strength." The truth is, when we get hit emotionally—another name for trauma—it can be just as devastating as being injured physically. We dare not minimize it; we have to deal with the trauma.

RATIONALIZATION

Rationalization is when people make excuses for offenders—or offenders make excuses for themselves. They make such comments as, "Hey, my parents did the best they could. They had a difficult childhood themselves." The supposition is that the excuse makes the abuse acceptable. The truth is, *there's no excuse for abuse.* That statement may appear to be obvious, but it isn't to someone who suffered through traumatic childhood events, especially if family members were involved.

Time after time, I've heard men and women make excuses for those who abused them sexually as children: "If I'd been more submissive, maybe this wouldn't have happened." "If I hadn't done this or that, maybe it wouldn't have happened." I repeat, there's no excuse for abuse. Children have little, if any, choice about what takes place in their lives; they're dependent on adults.

In our society, men who, as children, were sexually abused by a woman, can find themselves in a Catch-22 situation. "Oh," some unthinking male might say to them, "that wasn't abuse; you were just getting educated as a man. That was your first 'score.'" But usually the man who was victimized never says a word because, as a male, he's told in one form or another, "That was a good thing. Men like that kind of stuff." But he was a child at the time—and there is *absolutely* no excuse for abuse, no matter how twisted and distorted our society may perceive male sexuality.

DISASSOCIATION

This emotional parasite is probably the most difficult to see in our lives because, in blocking out the pain, we lose sight of the problem. When the pain arrives, we choose to go somewhere else mentally. This is another survival response to severe situations.

I remember being in a very difficult situation while flying one time. I had a heavy load on board, so I couldn't maneuver my aircraft very well; the enemy on the ground was starting to get a lock on me. The instruments in the cockpit told me that radar-controlled guns as well as surface-to-air missile sights were searching for me. On top of that, I started to have a problem with the fuel pump. Every warning light in the cockpit seemed to light up!

In the midst of that life or death pressure, I distinctly remember saying to myself, *You know, if another light turns on, I could get a free pinball game.* I started laughing in the midst of the craziness. In order to maintain my sanity I was telling myself, *This is all just a pinball game; I'm not really here.* I had learned that if pain showed up, I'd make sure that I wasn't there mentally.

When we disassociate, we watch what's happening to us as an outside observer. This can be a powerful mental survival response, but the problem is in what we do with the memory once the trauma is over.

THE HUMAN COMPUTER

So, what do we do with such potent mental parasites? How do we deal with the issue of trauma when it becomes entangled with our sexuality? Before we answer that question directly, let's look at one of God's most incredible creations—the human brain. I've taught astronomy at the undergraduate level, and have been fascinated with cosmology (the origin of the cosmos) most of my academic life. But absolutely nothing approaches the complexity and beauty of the human mind.

In his treatment of patients afflicted with epilepsy, Dr. Wilder Penfield, a Canadian neurosurgeon, made a fascinating discovery. His work involved surgically exposing and electrically stimulating brain tissue in fully conscious patients. His initial goal was to find the portions of the patient's frontal lobe that caused epilepsy. In the process, he discovered what he termed a "double consciousness" phenomenon.[2] Penfield declared, "Something else finds its dwelling place between the sensory complex and the motor mechanism.... There is a switchboard operator as well as a switchboard."[3]

This discovery has tremendous implications for dealing with trauma issues. Dr. Penfield realized that the patients were not only aware of their immediate surroundings—of the operating room, the surgeon and his assistants—but also of a suddenly reenacted scene from the past. As he placed the electrodes to the patient's brain, each would recall a scene so vivid that it included sounds and even odors that had been part of that incident. Each patient was, in effect, objectively watching a rerun of a scene from his or her past; at the same time, the subject's brain was directing the recording of an equally complete record of the events occurring in the present situation. As Penfield put it, "If we liken the brain to a computer, man *has* a computer, not *is* a computer."[4]

Penfield's research emphasizes the fact that man is not just a collection of biochemical elements that have evolved into an impressive computer. Man has a mind that operates an incredible computer that records everything in detail.

Our brains constantly scan our environment. The brain takes note of what's going on around us and, specifically, what we're doing. It records our feelings at the moment (*I feel great today*), as well as our body sensations (*This chair sure is hard*) and, finally, our comprehension of what's taking place (*What's this guy getting at?*). It stores that information on a continuous basis. We've all had the experience of the brain reminding us of that stored information when a sight, sound or smell suddenly takes us back to an incident that happened when we were kids.

Now let me take the computer analogy a bit further. Figure 7 on the following page illustrates how our brains store memories like a computer stores information.

This mental recording process goes on continually in our "hard drives." But what if something truly traumatic impacts our lives as children, such as Dad begins to beat Mom in the next room in the middle of the night? (That happened several times when I was a little guy.) It absolutely terrifies us!

Or suppose my brother begins to molest me at night, and when he hears Dad coming down the hall to say goodnight, he says, "Don't tell Dad. He'll beat both of us again."

The list of potentially traumatic incidents is endless in our fallen world. Whatever the problem is, it just doesn't fit with anything we've had to deal with before. It doesn't fit on our emotional and mental hard drives. Instead, it goes on what could be called the trauma disc. When this happens on a repeated basis as we grow up, we end up with a lot of gaps on our hard drives or life disks. There are a lot of things that just seem to be missing from our recollections of

THE BRAIN'S INTERNAL COMPUTER

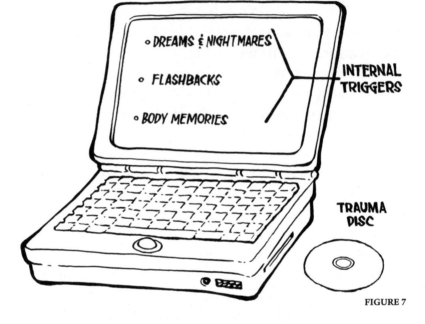

FIGURE 7

the past. The rearview mirror may be huge, but we're not even aware of it. We think that's just the way life is.

I thought it was normal not to be able to recall much of my grade school and junior high years. I was amazed when my wife could share detailed memories about her past. Penfield's research tells us that her experience was normal, but mine wasn't. It wasn't that my wife instantly recalled every detail of her past, but many events came easily to her memory. For me, those memories were blocked. The problem was that because I couldn't handle it as a kid, the information was on my mind's trauma disc. It needed to be downloaded onto my life disk.

In His wisdom, God has so constructed our brains that, when it's time, He will enable us to deal with the trauma. When, because of the parasites of trauma, we refuse to deal with the trauma, we're stuck with horrific emotional pain. That's when we can do things we don't understand, because the trauma discs have kicked in. Some folks have an entire library of them. As a result, we can end up acting "crazy."

WAKE-UP CALLS FOR HEALING

For some of the American soldiers in Vietnam, sex was a way of escaping the war. Every time we'd get out of the country, some guys would go crazy sexually. They tried to escape the horror of war through all kinds of high-risk behavior. They engaged in sex in ways that kicked off their systems the same way amphetamines would, in order to dull the pain. Once they got back to the States, they could find that same experience only by being violent.

Women can be just as vulnerable. If their first sexual experiences were under violent conditions, they may have felt pleasure in the midst of the pain, while also feeling responsible at the same time. As adults, these women can end up feeling that the only way they can be orgasmic is when a man hurts them. Dr. Carnes points out that this kind of arousal accesses a neuropathway that's very compelling. If the brain adjusts to it, a woman then needs that kind of stimulation to feel normal.[5] Translation: She ends up acting crazy and possibly destroying herself and others in the process.

So, how does the gospel—the Good News—fit in all this? Those crazy times are actually wake-up calls from the Holy Spirit for healing within. Paul gives a wondrous description of the Holy Spirit's work in the life of a follower of Christ:

> The Spirit helps us in our weakness. We do not know what we ought to pray for, but the Spirit himself intercedes for us with groans that words cannot express (Rom. 8:26).

Paul's use of the word "weakness" is deliberate and powerful.[6] This passage graphically describes how the Holy Spirit can bring us to healing, no matter how deep the trauma. The phrase "helps us in our weakness" is composed of three words run together in the Greek which mean "bears alongside of, instead of, the load." Paul was pointing to the fact that the Holy Spirit will come alongside us in the midst of our deep, personal pain. And, instead of our having to carry this pain, shame and guilt, He carries it for us. Our part in the process is to recognize that the Holy Spirit wants to help us in the midst of our craziness. That's why the issues of denial, minimization and rationalization are such killers when it comes to our sexual bondage. They set us up to carry the ever-increasing load of pain ourselves.

DREAMS AND NIGHTMARES

In His grace, God sends wake-up calls into our lives when we're battling with past trauma. One of the most common is dreams and nightmares. We all dream nightly. In fact, we spend a significant period each night in Rapid Eye Movement (REM) sleep. Most of us have seen a dog go through REM as he lies asleep on the floor. His eyes are closed, but we can tell they're moving, and the facial expressions indicate that he's dreaming. We do the same thing—except most of us don't dream of chasing cats. Dreaming is so crucial to our mental health that if someone awakened us every time we started to dream, it wouldn't be long before we'd start experiencing some significant emotional distress.[7]

God can use our dream cycles to bring to our attention that it's time to deal with past trauma. That's what I experienced in my life. (When I refer to dreams and nightmares, I am referring to the ones that frequently wake us up in the middle of the night.) Those dreams can be telling us that the Holy Spirit wants to bring a deeper sense of wholeness and healing into our lives.

I was fine for a period of time after I returned from Vietnam, but then I began to have dreams and nightmares. They weren't significantly disturbing at first, but they began to increase in intensity, until I was waking up in a cold sweat. The Holy Spirit was bringing to the surface the trauma that lay deep within my soul. I love how Paul continues his comments in Romans 8:27: "And he who searches our hearts knows the mind of the Spirit, because the Spirit intercedes for the saints in accordance with God's will."

I gradually began to realize that the Holy Spirit was interceding for me and through me. As I yielded to His work by reading my Bible each night as I went to bed and allowing Him to lead me in prayer, and as I began to have my wife pray over me each night and made myself accountable to other men, things started turning around. At first I felt like I was going crazy, but I came to realize that in the crazy times, the Holy Spirit had never been closer.

Those were difficult days. I hated feeling so weak, but one of the major problems I had was hiding the wounds within and pretending that I was always strong. Those days were difficult but necessary, because, since then, I've had no more nightmares. But I had to recognize that God was bringing wholeness to my life by taking what had been thrown onto the trauma disk of my mind and helping me integrate it onto the hard drive of my daily life. What was interesting is that Vietnam wasn't the total focus of the process; it was just a doorway into all the other stuff that had been thrown onto my trauma disk. I came to realize that I had been working at surviving most of my life; Vietnam had been just another part of that long pattern of pain, a pattern I had attempted to medicate with sexual addiction.

FLASHBACKS

Flashbacks are another common wake-up call from the Holy Spirit. These incidents occur when we're awake and something triggers the trauma disc.

I was coming out of a building at seminary one day, walking with a large group of students. It was lunchtime, and I was trying to process the overload of information I'd just taken in from the lecture. I was feeling the rising stress of trying to figure out how I'd ever accomplish all the work assigned by the professors. Just as the crowd of students surged out of the building and headed out across the campus, the local fire station siren signaled that it was noon. This was standard practice in the small farming community where the seminary was located. But in an instant, I was no longer in Wilmore, Kentucky; I was back in Vietnam.

The last time I heard a siren like that was in the midst of a rocket attack. If soldiers didn't move quickly to find cover, the survivors would be sending them home to Mom in a body bag. I exploded out of the crowd of students and raced toward the protection of the large metal garbage container next to the building. I'm sure I looked more than slightly weird to the students who watched me run into and then crawl out of a garbage can—once I remembered where I actually was.

It's important to emphasize the fact that I wasn't just remembering Vietnam. When the siren went off, *I was there*. I chose a humorous incident to make my point, but things quickly stop being funny when moments of trauma are attached to our sexual-response cycle, such as when a husband touches his wife in the middle of the night and she suddenly is shocked back into a moment of sexual abuse as a child. Nor is it humorous when a husband flirts with other women because he's reacting to his fear of being a homosexual based on a homosexual encounter he had with his roommate in college years ago.[8] These are all wake-up calls from the Holy Spirit for wholeness to come to our lives, to begin the challenging but necessary process of dealing with the trauma disks in our minds.

I want to underline how all of this fits with God's vision in our lives. We can never see God's vision clearly if the trauma of the past blocks our perspective. We first have to deal with the rearview mirror.

BODY MEMORIES

A third category of wake-up calls is the unusual manifestation of body memories. When one man came to counsel with me, it was a make-or-break time for him. His wife had reached the end of her ability to tolerate what was going on in his life. He was lying and covering up inappropriate sexual behavior. The man deeply loved the Lord, but seemed unable to free himself from the vicious grip of his bondage. To complicate matters, the inappropriate behavior involved a female relative. His past was a tangled jungle of family of origin issues and out of control sexual behavior that frequently involved a relative. He sincerely wanted to change, but there seemed to be something blocking every move he made toward wholeness.

After several counseling sessions, he began our time together with the comment that he felt as if he had been beaten with a stick. He hurt all over. For some reason I sensed the Holy Spirit was at work in this physical problem. I asked him if he had ever been beaten with a stick as he was growing up. Tears began to flow down his face as he told of the time during his adolescence when, over some minor infraction, his father stripped him naked in front of his brothers and sisters and beat him with a stick. That moment from his past was filled with sexuality, shame, terror and humiliation. I asked if the physical symptoms he was experiencing were anything like what he had felt as a young man. He could only nod his head in agreement because, once again, he was so ashamed over what had taken place. The Holy Spirit was helping him to remember the point of trauma that not only deeply shamed him, but also affected his sexuality and family relationships.

The proof of that evaluation was the fact that after that counseling session he never fell back into the sexual bondage that had seemed to have a death grip on his soul. He finally was able to grasp a vision of what God could and would do in his life. Paul wrote of the necessity of the great healing work the Holy Spirit does in renewing our minds (see 2 Cor. 4:16; Eph. 4:23; Col. 3:10).

FROM BITTER WATERS TO SWEET

God led the people from the bitter waters of Marah to the fresh, clear springs of Elim, and "they camped there" (Num. 33:9). God never planned for His people to live by bitter waters; all along He was bringing them to life-giving waters. But first they had to go through the bitter waters of Marah. Our problem is that we camp out at Marah instead of Elim. We can be trapped by our past and be unable to see what God has ahead for us when we don't understand how to deal with trauma. We need to understand very clearly that *God's purposes for us are always greater than our problems.* If we let Him, the Holy Spirit will come alongside and carry the problems that would bury us. But it all takes place through the bitter waters of healing.

Notes
1. Jamie Buckingham, *A Way Through the Wilderness* (Grand Rapids, MI: Zondervan, 1983), p. 59.
2. Wilder Penfield, *The Mystery of the Mind* (Princeton: Princeton University Press, 1975), p. xiii.
3. Wilder Penfield, *The Physical Basis of the Mind* (Oxford: Basil Blackwell, 1950), p. 64.
4. Penfield, *The Mystery of the Mind*, p. 108.
5. Patrick J. Carnes, *The Betrayal Bond* (Deerfield Beach, FL: Health Communications, 1997), p. 11.
6. Kenneth S. Wuest, *Word Studies in the Greek New Testament* (Grand Rapids, MI: Eerdmans Publishing, 1966), p. 140.
7. Kagan & Havemann, *Psychology* (New York: Harcourt Brace Jovanovich, 1976), p. 262.
8. Les Parrott, *High Maintenance Relationships* (Wheaton, IL: Tyndale House Publishers, 1996), p. 185.

CHAPTER **12**

Values: The Titanic Challenge

I can always tell when a man is ready for a breakthrough in his battle with a sexual bondage. It begins to take place when he finally has a handle on God's plan for his life, when a God-given vision has truly become part of his thinking. Unfortunately, that's not the end of the struggle. Dealing with sexual bondage is never a quick-fix situation, even if we use religious language to describe it. That's why Peter stressed the absolute necessity of building strong values into the core of a man's being to keep him from cracking under pressure: "If you do these things, you will never fall" (2 Pet. 1:10). The values of a God-given vision must be lived out. A man may have a great vision, a great ability to fly high; but without strong values, he'll experience an internal failure because of the relentless sexual pressures.

A CLOSE CALL

I heard that unmistakable sound as I sat in my office overlooking the runway. I whirled around in my chair just in time to see Chuck's ejection seat fire him out of the back seat of a crippled aircraft prior to impact.

Chuck Scott had become a close friend, but it didn't start out that way. When I first tried to talk with Chuck about Christ, he had responded with a rapid-fire volley of expletives. But the Lord wouldn't let me quit on him, so I stuck a book that had meant a lot to me into his mailbox at the squadron. The book told the true story of a man who risked everything to follow Christ. Chuck grabbed his mail as he went out for a flight, but because of bad weather, he and the other pilots were grounded on the aircraft carrier with little to do but read. By the time Chuck finished the book, he had committed his life to Christ. We became closest friends, and Chuck's love for the Lord and his maturity grew rapidly.

The whole crash scene and Chuck's ejection occurred in just seconds, but it seemed to run in slow motion as I watched. Would the student make it out of the aircraft in time after Chuck ejected? If they both made it out, would their chutes open before they hit the ground? Those questions raced through my mind as I watched the drama unfold before me. My eyes riveted on the two figures now flying through the air with chutes streaming out behind them. The front end of the aircraft slammed into the runway below them. Fortunately, a crosswind blew them away from where the ball of flames would soon erupt below them. With no more than 100 feet of clearance, Chuck's chute blew open, and the student's opened with even less clearance. It was the closest call I've ever seen in an ejection, but both men were alive!

BEING ALERT TO OUR LIMITS

We lost an aircraft, but not the pilots. Others hadn't been so successful. Several squadrons had recently lost pilots as well as planes because the pilots had waited too long to eject. After the initial investigation into Chuck's accident determined that no pilot error was involved, the squadron commander asked Chuck to share with all the instructors and students how he was able to react so quickly in a very difficult situation. I'll never forget the scene.

Because I was serving as a safety officer, I presented Chuck with the ejection handle he had pulled to fire himself and the student free of the aircraft. We had framed that handle for him. After some preliminaries by the commanding officer, Chuck was asked to describe how he had managed to deal with such a catastrophic failure. The cause of the accident was a metal failure of one of the load-bearing rings in the engine. The engine failed and flew apart, throwing turbine blades through the vital inner workings of the aircraft. All the electrical instruments had gone dead, and the plane had lost hydraulic power. This all took place when Chuck was in the final phase of the landing, after the student had incorrectly induced a high rate of sink in the approach. When Chuck overrode the student's mistake by applying power, the engine disintegrated.

Everyone in the ready room was all ears. How had he managed to react so quickly and so precisely? Chuck didn't miss the opportunity or back down from his commitment to Christ. "Gentlemen," he began, "this morning as I was reading my Bible and praying before coming to work, I sensed Jesus graciously telling me to check the Natops Manual." The Natops Manual was the technical "bible" for flying our training aircraft. Chuck had noticed that students in an aircraft would often develop a high rate of sink while on a final landing approach. So, because of the Lord's prompting, he figured out exactly where the point of no return was. If he was below a certain altitude with a certain rate of sink and the airplane didn't respond, then he knew it was time to part company with the aircraft.

That's just what had happened that day. Now that Chuck had everyone's attention, he went on to share his faith. I watched the responses of the men in the room. No one seemed offended; in fact, several were nodding their heads in agreement. That day signaled a spiritual turnaround for sharing the gospel in the squadron. Men became very open to listening to biblical truth. And it all took place because one man stood for his values without apology and was honest about himself.

Chuck had clearly figured out where his limits were. I had seen so many fighter pilot types get into serious trouble or even kill themselves because they wouldn't acknowledge their limits. And

I'm not just talking about running some plane into the ground, but about running marriages into the ground—or health or kids or whatever. But it isn't just fighter pilots who act like that. In fact, that sort of behavior seems to come naturally to most men. Humorist Dave Barry put it well:

> It is a well-known fact that a male with even a moderate testosterone level would rather drill a hole in his hand (which he probably will) than admit, especially to his spouse, that he cannot do something himself. Put an ordinary husband on the Space Shuttle, and within minutes he'll be telling his spouse that he'll repair the retro thruster modules...I personally have destroyed numerous perfectly good rooms by undertaking frenzied testosterone-induced efforts to fix them up despite the fact that I have the manual dexterity of an oyster.[1]

Peter declared that, to our basic faith, we need to add not only good character and spiritual understanding but also alert discipline and passionate patience. In the original language, both of these words carry a tremendous emphasis on the priority of godly values. Alert discipline is a translation of the word *egkrateia*, which literally means the ability to get a grip on one's self.[2] Today's popular term "get a grip" would be a great translation. It's the picture of a person who, despite the intensity of the passions or emotions involved in a situation, holds to his convictions. It is a picture of *integrity under pressure*.

The term "passionate patience" comes from two Greek words that mean under and remain. It isn't a grin-and-bear-it term, but a picture of someone who has the larger picture in mind. Hebrews 12:2 declares that Jesus endured the Cross for the joy set before Him. The term has to do with courageously facing the trials and tribulations life can bring our way because we've caught sight of something much greater than what we're going through. In the process, the difficulty is transformed by the vision that pulls us to higher ground. It is a picture of *integrity in the midst of personal pain.* Both these terms—integrity under pressure and integrity in the midst of personal pain—underline a deep challenge for all of us, because we all have a hard time being honest with ourselves at times, particularly when we're under pressure or in the midst of personal pain.

THE TITANIC COST OF COMPARTMENTALIZING

Another accident has captured the interest and imagination of the public for years. In 1912, the *Titanic* sailed from England. It was touted as unsinkable. Its construction involved a new development in ship building: compartmentalization. The hull of the ship was divided into many watertight compartments. The idea was that if a few of the compartments flooded, the ship would still stay afloat. But, as we all know, the concept didn't work as advertised. When the integrity of the hull was compromised, the ship was doomed, along with more than 1,500 passengers and crew members who went down with the vessel.

Dave Barry's funny comments about men's arrogance take on a whole new meaning when we realize how many people today make titanic mistakes in their personal lives. Those mistakes are easily seen as someone drowns in the grip of a full-blown addiction; yet compartmentalization has almost become the standard for our whole society. "What I do in my private life is my business and has no effect on the job I do publicly" has become a familiar refrain of our times.

In fact, it has become the rebellious call of politicians and leaders throughout our land. Does my private life affect my public behavior? Of course it does—what a silly question!

Why do so many leaders make such ridiculous statements? Because if we compartmentalize our lives, it allows us to hold conflicting values and pretend nothing is wrong. We can declare, "Christ is first in my life," yet still let our anger rage against those closest to us. "No problem," we say, "that's in another part of my ship. I just get angry at home, not on the job or at church." Or we can say, "I love my wife," and still flirt with someone on the job or visit the porno video store. Compartmentalization is a killer. We may even have a religious experience, but at some point we'll sink.

It may seem strange to ask why integrity is important, but that's part of the reason so many are caught in the web of sexual bondage. In our confused world, people don't know the basics of life. First, despite popular rhetoric, lack of integrity deeply affects those around us. Scripture states the truth in a positive manner: "The righteous man leads a blameless life; blessed are his children after him" (Prov. 20:7).

■ ■ ■ ■ ■ ■ ■ ■ ■

When integrity is part of our lives we end up rooming with God, and nothing can shake us up with God on our side. That's why it's so foolish to ask ourselves, Who will know if I do this? *The answer is obvious: God will. Real intimacy isn't possible without integrity.*

■ ■ ■ ■ ■ ■ ■ ■ ■

That verse deeply touched my heart the first time I read it years ago because, as I mentioned, I grew up in an alcoholic home that was fractured by repeated divorces. Consequently, I was lied to or disappointed continuously as I grew up, which made me a cynical young man. When I came to Christ, I realized that cynicism wasn't what my kids needed from me. If my family was to experience all God had for us, I had to develop integrity in my life. I love what Rick Warren said should be a husband's primary goal: to have those who know you the best respect you the most. Without integrity, not only will the ship sink, but we'll also take a lot of other folks down with us.

King David stated the most important reason for integrity—dwelling in God's sanctuary:

> Lord, who may dwell in your sanctuary? Who may live on your holy hill? He whose walk is blameless and who does what is righteous, who speaks the truth from his heart (Ps. 15:1-2).

David then went on to give an entire list of responses to daily life that could be summed up in one word: integrity. And, like Peter, he concluded the list with the proclamation that "He who does these things will never be shaken" (v. 5). Integrity is so important because it touches God's heart. David said that when integrity is part of our lives we end up rooming with God, and nothing can shake us up with God on our side. That's why it's so foolish to ask ourselves, *Who will know if I do this?* The answer is obvious: God will. And it isn't that He will *get* us because of what we've done. The problem is what it does to our relationships. Real intimacy isn't possible without integrity.

And lack of real intimacy keeps counselors' offices full. I've made a decision that no matter how large East Hill Church may grow, I'll never stop counseling. I can't counsel everyone, but I will avoid the trap of just being someone who speaks from a pulpit and doesn't listen to the hurts of folks one-on-one.

I once spoke with John Townsend about his counseling practice. John is a great counselor, so I wanted to gather some wisdom from him. I remember what he had to say about marriage counseling: The number-one problem he found in counseling troubled marriages was that at some point trust had been lost—and integrity is the foundation for trust. So the big question is, how do we get integrity? How does this issue of godly values get so far down into our lives that God's vision for us really can take place?

DEEPER ISSUES

One of the most fascinating things I learned about the *Titanic* was that when searchers discovered its wreckage on the floor of the Atlantic, they were able to answer some questions that had gone begging for years. The one that I was the most interested in, because of my accident-investigation background, was why the *Titanic* went down so rapidly.

The searchers were able to recover some of the steel plating from the hull along with the accompanying rivets. Detailed analysis revealed that the steel of the hull and the rivets contained a high level of impurities that significantly lowered their strength. And in the North Atlantic's cold waters, the metal became especially brittle.[3] Those impurities compromised the hull's integrity, causing it to be fractured easily by the impact with the iceberg. The engine in my friend Chuck's aircraft failed for similar reasons, because of stress cracks in the initial production of the part that gave way. Impurities in that part caused the plane to go down.

IMPATIENCE

Impurities in our lives can easily destroy our integrity. Essentially, this whole book is about sexual bondage, which is a litany of broken promises and lost integrity. But please remember that sexual bondage is a symptom of deeper issues. If we focus only on the outward behavior, we'll see people sinking in sin and be unable to figure out why they're going down so fast. We need to understand the emotional issues and battles behind the scenes that create the fracturing in the first place. So let's look at three familiar biblical stories that deal with emotional impurities that can weaken personal integrity.

Impatience is the first issue that brings emotional impurity resulting in a loss of integrity. We've all said and done things out of impatience that really compromised the values we hold dear. All we have to do is drive on a crowded freeway to turn our worship chorus from "I surrender all" to "Born to be wild"!

But few things frustrate us more than having God place us on "hold." At times it seems that God has some heavenly voicemail system, and we're lost in the shuffle. Our thoughts often run like this: *If God instantly brought the cosmos into being with just His words, why do I have to wait for three months to get a job? Why have I been waiting five years for a mate and there are still no prospects in sight? Why is this physical healing taking so long? If God is so loving, why does it seem like I'm constantly placed on hold?*

There's a story in 1 Samuel about a lady named Hannah who had been waiting years for God to give her children. For a Hebrew wife, one of the greatest tragedies was to be childless. To add insult to injury, her husband had another wife. (The other wife was the husband's idea, not God's. Sexual bondage has a long history.) This other wife constantly harassed Hannah over her childlessness. Can you hear Hannah's deep agony as she prays?

> In bitterness of soul Hannah wept much and prayed to the Lord. And she made a vow, saying, "O Lord Almighty, if you will only look upon your servant's misery and remember me, and not forget your servant but give her a son, then I will give him to the Lord for all the days of his life" (1 Sam. 1:10-11).

The Lord heard Hannah's prayers and gave her a son, who was named Samuel. Does the Bible list the names of the other wife's children? No. But Hannah's son Samuel was the first in the long line of the Hebrew prophets. Samuel was the man God used to anoint Israel's kings. Samuel had two books of the Bible named after him. Not a bad résumé, right?

So, why did God make Hannah wait? Why does He make anyone wait? Because waiting is one of God's greatest tools for our growth. God had to develop a Hannah before He could develop a Samuel. Paul stated the principle in Romans 5:3-4:

Let us exult and triumph in our troubles and rejoice in our
sufferings, knowing that pressure and affliction and hard-
ship produce patient and unswerving endurance. And
endurance (fortitude) develops maturity of character (*AMP*).

To be honest, I have never liked that passage, but through the
years I've discovered that what Paul said can help me pull myself
out of the pit of impatience which I so easily fall into. He said patience develops strength of character in us. Therefore, character
development, or integrity, starts with waiting.

■ ■ ■ ■ ■ ■ ■ ■ ■

*Demanding immediate gratification has become the American
way, but it isn't the way of God's kingdom. God isn't always
going to give us what we want when we want it.*

■ ■ ■ ■ ■ ■ ■ ■ ■

I hold a Higher Ground seminar for the new men in our church
several times a year. It's a time when I take them through the stages
of a man's life from God's perspective. One of the things I help them
understand right up-front is that the difference between a man and
a boy isn't physical, but emotional. A man has developed the capacity to avoid demanding immediate gratification—he can wait. He
can make sacrifices for something greater. He has higher causes
than his immediate needs. He can put his wife's needs before his
own. On the other hand, a boy has to have what he wants when he
wants it, which is why he's likely to go through a series of failed marriages, or end up in sexual bondage or deeply in debt or battling
uncontrolled anger. He has to have what he wants when he wants it.
Paul pointed out the priority of waiting as part of God's plan.
It's somewhat like the old Polaroid pictures, where we took the pic-

ture, then had to wait as the image developed before our eyes—it took a while. It's in those God-ordained waiting times that God's purpose and plan is revealed. Waiting is not an elective course in following Christ.

Demanding immediate gratification has become the American way, but it isn't the way of God's kingdom. God isn't always going to give us what we want when we want it. Instead He wants to give us more than we have ever dreamed or hoped for. Hannah is a prime example.

We haven't really learned to live until we've learned to wait. If we feel that waiting is wasted time, then at some point we'll look at our lives as being wasted and we'll throw our integrity right out the window.

The Bible is filled with stories of people who waited. Lazarus waited stone-cold dead in a tomb for four days! But it was worth the wait when Christ called his name. It's always worth the wait in Christ. And please don't forget this: Christ waited from eternity for you and me to turn to Him. But if we allow impatience to become part of the metal of our souls, at some critical point, our integrity will fail, and we'll sink.

FRUSTRATION

The story of Gideon in Judges 6 has one of the great one-liners in the Old Testament. Gideon was hiding from the Midianites in a hole in the ground used as a winepress. Basically, he was trying to figure out how to keep the Midianites from stealing his lunch. Then an amazing thing happened:

> The angel of the Lord came and sat down under the oak in Ophrah that belonged to Joash the Abiezrite, where his son Gideon was threshing wheat in a winepress to keep it from the Midianites. When the angel of the Lord appeared to Gideon, he said, "The Lord is with you, mighty warrior" (Judg. 6:11-12).

Then the angel of the Lord told Gideon that God was going to use him to take out the Midianites. Gideon didn't believe a word of it. So the Lord told Gideon, "Go in the strength you have. . . . Am I not sending you?" (v. 14).

Now, that was a confusing command to Gideon in the midst of his frustrations. But that's usually the way the Lord speaks to us. When we're down in a pit, He almost never begins with the thing that's bothering us the most. He didn't show Gideon how to keep his lunch out of his enemies' hands; instead, He spoke to him of his destiny. The Lord wasn't speaking to Gideon about *where he was* as much as He was pointing out where Gideon was *going to be*. And that was crucial information, because only a sense of destiny will enable us to be people of integrity when the tough times come.

When everyone else on the job is cutting corners and telling half-truths to make a sale, when friends in the classroom are cheating to pass the test, when a marriage starts to feel like it's expendable because we're getting nothing out of it, when the urge to visit the adult bookstore or the sex sites on the Internet hits—those are the times when we better have a sense of destiny in our souls.

Until we know the Lord is with us, we can spend our whole lives trying to make a loaf of bread instead of making a difference in our world.

The great one-liner isn't the angel calling Gideon a mighty warrior; that's simply humorous. The real punch line is when Gideon is told, "Go in the strength you have." I can just picture Gideon jumping up and down in the hole, shouting at the Lord, "You have to be kidding! I'm so frustrated I can't see straight. What do you mean, the strength I have?" But that's the point, isn't it? God challenged Gideon to understand God's purpose in the midst of his frustration.

Our lives are "Father filtered"—meaning that anything that comes into our lives, whether positive or negative, has been allowed by God for His purposes—if we've honestly said yes to God. Our frustrations come with meaning in them, not just mayhem. Besides that, God isn't going to do something great with someone who isn't frustrated. God-given frustration gives birth to a passion that can change things. If we want to understand our God-given calling, we must first look at our frustrations. What are we frustrated with that we know could be better? What bothers us about our present situation that doesn't just involve our comfort, but the needs of others? Once we answer those questions honestly, we start to catch sight of our God-given calling. Our frustrations can ignite our calling!

Looking back on my early days of church attendance, I have to chuckle. It wasn't very funny at the time, because I didn't understand that the Holy Spirit was trying to communicate something to me regarding my frustration and my calling. As I've previously mentioned, when I first came to church it didn't take long for me to decide it wasn't for me. They hadn't a clue what to do with the baggage I was carrying from Vietnam. When they talked about family, it was always within the context of Mom and Dad and two great kids—you know, the nice Christian nuclear family. My family had been nuclear all right—thermonuclear! The church just didn't get it. They were acting as if *Leave It to Beaver* was still the norm. My family was more like *The Simpsons* or *Beavis and Butthead*.

Then I slowly began to realize that the frustration was God's call on my life. I was hearing a call to be part of a church where the people didn't have to act like they had it all together; where folks would openly deal with their past hurts rather than learn the religious language of denial. How about a church for real people who were messed up, like me? That was what Christ was calling me to. And I said, "Sign me up for that one!"

Romans 8:28 is an incredible promise. Unfortunately, it's frequently misquoted and taken out of context. Here's the way it's often quoted: "All things work for good." But that's not what the verse says. It isn't correct unless we quote the entire thought:

And we know that in all things God works for the good *of those who love him, who have been called according to his purpose* (emphasis added).

This verse applies only to those who have responded to God's call. If we've said yes to follow Christ, we're called of God. It isn't something reserved for preacher and missionary types. He has called us. We've heard His voice:

- so strong it pierced the darkness of our lost condition;
- so penetrating it pulled us away from our selfishness; and
- so compelling it called us to look up from the pit of our frustrations to the high and holy calling of God in our lives.

And there's no pit more frustrating than sexual bondage. By His grace, however, we can find ourselves saying things like:

- "I would've fallen back into that pit of sexual bondage, *but He called me.*"
- "I would've stayed defeated, *but He called me.*"
- "I would have given up, *but He called me.*"

If we allow our frustrations to rule our lives, we'll sink. But if we allow God's call to rule our lives, nothing can take us down!

DEFEAT

The final scene we'll look at is a very familiar incident in the life of Christ and the disciples. I have a watercolor of the scene in my office at home, because it's a situation that I frequently find myself caught in. The picture reminds me of one of the most important truths for a man of integrity:

> So it was, as the multitude pressed about Him to hear the word of God, that He stood by the Lake of Gennesaret, and saw two boats standing by the lake; but the fishermen had gone from them and were washing their nets.... When He had stopped speaking, He said to Simon, "Launch out into the deep and let down your nets for a catch." But Simon

answered and said to Him, "Master, we have toiled all night and caught nothing; nevertheless at Your word I will let down the net" (Luke 5:1-2,4-5, *NKJV*).

I absolutely love Israel's Galilee region. Every time I travel to the area, I get up early in the morning, at least once, to sit on a hillside and look out over the lake. I can almost see Christ teaching the multitudes along the shoreline, with the fishing boats beached nearby. But on that morning depicted in Luke 5, things were not going well for the future disciples. They had fished all night and caught nothing. They were washing their nets as Jesus passed by, leading an ever growing crowd. Washing nets in the morning was standard procedure for commercial fishermen if they had a boat full of fish. But their boat was empty. Still, they were washing their nets, because they had decided that nothing else was going to happen. They had decided to give up—to quit.

How often I've seen men come into my office with such feelings of defeat. It doesn't take long to figure out they're washing their nets. They've made appointments because their wives basically forced them, but they've given up. They don't come out and say it openly, but there is a quiet conviction in their souls that change isn't possible in their situations. When they reach that point of defeatism, integrity is impossible. On the outside they may seem to be the most honest men around. They'd never lie or steal or be dishonest in their businesses. But they've lost integrity at the most important point of their lives—their self-respect. They're just washing nets.

It can be such a subtle change in a man's heart, just a click on the inside, unnoticed even by himself. But the change is monumental, because he's quietly decided to quit. I always have one question for such a man: "Who told you God was through with you?" We may have given up, but God hasn't given up on us. It's over when God says it's over, and He'll *never* give up on us!

That's why Jesus, after He was finished teaching, told Peter to launch out into the deep. He was getting Peter out of the shallows.

Peter's life was beached, and Jesus was getting him back into the game. "Quit fiddling with your nets," Jesus was saying. "Let's catch some fish!"

Peter's response to Christ is typical of someone who's fighting with a sense of failure and discouragement—he restated the problem: "Master, we have toiled all night and caught nothing." His words indicated that he felt as if Jesus were saying he hadn't really tried.

Sounds a lot like the most common reaction I get from people I'm counseling: "But, Pastor Ted, I've tried everything to get free from this bondage." They're not so much rejecting my counsel as doing battle with a sense of deep failure.

- "Don't tell me my marriage can turn around; it's hopeless."
- "Don't tell me my children can get better; we've tried everything."
- "Don't tell me there's hope for me; I'll never be free from the grip of homosexuality."

You name it, I've heard it. You name it, I've seen Christ change it!

With weary shoulders and a battered spirit, Peter said, "Master, I've worked all night and I'm tired." When we say things like that, we're implying this: "Jesus, I should have had some results by now. I know things at home should be different, but they aren't. I ought to be out of debt by now, but I'm not. I ought to be free from this thing that drives me to the sex shops on the Internet, the adult bookstore or masturbating when I'm lonely or bored. Master, I've tried, but I'm sick and tired of trying. After all I've been through, I should have something to show for it by now. I've gone to Promise Keepers, and I've repented a thousand times. I've gone to the altar and declared that things were going to be different. I've joined a small group. I have prayed, toiled and tried. Frankly, I've quit."

Hell jumps for glee. "I have him right where I want him," Satan cackles. "I've polluted his God-given dream with a sense of failure and defeat. It's just a matter of time before he turns from God's call and throws away his integrity. I have him in a hole, and I'm going to nail the lid shut!"

"I have toiled all night," Peter groans. And hell smiles.

"I have toiled all night and caught absolutely nothing," Peter moans. And Satan grins from ear to ear, like the Grinch who stole Christmas.

"I have toiled all night and caught nothing, so I decided just to wash my nets and quit," Peter mutters. By now, the devil is congratulating himself on his marvelous destructive powers. His pointy ears flap furiously as he jumps up and down in celebration of his villainous efficiency.

Then Peter totally messes up hell's plans with just one word: *nevertheless.*

- "I've failed so many times, Lord; *nevertheless,* at Your Word, I'll try again."

- "I've been battling this sexual bondage since I was a kid; *nevertheless,* I'll war against it once again at Your Word."

- "The world tells me that being a homosexual is something I can't change, that it was the way I was born; *nevertheless,* Lord, Your Word says I can change."

Nevertheless. Peter finally figured it out. "Lord, all I really want to do is follow You; therefore, I can't fail. I have absolutely nothing to lose!" A man who realizes that fact will never sink. His integrity won't crumble under pressure. He can't be bought or sold. He belongs to Christ. He will be a man with a God-given vision, impassioned with God-given values. It doesn't matter how long he has to fight the battle; he will keep getting back up and declaring a divinely inspired "*Nevertheless.*"

Notes

1. David Barry, *Dave Barry's Complete Guide to Guys* (New York: Random House, 1995), p. 40.
2. Horst Balz and Gerhard Schneider, *Exegetical Dictionary of the New Testament,* vol. 1 (Grand Rapids, MI: Eerdmans Publishing Co., 1996), p. 377.
3. "The Titanic," Discovery Channel Special, June 1998.

CHAPTER 13

Kingdom Toughness

By now it has probably become obvious that coming to real sexual well-being takes toughness. In this fallen world, there's no way we can hold onto God's vision for our lives and contend for Kingdom values without a real streak of tenacity in our souls. Of course, with my background, toughness shouldn't be a problem. Actually, I picked up a number of nicknames or call signs through the years, from Captain America to Bull—Bull being the one that really stuck because of my propensity to plow through something and not quit. Yet I have discovered that toughness as defined by the world is something very different from what God calls us to in His kingdom.

As we saw previously, the apostle Peter declared that if we build certain traits into our lives we'll never fall—we'll build Kingdom toughness within. We looked at the issue of vision as found in the terms "good character" and "spiritual understanding." Then we studied the issue of our values as found in the terms "alert discipline" and "passionate patience."

Now we come to the term "reverent wonder." Several commentators have declared that, because of its depth of meaning, this word *eusebeia* is difficult to translate, if not untranslatable.[1] This means that a one-word translation into English won't do it justice because the word has more than one focus or definition. It is a picture of someone who is not only rightly related to God, but also rightly related to his fellow man. Some might suggest that statement is obvious. If you are rightly related to God you will be rightly related to others.[2]

However, we can't assume that if we're rightly related to God it follows we are also rightly related to others. The tension of that dual focus requires some significant spiritual stamina. A lot of folks may love God, but have nothing but trouble with people. Conversely, I meet lots of folks who can get along with others fairly well, but are profoundly out of alignment with God. When either of those two points are out of balance, we will have great difficulty sustaining a God-given vision. We may have a great personal value structure, but it will never affect our world.

So, how do we respond to Peter's challenge? How can we live with a sense of reverent wonder? How can we have a spiritual toughness that enables us to stay in right relationship with God and people? Remember, if there is one thing that sexual bondage does, it totally destroys our relationship with God and others. We end up using people and hiding from God. So, the obvious answer is: It has to start with God.

RECOGNIZING AUTHORITY

The student in the back seat was "under the bag," as we were boring holes in the South Texas sky in an instrument-training flight. Being under the bag means he had to pull a curtain over his cockpit and fly the aircraft by instruments. It's a tedious and tension-filled part of flight training. It's tedious because instrument flying is by the book: details, details, details. It's tension filled because flying a high-performance jet aircraft purely on instruments is a lot like learning to tap-dance on a hardwood floor covered with ball bearings. The aircraft is inherently unstable, so if we lose our concentration, even briefly, there's no telling where we'll end up.

That night, I had a student in the back seat who was all over the sky. I finally got tired of air traffic control calling us and wondering where we were headed. So I quietly trimmed the aircraft up so that it would fly straight and level for the next couple of minutes. The student apparently was stunned by the fact that he wasn't fighting the aircraft anymore and didn't say a word. So I sat back—if you can do that while seated on a rock-hard ejection seat— and looked at the night sky. I'd never really done that before, because there was usually something screaming for my attention. But that late at night the air traffic was minimal, the student wasn't getting into any more trouble and the plane had calmed down, so I just took a few minutes to look around.

Sitting in the front seat at 30,000 feet, I felt like I could see forever. The Milky Way was like a rich carpet of stars poured out across the heavens. The ground below was sparsely populated, so the few visible lights seemed to blend into the light of the stars above me. It was like sitting in the middle of a huge sphere, with all of God's creation lifting praise to Him!

Then I sensed the Lord gently speak to my heart: "I'm coming back soon." It was just a phrase, just one sentence, but it exploded in my heart like a sonic boom.

Up to that point, I'd come to know Jesus as my Savior, my Messiah and my Friend. But that night, for the first time, I came face-to-face with the fact that He was also my Lord—my commanding officer. That's not a popular concept these days. We tend to want to see Jesus only as the One who blessed the children and lifted up the broken and downtrodden. But we need to remember that He is also the One before whom the apostle John fell on his face like a dead man:

> His feet were like bronze glowing in a furnace, and his voice was like the sound of rushing waters. . . . and out of his mouth came a sharp double-edged sword. His face was like the sun shining in all its brilliance (Rev. 1:15-16).

Kingdom toughness and tenacity begin to take root in us when we realize we're under God Almighty's loving authority. The centurion who approached Jesus on behalf of his ill servant was one of only two people in the New Testament Jesus specifically pointed out as examples of great faith. His coming to Jesus was quite a risk, because he was a commander in the army occupying Israel at the time. The Jews hated the Romans, and many considered Jesus a rabbi—and who's more Jewish than a rabbi? Christ's response to the centurion's request, however, was characteristically gracious. He immediately volunteered to go to the man's house and heal the servant. Then the centurion made a startling statement: "Lord, I do not deserve to have you come under my roof. But just say the word, and my servant will be healed. *For I myself am a man under authority*" (Matt. 8:8-9, emphasis added).

In response to the centurion's statement, Jesus made the declaration that He hadn't seen such great faith in all Israel. That must have set the Pharisees' teeth on edge!

This man clearly understood the concept of authority. It was part of his daily life as a military commander. And he understood God's authority over him. In the midst of a battle situation, when people's lives are on the line, the commander doesn't have time to explain his orders, or for dialogue and analysis. The correct response is simply, "Yes, sir," and then do an about-face and get on with the job.

There are times when the Lord won't explain His orders. There are significant issues of our lives on the line, and the Lord isn't giving us a lot of details about His reasons or methods. But He's made it very clear how we should respond. The question is, Will I be a person under God's loving authority or not? At such moments, Kingdom tenacity is either built up or destroyed.

There have been many times, as I've helped people at war with their sexual bondage, when I realized they had come to a turning point. One of the most crucial turning points is whether or not they will accept God's authority over them. I try to explain the reasons for God's sexual guidelines, but it always comes down to whether or not they will comply. In nearly every case, at some point, what God has asked them to do in the healing process doesn't make sense to them. Will they respond to God's loving authority by saying, "Yes, Sir," and then get on with the task, or not? If they don't, they'll never have any staying power in the midst of the battle.

Job is probably the greatest example of a man who submitted to God's authority, even when he didn't understand what was going on. The guy went through a hellish experience. He lost everything in a matters of hours. Even his wife slam-dunked him by suggesting he ought to just curse God and die. Then his friends showed up, and all they could do was suggest that he had caused his own problems because he had sin in his life. With friends like that, who needs enemies? Fortunately, the book tells us up-front what's actually going on. Satan declared that the only reason Job followed God was for what he could get out of Him. God responded by saying that wasn't true, and gave Satan the chance to try and prove his point. Job was on the line and didn't even know it.

Finally, after patiently listening to his "friends" tell him he was the problem, Job took God to task. He told everyone what he knew about God and, by the time he was through, it sounded like he knew more about God than God Himself. Then one of the great confrontations of the Old Testament took place:

> Then the Lord answered Job out of the storm. He said: "Who is this that darkens my counsel with words without knowledge? Brace yourself like a man; I will question you, and you shall answer me" (Job 38:1-3).

God basically said to Job, "I'm going to talk to you like a man, so cinch up your pants and let's have at it." In all His discourse, God didn't answer a single question Job raised. The point that God made was that Job had forgotten whose authority he was under. Fortunately, Job eventually said, "Yes, Sir," did an about-face and got on with his life, no matter how tough it may have been. Those moments always change us, and we see that truth in Job's statement about what happened: "My ears had heard of you but now my eyes have seen you" (Job 42:5).

Kingdom tenacity comes only from such moments. At some point, freedom from sexual bondage comes down to a decision about who's ultimately in charge. These are warrior moments, times when, like Paul, we hear the Lord telling us, "My grace is sufficient for you" (2 Cor. 12:9). Once we accept that fact, we suddenly realize that our understanding of God has radically changed. We come to see Him as the Lord God Almighty. As a result, we can't quit, because we're under authority.

STAYING IN THE BLESSING

To be someone who lives within God's authority, we also need to decide to walk in the blessing God has set aside for us. If we've said yes to Christ the Son, then God the Father has set His heart to bless us. The enemy knows that, and it deeply troubles him. He would love to get his hands on us, but in order to do so, he has to get us out of the place of blessing.

The parable of the prodigal son is not only one of the best-loved stories Christ told, but also one of the clearest pictures of one who comes out of bondage and of another who stays in bondage. In a previous chapter we looked at the father's response to the son. Now let's look at the prodigal's response to hell.

The prodigal was born into money. He had servants, a big house, the works. But it wasn't enough for him. It never is for the person who insists on being in control. So the son essentially said to his father, "Father, it isn't enough that I'm living in a place of blessing. I want to do what I want to do. I want to be in total control." Eventually, he would have been in control anyway. But he decided to step out of his place of blessing to be in charge *now*. The approach of someone in bondage is always the same: *I want what I want—now.* And the enemy's approach is always the same: to move us out of our place of blessing, our place of covenant agreement with God.

That's why, as husbands and wives, it is absolutely imperative that we stay in the blessed place of marriage, that we invest our lives in the covenant of marriage. Many Christians today don't even think of marriage as a biblical covenant. And it seems things haven't changed a lot. Some folks back in Old Testament times forgot that fact as well:

> You ask, "Why? [things are going so bad in your life]" It is because the Lord is acting as the witness between you and the wife of your youth, because you have broken faith with her, though she is your partner, the wife of your marriage covenant (Mal. 2:14).

First of all, a biblical covenant is built on God's sovereignty. We're again dealing with the principle of authority, and God is supreme in all of His covenants. That's why a marriage begins to move away from God's blessing when one or both parties turn away from acknowledging that God is in charge. The Lord knew what He was doing when He gave each of us the mate we have, and a marriage is not just about the person we vowed to love, honor and cherish. It is also about the vow we made before God on our wedding day.

God designed marriage to be a shelter in the midst of the storms, not the center of the storm. He gave us our mates because He knew it wasn't good for us to be alone. So we shouldn't disagree with the gift that God designed to be His place of blessing for us. Whenever a married man has a severe battle with sexual bondage, it's always preceded by a deterioration in his marriage. A man always walks away from God long before he walks away from his wife.

Second, covenant is God's means of growing us up. I remember counseling a distraught husband not too long ago. We had developed a friendship through the years, so I could be straightforward with him. When he said, "Pastor Ted, my wife is crucifying me," I simply responded with a slight grin and said, "I thought you wanted to be like Jesus." A great marriage isn't rooted in psychology or communications techniques, though those may be helpful; it's rooted in solid theology.

In Ephesians 5, Paul gives clear, practical suggestions for a good marriage. Frequently the context from which he's speaking is totally forgotten: "I am talking about Christ and the church" (v. 32). The only way marriage will ever work to its full potential is by getting our eyes on Jesus. Marriage's ultimate purpose is not just for intimacy to take place, but that there might be real character growth. How we treat our mates will affect our character for eternity, and that's why sexual bondage is so incredibly devastating.

Our enemy understands that fact very well, which is why he wants to get us out of the house, out of covenant blessing. His strategy has changed little down through time, even all the way back to when God's people first entered the Promised Land—the place of blessing God had set aside for them. From the start, sexual bondage was one of the enemy's primary weapons for getting God's people out of the blessing.

The king of Moab employed the false prophet Balaam to curse Israel (see Num. 22–25). But no matter how Balaam tried to say it, God wouldn't allow him to curse His chosen people. God was committed to blessing them. Finally, Balaam came up with the idea of getting the Israelites to curse themselves through sexual bondage: "The men began to indulge in sexual immorality with Moabite women" (Num. 25:1). It's a tactic as old as hell, and very deadly if we don't know how to deal with it. The enemy knew the only way he could get his hands on the people of Israel was to get them to walk away from God's covenant blessing for them.

He also knew the only way he could get his hands on the prodigal son was to get him out of his father's house. So he sent a restlessness into the prodigal's soul. Today we call it boredom. I've watched so many men walk right into a pigpen because they felt bored, or they just got too busy and let their marriage die. They were driven by a restlessness to achieve, to have a new thrill, or a restlessness within because they'd never faced their deep hurts. That's why one of the smartest things we can do is stay in the marriage—even if we feel like our spouse doesn't appreciate us, or we feel wounded and discouraged. Instead of leaving the house, we need to let a passion for God's blessing give us a tenacity to hang in there.

The major mistake the prodigal made was to leave home and play right into the enemy's hands. He listened to the enemy's siren call: "Come on out and play. Come on out. I want you, but I can't quite reach you." So many men have fallen for the same trap:

> Come on out. I've been trying to discourage you in this marriage, to get you emotionally drained, so I can get a death grip on you. Come on out of the Church. You're single, and the Church is filled with married people who don't have to deal with the sexual frustrations you have. If you were married, you wouldn't be having this struggle. I can't quite get a clear shot at you when you're in the Church. Come on out.

So the prodigal son packed his bags and headed for the bright city lights—out of God's will and out of the house. Initially, he had a blast—and for a time, he was still blessed! You see, that's the backside of God's grace. We can be blessed at the same time we're wrong. So the son was telling himself, *I have the best of both worlds. I'm doing my own thing, and God is still blessing me.*

But if we stay out there long enough, we'll lose everything that really matters: wife, kids, job, integrity and self-respect.

Remember what happened next? A famine swept the land. The enemy was closing in for the kill: "Come on, I can't get my claws in you without your help. Come on, let's make a deal; you're so close I can smell the stench of the pigpen on you."

That's when the Jewish prodigal attached himself to a pig farmer. (We know where we really are by the people we hang around with when we're in trouble.) So the son ended up in the pigpen, up to his armpits in slop. Hell was throwing a party because of what they'd done. Satan had him right where he wanted him. It was time to toy with the boy, like a cat does with a wounded mouse before it devours the victim. One more step and it was finished. The prodigal was doing things he never thought he'd do. We know hell has a claw in us when we find ourselves doing things we never thought we'd do, saying things to our mates that never would have entered our minds when we stood at the altar and exchanged vows, and accepting things as OK that not too long ago would have deeply troubled us. When that starts happening, *we're in the pigpen*!

The critical moment for the prodigal was at hand. Hell leaned forward for the kill; then something happened:

> And he would gladly have filled his stomach with the pods that the swine ate.... But when he came to himself, he said, "How many of my father's hired servants have bread enough and to spare, and I perish with hunger!" (Luke 15:16-17, *NKJV*).

I love how the *NIV* expresses it: "When he came to his senses...." But what brought him to his senses? The answer is found in an awesome expression of God's sovereign love: The prodigal *would have* filled his stomach. In other words, he *almost* ate pig slop. We may never have told anyone about it, but there have been some "almost" moments in our own lives, times when we were so lonely, so down, so tempted that we *almost*... we were on the verge, but we didn't; and it wasn't a matter of our willpower that stopped us.

Those moments are important to remember. I recall a gentleman who became something of a mentor to me. While I was in charge of a counseling ministry at a local church, I asked him about various counseling techniques, and what to watch out for in counseling. His response startled me. He said, "First of all, watch out for yourself." He went on to tell me about a counseling situation in which he became attracted to a young lady he was counseling. To make matters worse, she was pushing every button he had. He knew he was getting into trouble, but he seemed unable to stop himself from moving toward the pigpen.

At his lunch break before the counseling appointment, he found himself crying out to God, "Help, Lord!" Determined to keep it on a professional level, he went on with the appointment. And that's what happened: He kept it strictly professional. With great relief, he headed toward his car after the counseling session. But the young lady was waiting there for him. As she enticingly leaned up against him, the only thing he could do was give a half-hearted smile. Suddenly, the woman's whole demeanor radically changed and she walked away. My friend couldn't figure out what happened until he got in the car and looked in the rearview mirror and smiled. There, between his front teeth, hung a huge piece of spinach. He knew he'd brushed his teeth after lunch. Apparently, God had sent a "spinach angel" in response to his cry for help.

I'm so grateful that the Father has given me such a great family, such tremendous kids, such a lovely and gracious wife. He has forgiven me so much. He has allowed me to minister in His name. But if I stop and think about it for a moment, one of the things I'm most grateful for are the almosts, for those times that, if I'd kept going, I would've lost everything. If the enemy had pushed one inch farther, I would've collapsed. If the temptation had been one degree more intense, I would've melted. If the Lord hadn't been sovereign on my behalf, I *almost*...

The God-given almosts enable us to change our minds. Sometimes we can't change our circumstances, but we *can* change our minds. Sometimes we can't change our marriages—in fact, most of the time we can't—but we can change our minds. We may not be able to change our response to sexual bondage in our lives right now, but we can change our minds. And, like the prodigal son, that decision eventually will change everything. Kingdom toughness ultimately isn't about us, but about the Lord. He will always work tenaciously on our behalf so that we may come to our senses. We can't quit, because God has decided to bless us!

CHOOSING TO BE GRATEFUL

There's a surprising final and most important element in Kingdom toughness: We must choose to be grateful. In his analysis of why the first generation of Israelites delivered from Egypt totally wilted in the wilderness, Paul makes an interesting observation:

> Now these things occurred as examples to keep us from setting our hearts on evil things as they did. Do not be idolaters, as some of them were....And do not grumble, as some of them did—and were killed by the destroying angel (1 Cor. 10:6-7,10).

Paul was saying, *Don't let yourself go down the road of complaining and grumbling—it leads right into the enemy's hands.* Why would God make such a big deal out of complaining? For the simple reason that complaining or grumbling is a character issue more than it's about circumstances.

Who's responsible for the joy and gratitude in my life? That's one of the most important questions we'll ever answer. Actually, there's only one appropriate answer: me. I must take responsibility for my response to life. I can't leave it to my boss, my mate, my kids, neighbors or friends. I'm the one who's ultimately responsible. It's true that the people around me can deeply affect me, but the bottom line is, I determine how it all shakes out.

If we wait until the boss—or on the opposite end of the scale, the employee—says "thank you" before we're grateful, we're in for a long wait. We can spend some of the best years of our lives waiting for our kids to appreciate us so we can be grateful for them. They really can't appreciate us until they have kids of their own. We can spend years in a miserable marriage because we're waiting for our mates to finally appreciate us, but we're wasting our life waiting.

Gratitude is *our* responsibility. If we miss that fact, we'll miss some of the most precious gifts God has given us.

For some unknown reason, I decided I'd bend the rules a little one day, which is never a very smart move—especially under pressure. I decided to ignore the fact that one of the boost pumps wasn't working in the aircraft as I started it up. The plane had a backup boost pump anyway—no problem. Besides that, if I started over with a new aircraft, we'd lose our target time. I was leading a flight of four aircraft. I had an instructor under training in my plane, with three students on my wing. We were all headed to the target range for a bomb hop. We finally got airborne, and the students managed to get into flight formation. Everything was going just fine. I called in to the target and got clearance. I made my first run, and guess what? The other boost pump went out, which meant that in about two minutes I'd be flying an aircraft with nearly a full fuel load and no way to get the fuel to the engine. In other words, I'd end up manning a very heavy and very fast *brick*!

As I clawed my way skyward, trying to gain some altitude, the handwriting was on the wall. There was no way I could make it back to base, and my evaluation of the situation was confirmed as the engine began to flame out due to fuel starvation. By the book, I had only one option: eject. This type of aircraft, with this fuel load and no power, couldn't be "dead-sticked" into a landing. The sink rate would be way too high. The safety manual clearly stated that we wouldn't make it, and I knew it. The instructor under training in the back seat knew what the book said also, which was why he was positioning himself to eject. I looked in the rearview mirror and signaled for him not to move. I was going to find a way to land this thing—I didn't care what the book said. I got us into this situation by my own stupidity, and I'd find a way out.

I called the air traffic controller in my best Mr. Iceman voice. (I listened to the recording afterward and discovered I sounded more like Mickey Mouse wearing a pair of shorts three sizes too small.) I declared an emergency and said I'd have to land at the outlying practice field. Then I asked if he'd please give me vectors to the field. To make a short story even shorter, because it's impossible to stay airborne very long when flying a brick, we headed down—and I mean *down*. By God's grace—and that's the only explanation I have for how we made it—we ended up sitting at the far end of the runway after using every available inch to stop. As we sat there waiting for the emergency vehicles to catch up with us, I looked down at my hands. They were shaking; I'd never seen them do that before.

At that moment I was grateful—grateful for life, for my wife, for God's goodness. I think it was the first time I really stopped taking life for granted. I realized life was a gift.

■ ■ ■ ■ ■ ■ ■ ■ ■ ■

Whenever a married man has a severe battle with sexual bondage, it's always preceded by a deterioration in his marriage. A man always walks away from God long before he walks away from his wife.

■ ■ ■ ■ ■ ■ ■ ■ ■ ■

A little over a year ago I had to let go of my wife's hand as she was wheeled into surgery. It wasn't supposed to be serious, but there were no guarantees. Once again, I realized with a new depth of understanding how our life together is such a great gift. It isn't a right; it's a gift, a very precious gift. We mustn't take the fact that we're alive for granted. If we're honest with ourselves, we have to admit that every moment is a gift from God—an expression of God's goodness. Who am I going to make responsible for the joy and gratitude in my life? It has to be me. I can't hold anyone else accountable.

Today is the day I need to decide to walk in gratefulness, not when things finally work out the way I want in the future, because that idealized future rarely comes in a fallen world. I remember calling a dear friend not too long ago. He's one of the most grateful men I've ever known, and that's why he's always such a delight to be around. When we moved to Southern California for a short period years ago, we stayed with him and his wife for a couple of nights until we got settled. Diane and I were startled out of a sound sleep in the middle of the night by cries of agony coming from the other end of the house. My friend's wife was struggling with another night of fierce pain from an auto accident that had caused severe nerve damage.

Our friends never denied their problem, yet Butch was one the most grateful and loving men I've ever met. Even when I called him recently to tell him how much I appreciated him, he didn't complain about the fact that he's now battling a rare form of bone cancer that causes him a lot of pain. All he could say over the phone was how grateful he was for our friendship.

I kept thinking, *I'm the one who should be grateful.* In watching Pastor Butch, I finally caught a glimpse of who I was called to be. Butch just loves people, and Christ's healing power flows through him. I remember saying to myself, *Jesus, that's the kind of pastor I want to be.*

I'll never forget the question I faced that night we spent in his home. I examined my life and all that I had and, as I looked at the ceiling, I asked myself what I was waiting for before I became a grateful person. If I think something or someone is going to come along and make me grateful, I'm sadly deceived. So, when am I going to practice gratitude? It's my call.

And that's the truth for all of us. We don't have yesterday, and we don't have tomorrow—we only have today. It has to be me, and it has to be now!

You might be saying to yourself, *Well, Ted, that's hard for me to swallow because of my huge disappointment.* As we've seen, a deep pain in our hearts is very difficult to deal with and can even set us up for sexual bondage. It can wear us down. But grieving is a healthy response, which is why it's so important to realize the nature of the woundedness within, and then grieve over it and deal with it. But we can't let that pain have one more inch of our souls than necessary. We mustn't let the wound keep us from receiving God's gift of gratitude that lies at the very core of a life characterized by Kingdom toughness.

Someone might ask, *If God wants me to be grateful, why doesn't He just remove all the bad stuff and give me what I want?* A wise parent understands the foolishness of such an approach. We don't raise grateful kids by giving them everything they want. What we raise by indulging desires are self-centered kids who will have lots of difficulties. An attitude of gratitude is always developed in the midst of difficulty. In fact, a grateful heart can't be produced without trials.

Gratefulness is a discipline developed through pain that comes with remaining faithful to the vision God has given and the values we hold dear. But it isn't another name for denial.

For example, I can look out my window on any given day, and I may see a beautiful clear blue sky, or it may be miserable and rainy. I can look around and study my surroundings, whether I'm sitting in a mansion or in a run-down shack. Regardless of the circumstances, I have every reason to be grateful—*I can see.* A lot of people don't have such a gift.

The watch on my arm tells me that I've been given another minute, courtesy of God. We can't create a single moment; only God can do that. I've been given another opportunity to make a difference in my world, no matter how small or insignificant, or how impossible it may appear right now. With Christ in me, I can make a difference.

The wedding ring on my hand reminds me that I've been given another gift—and I'm not referring to the ring. There may be moments—however brief—when I don't like the gift quite as much as I usually do. But as imperfect as my gift may seem, it's a gift nonetheless. At the very minimum, that marriage commitment challenges me to grow emotionally and spiritually, on a daily basis.

For those of us who live in America and are part of what's called "the middle class," we are in the top 10 to 15 percent in the world financially. Sure, we may have car payments, house payments and credit card bills, but most folks on this planet would love to have problems like that.

Quitting doesn't make any sense when we realize all that God has done for us. We have all of this and heaven too! Once that truth grips our hearts, a determined, godly sense of toughness begins to take root in our souls. If you don't believe me, just talk to my tough and loving friend Butch. He'll make you a believer!

Notes

1. William Barclay, *The Letters of James and Peter* (Philadelphia, PA: Westminster Press, 1997), p. 303.
2. Lawrence O. Richards, *Expository Dictionary of Bible Words* (Grand Rapids, MI: Regency, 1985), p. 315.

CHAPTER **14**

Lord of the Mulligans

Christmas was a great time of year, but it didn't make a whole lot of sense to me. The songs we sang at Christmas were warm and traditional, but to my mind a little weird. "Sleep in heavenly Peas"? Those awful green things were bad enough on a dinner plate—but sleeping in a bed full of them? This is a bit strange. "God and cinders reconciled"? This was perhaps the most baffling line of all. What did God have to do with a pile of ashes?[1]

Scott Richardson wrote that paragraph concerning his confusion about Christmas when he was 13 years old. As a 13-year-old, I didn't have even that clarity about Christmas. I remember, several years later, the last Christmas I spent with my family before I left for flight training. I bought my stepfather a bottle of Jack Daniels, in a special holiday edition gift bottle, of course. We sat by the tree afterward and polished the bottle off together. It was a great Christmas as far as I was concerned—one of the best I could remember. Before, Christmas had always been a time of intense family tension. At least this latest stepfather got drunk with me, instead of just screaming at me.

When I returned from Vietnam and heard Christmas carols for the first time as a Christian, I was amazed. I'd been listening to those songs since I was a kid, usually as background music while we went shopping. But now I realized what those carols were about, and I was overwhelmed with joy. They were incredible! Then I heard the "Hallelujah Chorus" from Handel's *Messiah,* and tears welled up in my eyes. I was stunned by the glory and graciousness of the song:

And his name shall be called Wonderful, Counselor,
the Mighty God, Everlasting Father, the Prince of Peace
(see Isa. 9:6).

The reason the chorus is so profound is that Handel was directly quoting the Old Testament prophet Isaiah, who spoke of the Messiah's nature hundreds of years before His coming. I discovered in subsequent years just how beautifully Handel had described my Savior.

As I've mentioned several times, I hardly ever went to church as a kid, and what I heard about it didn't sound very appealing. It seemed to me that the Baptists didn't like the Catholics; the Catholics were suspicious of the Pentecostals; the Pentecostals thought the liberals worked for the devil; and the liberals were convinced the Pentecostals were brain-dead. It was as if they all had their own little god warring for attention; therefore, they didn't need each other. I think what disturbed me the most was that it seemed to me they didn't really like people, but they loved their various doctrines. I know my perception was distorted, but that's the way I saw it as a kid.

Discovering the Wonderful Counselor

Still, there were two things that wouldn't let me walk away from the question of who God really was. First, I didn't know much about God, but somehow I'd heard the outrageous claims of Christ: "I am the way and the truth and the life. No one comes to the Father except through me" (John 14:6). The guy claimed not only to be God, but that He was the *only* way to God!

I was smart enough to realize that if the Hindus were right, I had nothing to worry about because, from their perspective, any sincere seeker would be fine. If the Buddhists or any other eastern religion were right, the same conclusion would be true. If the Universalists were right, we'd all end up in heaven anyway, so it didn't matter. If Christianity was a hoax and we all just turned to dust when we die, then even that didn't matter. But if this Jesus really is the Wonderful Counselor, the Mighty God, the Everlasting Father, the Prince of Peace, then I had to deal with that issue.

At a much deeper level, I couldn't walk away from the question of who God really was because of what I'd experienced as a kid. Years ago, when Mom was on her third or fourth husband (I still loved her deeply), it hurt me tremendously every time I would hear them yelling and screaming at one another. In those moments, I frequently took my rifle and headed for the hills.

We lived on a huge sheep and cattle ranch at the time. Sometimes I'd spend all day up in the hills. At the time, I was only about as tall as my rifle, but my dog and I thought we were something else. One day, as I sat on a hilltop overlooking the ranch, I started talking to God—really talking. I told Him about my hurts and hopes, about my dreams and doubts. And, amazingly enough, He talked to me! Oh, not in an audible voice; it was a voice within. But instinctively, I knew it was God. Kids don't get as confused as adults about such things. As a kid on that hillside, I discovered that His name is Wonderful Counselor.

When Isaiah referred to Christ as the coming Wonderful Counselor, he obviously wasn't referring to the arrival of a clinical counselor. The Hebrew word he used for counselor was *yaats*. It refers to someone who speaks purpose into our lives—God's purpose.[2]

That little boy on the hillside eventually found himself carrying a rifle in Vietnam. I was trained as a fighter pilot, but when I showed up, they were losing platoon commanders quicker than they were losing pilots, so they gave me a rifle and said, "There's your platoon." Only the Marine Corps does things like that. But after a while there was a pilot shortage, so I was flying again.

It didn't take long before the total insanity of the whole situation started to get to me. After a rather scary night mission, I was headed home to relax. As I set the plane up for the landing approach phase, I started picking up ground fire from the villages surrounding the base. These were people we were supposed to be defending. This was nuts!

Finally, after several months of ever increasing, similarly crazy situations, I found myself on my knees. I'd just finished reading the letter and book my wife had sent me. Earlier that day, I'd been involved in another crazy situation in which I had to kill some of the "enemy" at close range. I use the word "enemy," but at times we couldn't be sure if they were the bad guys or just some farmers trying to scratch out a living in this free-fire zone. In other wars the lines had been much clearer, but in this war the lines were really getting blurred.

I was once again about half drunk as I read the letter and book, but I was thinking clearly enough to realize that my plans for personal glory were going nowhere fast. I was struggling with failure of the worst kind—the death of a dream. I felt like saying, "Lord, what can You do with someone like me? I've messed up so many times." But that night, as I've explained in earlier chapters, I was reacquainted with the Wonderful Counselor—the Lord of the second chance.

COMING OUT OF HIDING

We've looked at the importance of *vision*; that night I had to acknowledge the death of my own personal vision. We've studied the priority of meaningful, God-given *values*; that night I had to face the bankruptcy of my values. I was a good guy by every standard I could come up with, yet I was dying on the inside. I was tough and getting tougher, but it was a toughness of the flesh. That night,

God began to build a Kingdom toughness in my soul that would eventually bring me out of my alcoholism and addictions. But all of that was only possible because I came to understand and experience Kingdom tenderness.

The last two terms Peter used in his description of things that will enable us to avoid falling are very familiar: *phileo* and *agape*. Translators have transliterated these terms into English because they've become so familiar. Phileo is the word from which we get the name Philadelphia, which means city of brotherly love. Agape has become the name of Christian musical groups, publishers and a number of other Christian enterprises.

The problem with the familiarity is that the terms become essentially meaningless, which is a tragedy because, without these truths as part of our lives, we'll never understand Kingdom tenderness. What was Peter referring to when he used these terms? We need to return to the time in his struggles when they first deeply affected his life, but this time from Christ's perspective:

> Early in the morning, Jesus stood on the shore, but the disciples did not realize that it was Jesus. He called out to them, "Friends, haven't you any fish?" "No," they answered. He said, "Throw your net on the right side of the boat and you will find some" (John 21:4-6).

This is a striking scene for several reasons. First, we have a bunch of fishermen admitting the truth—that they haven't caught a thing. That in itself is amazing! Next, Peter didn't immediately figure out that it was the resurrected Christ standing there. Peter was in nearly the exact same situation as he was in Luke 5, and the same miracle took place. Yet he didn't get it until John pointed out to him who was on the shore. He was too busy hauling in the fish, too busy with business. Ever done that? I sure have.

But once Peter realized who it was that had directed them in their great catch of fish, he responded in characteristic fashion.

He jumped overboard and started swimming ashore. Once on shore he discovered that the Creator of the universe, the risen Christ, had fixed him breakfast.

John included an interesting little detail in the story that can easily be missed, but it isn't there by accident. John noted that there was "a fire of burning coals" (*anthrakia*) on shore. The only other place that word appears in Scripture is in John 18:18—the time in the courtyard when Peter denied ever knowing Christ. Peter was warming himself over a fire of burning coals when they asked him if he knew Jesus. In essence, Peter's response was, "I don't know the guy. He means nothing to me." What was going on here? If Peter was going to receive the Lord of the second chance, he would have to face the truth about who he was and what he'd done. The noose of denial would have to be removed from his soul. To receive the Lord of the second chance, we must begin by facing the truth about ourselves. We must stop hiding, and that's tough; we can hide in so many ways.

I recently read a true story about a man who shoved his way to the head of the ticket line after his flight had been canceled. "I have to get on the next flight, and it has to be first class," he bellowed to the agent.

"I'll be happy to help you, sir," she replied, "as soon as I serve these folks in front of you."

The passenger was irate. "Do you have any idea who I am?" he shouted.

Without replying, the agent picked up the airport intercom and announced to the whole terminal, "May I have your attention, please. We have a passenger who doesn't know who he is. If anyone can help him reclaim his identity, please see the agent at gate six."[3]

Most of us probably wouldn't do something as selfish as that man did in a public setting, but we've thought about it. We've demanded our way in a more indirect manner, all the while hiding from God's work in our lives in the midst of a frustrating situation. But the amazing part of the whole thing is that God, unlike the ticket agent, lets us get away with it.

It began in the first pages of Scripture, after Adam and Eve decided to do their own thing (see Gen. 3). They decided not to do God's will, but to push to the front of the line and have their own way. Then they hid in the bushes of their own shame. They didn't hear God speaking through the public address system about how rude they were; instead, they heard their Father's tender voice calling out, "Where are you?" That question has always struck me as rather humorous, as if there were a bush they could hide behind where God couldn't see them. God allowed them to hide. Yet at the same time, He challenged them to realize where they really were.

God allows us to hide—at least for now. A final day of judgment is coming when we'll all stand before Him, totally unable to hide anything, but He doesn't force us to stand openly before Him now. As a result, some of us have been hiding areas of our lives for a long time, and that's what causes bondage. Hell always grows strong in secrecy. Some of us carry burdens of guilt; others hide behind a thorny bush of anger, or our business or careers or even all kinds of ministry activities.

■ ■ ■ ■ ■ ■ ■ ■ ■

Some of us have been hiding areas of our lives for a long time, and that's what causes bondage. Hell always grows strong in secrecy.

■ ■ ■ ■ ■ ■ ■ ■ ■

Through the years, East Hill Church has helped many pastors and spiritual leaders come to health after they've morally fallen. The hardest part of the whole process is getting them to come out from behind the "bush" of being a pastor. Their whole identity has become entangled in ministry. They don't even realize they're hiding from God in the pastorate. But at some point they have to trust God and acknowledge the truth about themselves. Otherwise, they'll never experience the joy of being touched by the Lord of the second chance.

DO YOU LOVE ME?

As Peter stood before the fire where his risen Lord had cooked him breakfast, he was remembering the greatest failure of his life. He was an expert at failure. At some point all of us have such a failure, and it feels irredeemable and unforgivable. Peter remembered standing before the fire and not once, but three times, openly, blatantly, denying the One who loved him more than anyone else.

Ever done that? I have. I remember vividly the sequence of relapse I went through in the journey out of pornography's grip. "Relapse" is a nice sounding term, but it's the same thing Peter did by another name. The only difference is that we end up standing before the flames of our own woundedness and lust as we deny the One who totally loves us. We end up betraying our best Friend as we go back to the very thing that would destroy us. I did it many times.

But now breakfast was over, and Jesus and Peter stood before the fire. Peter was silent. He knew what was coming. He stood like a condemned man before the judge. There was no need for a trial; the evidence was indisputable—it screamed for his conviction! Then Jesus did something amazing, so amazing that few folks grasp the magnitude of the question, instead reading an accusation into Jesus' words: "Simon son of John, do you truly love me?" (John 21:16).

Jesus didn't ask Peter if he was going to do it again, nor did He seek to find out if Peter was sorry for what he had done. He didn't interrogate Peter to find out if he was going to try harder next time. He asked him if he truly loved Him.

Haven't we all, at some point in time, asked someone if he or she really loves us? If we're married, we have.

Thirty years ago, I put a letter in a mailbox in Joliet, Illinois. It was a cold wintry day, but the letter was filled with warmth. It was a marriage proposal to a beautiful young lady in California. The question in the letter was, "Do you love me?" We had met and dated for only a couple of months in college, but I knew she was the one for me. So I mailed the letter and waited for her reply. I waited and waited. Then I waited some more. Finally, after two days, I couldn't stand the suspense anymore, so I called her. I had to know her response.

"So, what do you think?" I asked. "Do you love me?" There was a long pause on the other end. I couldn't believe it; I thought she would be shouting and screaming for joy, saying things like, "Hey, you big hunk, I can't wait to get out there and marry you!" Eventually she did get around to declaring her love for me, but it took her a couple of months to get to Illinois.

I felt so vulnerable during that phone call. We all do in a situation like that. Jesus made Himself vulnerable in the conversation with Peter. Get hold of that: Peter was ready to duck, knowing he deserved to be backhanded. But he heard Christ ask if he loved Him. When we ask a question like that, we *all* put our heart right out there on the line—even God!

Jesus wasn't vulnerable only when He came to Earth and lay in a manger, or when He was faced with the failures and humanness of the disciples, knowing one of them eventually would betray Him. Nor was the cross, where He made himself vulnerable to everyone's sin and suffering, the only place of His vulnerability. Jesus' entire life on Earth was one of unguarded servanthood to lost mankind. "Do you love Me?" is a constant expression of Christ's heart.

And that simple question changes everything. It changed my relationship with Diane, the girl in California who eventually became my wife. And it's been changing my relationship with my Savior.

I've been reading a number of the writings from early Church history. As I did so, I realized once again that one of the things they did regularly was confess their sins. Christian psychologist and author Larry Crabb recently observed that modern psychotherapy arose partly in response to the void in the Christian community left by the Protestant insistence on private confession. Crabb said that religion has come to be seen as a personal matter between individuals and God. One difficulty with that philosophy is that we end up being less than honest with ourselves as well as God.[4]

One morning, during a time of prayer, I paused and thought through the previous day and couldn't come up with anything to confess. I therefore assumed I must be doing fine. Then Jesus spoke to me in that same voice I'd heard as a kid on a hillside when I was pouring out my pain and personal hurt. He simply asked, "Do you love Me?"

The question crushed me. I'd just prayed about a situation (I have to admit I'm embarrassed to put it in print) in which I thought our church was being ignored by our denomination. Churches from other denominations would ask me for help in ministering in the area of sexual bondage. We'd even received praise and requests for help from many sectors of the community outside the Church. We were reaching thousands of unchurched folks and seeing them come to Christ; yet I felt our denomination acted as if we didn't exist.

Did you notice the critical pronouns in the last three sentences? "...would ask *me* for help" and "...*I* felt...." Those two words are dead giveaways. Ted was worried about Ted's kingdom, not God's. I was preoccupied with my own adequacy and recognition. When we serve God and try to get others to affirm us at the same time, we end up playing games, hiding from God and not even realizing it.

As I said, when Jesus asked me if I loved Him, I was crushed. That's when I realized the important question isn't "Am I OK?" If I was looking for Jesus to tell me I'm adequate in and of myself, of course I'm not—and neither was Peter. I needed to change the question from "Am I OK?" to "What can I give?" That, of course, was the question Peter was challenged with.

The truth about me is that sometimes I get so full of myself, I can't see Jesus. I get so self focused that I don't know if I really love Him. I end up just as Peter did, looking at the ground, probably moving some dirt around with his soggy sandals and saying, "Lord, You know." *Lord, when I get my head on straight and my heart isn't so pol-*

luted, I really do love You. And I want to love You—at times more than any-thing else in my life. But, Lord, I really don't know the truth about my heart most of the time. Yet You do, and that's why Your name is Wonderful Counselor, the Mighty God.

"Simon [Peter] son of John, do you truly love me more than these?" That was actually the full question Jesus asked. It wasn't a performance question. Remember, Jesus is the one who built the fire and made the breakfast. The words match the glowing embers of the fire. Prior to the denial, Peter had boldly declared that he loved Christ more than the other disciples and would never forsake Him. Jesus was taking him back to the worst failure of his life, not to condemn him, but to give him hope and to forge a new depth of relationship between them.

I can picture Peter's head hanging even lower. I've been there. I'd been in the ministry for more than 20 years, and to realize how self-centered my prayers had become was withering. I'd forgotten a very important truth: The urges of the flesh don't disappear just because we've addressed the bondage and dysfunctions of our past. I was no longer an alcoholic or bound up by pornography, but I still had to deal with my flesh.

Most of us know what happened next between Jesus and His downcast disciple. "Peter, go feed my sheep," Jesus said. I'm convinced there was an incredible smile across Jesus' face as He said it. Initially, Peter probably stood there dumbfounded. In fact, it seems he immediately began comparing himself with John: "What about him?" Obviously, Peter still had a long way to go, and so do we. But Peter was on his way. Jesus basically told him to get off the bench and get back into the game.

TAKE A MULLIGAN

After I was able to recover somewhat during my time of prayer, I heard Jesus say the same thing to me that He had said to Peter: "Follow me" (John 21:19). They weren't the words of a drill instruc-tor, but of the Prince of Peace.

The picture I saw as I heard those words was of an experience I had several years ago trying to play golf. (You'll have to pardon me. I know I'm supposed to like golf; after all, I'm a pastor. But the game drives me nuts! Chasing that little white ball around is an excellent way to lose your mind. Please, please don't make me chase that little white ball around—I hate doing anything that badly.) To make a long story short, I found myself out on the golf course. The friend I was with could really play the game, which only made me more nervous. I teed off, whacking the ball as hard as I could, which is probably part of the problem. It took off sideways, ricocheting through the trees like I was playing a pinball machine. I turned and looked at my friend standing well behind me—he knew how I played the game—with this serene smile on his face. "Take a Mulligan," he said.

"Take a what?" I asked.

"A Mulligan," he repeated. "You just tee another one up and start all over again." You know what I discovered? Golfers do it all the time! These guys make fishermen with their "fish stories" look like saints. I probably ended up using more Mulligans than strokes that day. It was a blast—for the trees, that is.

My initial response to his Mulligan suggestion was one of disbelief, but it didn't take me long to accept the gift. I knew what kind of golfer I was. At that point, I was so relaxed, I almost hit the ball straight.

Wouldn't life be a lot different if we took Mulligans? When our spouse does something that upsets or hurts us, wouldn't it be great just to say, "Hey, let's take a Mulligan on this one"? When someone cuts in front of us in rush hour traffic on the freeway, instead of reacting with rage, we could smile and say, "I think I'll give him a Mulligan on that one." When things get really heated with the kids and we say something stupid like, "I'm going to ground you for life," how about laughing a little and saying, "Sorry. Can I have a Mulligan on that one?"

Peter never got what he deserved or expected. Instead, he stood by his failure, admitting what he had done, and Jesus called for him to get off the bench and get back into the game. "Pete, let's take a Mulligan on that one, OK?" He's the Prince of Peace, because He's Lord of the Mulligans.

A Great Investment

A pilot never forgets his primary flight instructor. Mine was Captain Gunness. He was an old helicopter pilot who'd seen lots of action. I was so impressed with him I could hardly speak in his presence. Things started off well; Captain Gunness was a great instructor, and I learned quickly. Then things hit a snag about halfway through.

I'd had a terrible day. I was so far behind the plane, it was landing when I was taking off. I was all over the sky, and I just knew Captain Gunness was going to give me a failing grade. As we walked back to the ready room for debriefing, my head hung low as I waited for the ax to fall. About halfway across the flight line, as I walked beside my instructor, he called out to another instructor, "Hey, my student can fly circles around yours!"

I was stunned. He was talking to the instructor who had *the* top-rated student. I looked up at him, and he smiled and said, "I've invested too much in you for you to fold on me now. And you have what it takes." His words totally turned me around, and proved prophetic. Thanks to Captain Gunness, I ended up graduating at the top of the class.

I know it's less than a perfect analogy, but in a sense that's exactly what happened to Peter—not just once, but repeatedly. In Luke 5, Jesus told Peter to launch out into the deep, despite the fact that he hadn't caught a thing all night. They brought in such a catch that Peter found himself up to his belly button in fish. In fact, the boat started sinking because of the catch. Then Peter turned and said, "Go away from me, Lord; I am a sinful man!" (see v. 8). Jesus' response was along the lines of, "I can't let you quit, Pete. I've invested a miracle in you. You're going to end up fishing for men."

Then, on the mount of Transfiguration, Peter saw Christ in His divinity, talking with Moses and Elijah (see Matt. 17:3). So Peter came up with the bright idea of camping out on the mountain and building a shrine to all three. Maybe he was thinking of running a religious souvenir shop on the side. Whatever was on his mind, it would've been much better for him to have kept his mouth shut, but that wasn't his style.

Then the Father spoke from heaven and told Peter to be quiet and listen to His Son. I can just picture Peter saying to himself as they headed back down the mountain, "Why did I have to open my big mouth?" I can even hear him saying to Jesus, "You know, Master, I'm really bad at this disciple business. I must really have embarrassed You back there. Maybe I should throw in the towel." To which Jesus probably said, "Peter, the Father just gave you a revelation of what's to come. Heaven has invested in you. You can't quit."

Of course, the ultimate scene is the one with Peter standing on the shoreline, looking into the coals of the fire, remembering what he'd done. He'd already decided to quit, which is why he went fishing, and he was even failing at that. He was waiting for judgment to fall. Thoughts of how incredibly weak he was, and how he had betrayed his Lord, ran through his mind. He had given up on himself, which is why Christ stood before him with nail-scarred hands outstretched, saying, "There's no way you can quit. I just invested a resurrection in you. Nothing can keep you down now. Soon you'll be able to fly circles around hell!"

At its core, the gospel is about taking Mulligans, and God has been giving them from the very beginning. God went to Abram, who had laughed at God's promise and lied about his wife, and in Genesis 15 said, "Take a Mulligan, Abe; I haven't changed My mind about you."

God anointed a shepherd boy who wrote him love songs out in Israel's fields, and made him a king. Yet David committed adultery and murder. God came to him and declared there was going to be some painful fallout from his failures—"But how about a Mulligan,

Dave? I haven't changed My mind about you."

God called out to an overzealous Pharisee named Saul who openly mocked God's Son and hunted down His people. On the road to Damascus the Lord said to Saul, "How about a Mulligan, Saul? I'll even give you a new name."

God comes to people who are so tangled up with bondage that they're filled with anger and have lost hope. He comes to those who thought they were strong enough and smart enough to make it on their own, but now are busted and hurting. He comes to people caught up in our fast-paced world, so caught up in making a living that they're dying.

And to all of us, He says with a vulnerability that penetrates the toughest defenses we may have constructed: "How about a Mulligan? I'm not about to give up on you. If you have any doubts about that, just look at the Cross."

When the depth of His love hits our hearts, it will produce a very powerful thing in our souls: Kingdom tenderness. Because God has been so tender with us, we can be tender with ourselves and others. Then, as Peter declared in 2 Peter 1:5-7, we'll have the outflow of God's warm friendliness and generous love, which are the final pieces of a life that will never fall. We can't fall because Christ's love for us just won't let us quit. His tender hands keep picking us up and getting us back into the game.

Notes

1. Scott Richardson, *Myths The World Taught Me* (Nashville, TN: Thomas Nelson Publishers, 1991), p. 167.
2. *New International Dictionary of Old Testament Theology and Exegesis*, vol. 2 (Grand Rapids, MI: Zondervan, 1997), p. 491.
3. Ed Kittrell, *Funny Business* (Washington, D. C.: Georgetown Publishing House, October 1997), p. 6.
4. Larry Crabb, *Connecting* (Nashville, TN: Word Publishing, 1997), p. 98.

CHAPTER **15**

The Ultimate Challenge

Numerous authors have written books concerning the clinical aspects of sexual addictions, and even more books call for believers to seek holiness. But our ultimate focus is more specific than either of these categories. I wrote this book for one purpose: to persuade the Church to become a place of hope and healing rather than of shame for those fighting sexual battles.

Through the years, I've traveled and spoken throughout America, and I've made a discovery: Churches deeply reflect the character of their pastor, and that's especially true of a healthy church. Yes, I believe in the priesthood of all believers. Yes, the congregation should look to Jesus and not just to the pastor. But the pastor profoundly affects the spiritual nature and climate of the local congregation. I like to put it this way: When it comes to the flow of life and ministry in a church, the pastor is either the cork or the funnel! If the pastor doesn't lead the way on this issue, nothing lasting will take place.

If you're a layperson or a counselor on a church staff and really believe in what I've written so far, get a copy of this book into your pastor's hands. Don't try to start a ministry of this type without the pastor's direct support and approval. It's better to get on your face and pray for your pastor to see the desperate need than to do something on your own. Please take my word for it—it won't work without the pastor's support and leadership. Sexual bondage is deep in our society's nature, and hell will fight against such a ministry every inch of the way. Your church will need a united front to fight in this battle.

I said the pastor is, spiritually, either the cork or the funnel in a church. That means it all depends on which direction he's headed in his ministry. So, pastors, what are we ultimately trying to do as we lead the flock?

- Are we trying to build a large church?
- Are we trying to develop a thriving ministry?
- Are we trying to help folks get free from the hurts and hang-ups of their past?
- Are we trying to turn around the moral climate of our sin-sick nation?
- Are we trying to reach the lost?
- Are we trying to preach the Word?
- Are we trying to teach sound doctrine?

I've come to realize that pastors tend to answer those questions in light of their gifting and distinctive calling. In part, that's a healthy response. But if we're not careful, we can forget the ultimate task we're all called to, and we can confuse secondary battles with the primary one, which is to know and love God through Jesus Christ, and help our flock do the same.

The community of God has no higher calling than to seize the opportunity to experience God. Our fiercest battles are fought when we seek with all our heart to *trust* God so fully that we see every misfortune as something he permits and wants, to *know* him so richly that we turn to no one and nothing else to experience what our souls long to enjoy, to love him so completely and with such consuming passion that we hate anything that comes between us and eagerly give it up.[1]

That's what the Old Testament prophets called Israel back to again and again. And that's why they so frequently spoke against Israel's "whoring" after the sexual religions of the day (see Jer. 2; Ezek. 16; Hos. 3). We face the same challenge, except the sexual idols now are found on videotapes, Internet transmissions and movie screens, rather than carved from stone. The moment Israel stepped into the promised land, hell's most successful strategy was sexual bondage (see Num. 22–25). And because one of Satan's mottoes is "If it ain't broke, don't fix it," he's been using the same approach on today's Church with devastating effectiveness.

We pastors face a uniquely difficult situation. When people respond to Christ during a weekend service, we can't automatically begin to discipline them in the faith. Nowadays, people come to Christ with a lot of scrambled software from their past. They come with issues our predecessors never even heard of, like addiction, codependency, abuse, abandonment—and with almost no biblical background. Or, if they have a religious background, it's frequently deeply distorted with a performance mentality. We have a lot of other stuff to deal with before they can even begin to get a handle on dealing with their flesh. Perhaps pastors deep in the Bible Belt may not be dealing with these things yet, but that's the way our world is heading, so it's just a matter of time. Those are issues I have to deal with daily.

UNCUT STONES

He had anger and defiance written all over his face when he walked into my office. He was furious because his wife had left him. It took a while before he admitted that he had a bad temper and occasionally beat his wife. He was a boxer, and sometimes he carried home the anger of the ring. He'd grown up in the Church, but his family had been so abusive that—although he didn't recognize it—his concept of Father God was a fist in the face.

We counseled for quite a while before it became obvious that we weren't getting anywhere. I asked the Lord what I should do next. I sensed the Lord telling me to hug this angry man, to hold him in my arms and speak God's grace into his life. Looking at this tough-as-nails man sitting across the desk from me, I thought, *I don't think so, God.*

I initially chickened out; then, as we were wrapping up our session and he stood up to leave, I asked if I could give him a hug. The expression on his face was one of mild shock. Then he just stood there, so I moved toward him cautiously, put my arms around him and hugged him. It was like trying to embrace a telephone pole. Then something broke in the man as I began to speak of the Father's love. He disintegrated in my arms. While he was growing up, he'd been so emotionally beaten by his father that he'd never had a male authority figure embrace him and speak of God's love to him. I realized at that moment that I was dealing with one of God's precious uncut stones.

Moses gave the Israelites an intriguing command prior to their entering the Promised Land:

> Moreover, you shall build there an altar to the Lord your God, an altar of stones; you shall not wield an iron tool on them. You shall build the altar of the Lord your God of uncut stones; and you shall offer on it burnt offerings to the Lord your God (Deut. 27:5-6, *NASB*).

That might seem like an obscure passage, but it isn't. Actually, the concept of uncut stones appears frequently throughout Scripture. After the people of Israel finally crossed the Jordan River, one of the first things they did was build an altar of uncut stones, which was to be a memorial to the people of Israel forever, especially to the next generation (see Josh. 4). In his confrontation with the false prophets of Baal on Mount Carmel, Elijah constructed an altar of uncut stones and declared to the people, "Your name shall be Israel" (1 Kings 18:31). Peter proclaims in 1 Peter 2:4 that we're living stones, rejected by men (not polished), but chosen by God and precious to Him. At the core of Israel's encounter with God lies the concept of uncut stones.

I was able to respond to this physically strong but emotionally weak boxer I was hugging because I understood how he felt. I had faced my own "uncutness."

FACING OUR "UNCUTNESS"

A pastor needs to make four foundational decisions if his church is going to become a place of hope and healing. The first is to face our own uncutness. I've always been amazed at how easy it can become for pastors to play games. At times it seems as if the whole system drives us that way. Obviously, a spiritual leader must not be a person ruled by huge character flaws, which can lead to the trap of not dealing honestly and openly with them.

In part, the problem is caused by people's expectations, but in ministry we have to get free from people's expectations and courageously pursue God's purposes in our lives. One of the primary goals the Lord has for us is integrity and wholeness. We can't minister what we're not experiencing. And I have met few pastors who haven't had a significant struggle with their sexual desires and urges at some point in their lives.

The generation of Church leaders who will be appearing in this twenty-first century, almost without exception, were raised in homes that were hurting in some form or fashion. That's an explosive situation! But it's explosive in a good sense as well as bad. If the uncutness isn't dealt with, then somewhere down the road the bottom will fall out. There may be great preaching, rapid church growth, even signs and wonders, but eventually the foundation will collapse. The final result will be a world that sees scandals and hypocrisy when it looks at the Church, and will therefore remain totally ignorant of God's power to change lives. There is absolutely no way we are going to see our nation touched by God's grace or see real revival if the spiritual leaders don't lead the way.

The courts are forcing the Church to deal with the ministry's moral failures. And what could be more tragic than to have the world act as God's judge of the Church? We need leaders and churches that will become prophetic voices of hope and healing, because they've been healed themselves and are honest and open about it. Instead, we're becoming experts at writing legal policies to protect our organizations in case of lawsuits. We desperately need to face our own brokenness and uncutness. When we do, the results will be explosive. Scripture repeatedly declares that God will make us strong at our weakest points—if we'll yield to Him.

■ ■ ■ ■ ■ ■ ■ ■ ■ ■

We must face our own issues, no matter how painful the process; otherwise, there won't be any real godly power. We need ruthless honesty that exceeds our comfort zones and pursues God's heart, no matter the cost.

■ ■ ■ ■ ■ ■ ■ ■ ■ ■

We must face our own issues, no matter how painful the process; otherwise, there won't be any real godly power. We must find small groups where we can be held accountable and deal with our struggles without religious hype. We need a ruthless honesty that exceeds our comfort zones and pursues God's heart, no matter the cost. We'll find stuff within ourselves that we hadn't even noticed while we were busy ministering. But, in the terror of the journey, we'll discover a compassion and anointing that will enable us to build a place of hope and healing.

Generation X will be rising to leadership in the Church soon. But because of the self-centeredness of the previous generation, the "Xers" tend to come from dangerously shattered family backgrounds. Therefore, if the Xers are helped to face their uncutness—the hurts and wounds of their past—they'll be able to minister in God's power like no previous generation. God has never chosen problem-free folks to do His greatest works. The Bible reveals that He always chose those who were weak; then, through their very woundedness, He did His greatest works. We spiritual leaders *must* deal with our own uncutness.

Part of that is learning how to communicate effectively to people at a relevant level. As I wrote before, I hadn't grown up in the Church and didn't have a clue what a revival meeting even looked like, so you can imagine my reluctance when I was asked to be the keynote speaker at a revival meeting in New Mexico. I was totally lost as we started through the worship time. They asked me to sit up on the platform, where there was no hymnal—so I pretended to sing. As I looked out over the congregation I noticed two old guys jammed into the front row, singing at the top of their lungs—but each of them was singing a different hymn, and both horribly off-key. I thought, *Lord, this is terrible, what am I doing here?*

Then God spoke to my heart, "Ted, their songs touch My heart because they're communicating about My kingdom. I look on the heart, not on outward appearances." The Lord's comments dealt with my poor attitude—and then we experienced an incredible revival. God had done a bit more chiseling on my heart.

Why would the Lord make such a big deal about the makeup of the altars Israel was to construct as they entered the Promised Land? For 450 years the only buildings or monuments of real significance they'd seen were made of cut stone. There are still some standing in Egypt today. In fact, everything of spiritual importance was made with a hammer and chisel. That's why, in various places throughout the Old Testament, the Lord was very clear with Israel: "See those old stones lying on the desert floor? That's what I want you to use for My altar."

I can imagine the Israelites reacting just like me: "But, Lord, those stones aren't polished or finely cut. They're like two old guys sitting in the front row singing the wrong hymns out of key!" But God doesn't need men's polished efforts—He looks on the heart.

When it comes to Kingdom communication, I think a great place to start is with the promised ministry of the Holy Spirit. On the day of Pentecost two important things happened: First, tongues of fire appeared over the disciples' heads and they were given a supernatural ability to communicate—an outward *manifestation* of an *inward* change (see Acts 2:1-4). Second, the disciples, whose hearts had been cleansed and changed, began to move *outward* in a powerful witness to the world, as predicted by Jesus in Acts 1:8.

Communication can be a daunting process for a pastor. People speak an average of 120 words per minute, yet most listeners think at about 2,000 words per minute. That's why, after 24 hours, most people retain only 8 to 10 percent of what they heard. However, people do tend to remember anecdotes, illustrations and stories, which explains why Christ spoke in parables so often. To a speaker, those facts can be very frustrating until we realize that we communicate not so much with what we say, but rather by who we are.

I can't remember the details of a single sermon my spiritual father (Jack Carter) preached, but I'll never forget his spirit. I'll never forget sitting at his feet as he spoke in a home Bible study. He loved the Old Testament and the prophets, and as he shared their stories from the pages of Scripture, they came alive to me. I heard the thunderous voices of men who risked all to follow God: the passionate cry of Elijah and Ezekiel for holiness and for God's judgment fire to fall; the staggering intellect of Isaiah; and the searing tears of Jeremiah. My spiritual father *communicated* God's kingdom to me.

And that's what we as pastors and communicators need to do even as we come face-to-face with our own uncutness and submit it to God for His Master touch and refinement.

SPEAKING TO GOD-GIVEN DREAMS

Roy Disney told this true story of his brother Walt in grade school. The teacher had given the class an assignment of drawing something from nature. As the teacher moved down the aisles, checking on the students' progress, she paused at Walt's desk and commented, "Walt, those are nice flowers, but flowers don't have faces on them." Walt looked up and said, "Mine do." Flowers with faces, trees that could run and dance, an elephant with ears so big he could fly, a cricket that was a little boy's conscience and even a mouse that could talk—these were Walt Disney's dreams.

■ ■ ■ ■ ■ ■ ■ ■ ■ ■

*The Holy Spirit didn't come to the Early Church
just so that signs, wonders and miracles could take place.
He also came to enable each of us to express the
divine gifts placed within us from conception.*

■ ■ ■ ■ ■ ■ ■ ■ ■ ■

The second decision a pastor needs to make if his church is to be a place of hope and healing is to speak to people's God-given dreams. Scripture repeatedly points out that God has placed a message, a dream, a gift in every human heart. The Holy Spirit didn't come to the Early Church just so that signs, wonders and miracles could take place. He also came to enable each of us to express the divine gifts placed within us from conception. In fact, God declared to Jeremiah, "Before I formed you in the womb I knew you, before you were born I set you apart" (Jer. 1:4-5). Each of those folks sitting in the pews has a unique message to communicate.

But what does this have to do with the issue of sexual bondage? Remember the chapter that looked at the issue of self-control?

Real, bone deep, biblical self-control isn't possible without a God-given vision—without a sense of our God-given giftedness being released in us. Helping folks realize their God-given giftedness is one of a pastor's primary callings.

Some might say the example of Walt Disney is touching but doesn't apply, since it was a secular gifting. There is no such thing as a secular gifting. God is the giver of all great gifts (see Jas. 1:17). The only question is where we'll use those gifts—for God's glory or our own.

I remember speaking at a men's seminar and, right in the middle of a teaching, I sensed that I was to pray over a man sitting in the front row. As I started to lay hands on the man, I sensed he built race cars for a living. I asked him if that was true. His eyes opened wide and he nodded his head, indicating I was correct. I then asked him to raise his hands to God as I prayed for him. I simply prayed that the cars he built would be some of the best on the track—for God's glory. Tears began to stream down his face as I prayed. He looked up at me and said, "You mean, I can do that—build cars for God?"

I replied, "You sure can. With your wrench and welding torch, you can preach to guys I could never reach."

The reason I share this incident is that on that day, the day he first realized his God-given giftedness, the man was able to leave behind a smoking habit he'd battled for years.

As pastors, every now and then we need to remember that some of the greatest communicators in the Bible got off to a poor start. Peter frequently had one sandal or the other in his mouth. Paul literally bored one guy to death with his preaching (see Acts 20). And whom did Jesus choose for the first church staff? He put ex-hooker Mary Magdalene in charge of women's ministry. Impetuous sons of thunder, James and John, were given charge over youth ministry.

Am I campaigning for sloppy pastors? Not at all! We need to work with all our hearts, but do it in light of our God-given gifts, scrupulously avoiding the subtle and deadly trap of comparison.

We can't let ourselves get trapped into trying to pattern our ministry after a church we admire, or go to a seminar and copy what we've heard. We can appreciate the efforts of other ministries and learn from them; then we need to get on our faces and find out who we are and the gift God has given us. When we've done that, we can speak to the giftedness in the hearts of our people. They desperately need us to do that so they can come to freedom and health in their lives. We can help them throw the hammer and chisel of comparison out the window. So much of the emotional pain that's medicated through sexual bondage has to do with deadly comparisons from the past.

The Coast Guard recently helped a sailor whose boat was hung up on a sandbar. When they asked him what happened, he gave them a lengthy description of his boating experience, and then explained that his navigational chart failed to show the sandbar. Skeptical, the Coast Guard personnel asked to see his chart. It was a place mat from a seafood restaurant! Our flock doesn't need a seafood chart. They need to hear from God about the course He set for them before the beginning.

PROCLAIMING GOD'S GRACE

God's grace is the ultimate answer to the shame and guilt that drives people into sexual bondage. In order to have a church that is a place of hope and healing, a pastor must make the foundational decision to speak grace into people's lives. I remember when I first came to church and found myself thinking, *I know I'm messed up or I wouldn't be here. How about telling me how to turn things around in my life?* The presentations frustrated me. Negative sermons produce negative people. And exhortation without application only leads to one thing: exasperation!

It's sad but true: Churches are primarily known for what they're against in the community, rather than what they are for. The tragedy is that we can't lift people out of sin by putting them down.

Folks don't turn around if we nag at them. It doesn't work on you or me, and it definitely doesn't work on them. We're not called to make people feel ashamed; they're already dying from shame. More importantly, behind all the show, bravado and materialism, people really are looking for the gospel. If they can hear it in terms they understand, and aren't beaten down, they'll respond. And grace will produce a purity that legalism never could. Love will call forth a self-discipline that religion finds puzzling.

Does that mean we're going to ignore the consequences of sin? Are we going to avoid the fact that there's a heaven and hell? Not at all. I've never preached so much about sin as I have in the last couple of years. I've never mentioned hell so often. But the reason I can do that is because I talk about sin and hell *with tears in my eyes*. I never speak about the ultimate consequence of turning from God, of ignoring sin in our lives, without a catch in my throat or a tear in my eye. And it isn't about theatrics; it comes from a deep realization that except for God's amazing, incredible grace, we would forever be trapped in our sin. Worse yet, we could be playing religious games and hiding from our uncutness within. We could be pretending we never struggle deeply with sexual issues in our lives.

This is not an "us and them" issue. This is an issue about people who have been redeemed by a gracious God. The people caught in the gay lifestyle, the abortionist, the pornographer and the couple caught in adultery aren't the enemy. The enemy is the enemy! And our call is to help as many people as we can to get his noose off their souls. Which brings us to the next point.

BEING PREPARED TO PAY THE PRICE

On the surface this all makes sense. Of course we want to be a church of hope and healing. But are we willing to pay the price? Because that's the final foundational decision pastors need to make. We're talking about real healing and hope. And remember, folks who are caught in sexual bondage usually have wounded a lot of people around them, and probably will continue to do so for some time. They've become masters at deception and lying. In fact, in certain areas of their lives, they no longer even have a concept of the truth. Once these folks start working toward honesty and accountability, the challenge to walk them through it will drive us nuts.

If we're going to deal with past hurts and dysfunction in people's lives, the churched folks probably won't be comfortable with the level of honesty and struggle that's required. Besides that, the unchurched folks will start bringing their friends. They know little if anything about tithing or giving to a church, yet they'll put tremendous stress on our resources. If they have sexual bondage, they're usually in financial bondage as well. So, bottom line, costs will go through the roof, and income probably will not be able to keep up. More than likely, the church will end up undercapitalized and understaffed.

In addition, I usually find that pastors end up trying to pull off all of this during the most stressful time in their lives as a spouse and a parent. Ministering to this depth of hurt in people's lives puts a staggering strain on our lives, and we get little thanks for our efforts because, to be honest, a number of those we try to help won't make it. Even Jesus didn't have a perfect record with the disciples.

So why do it? I've asked myself that question several times. In fact, I was ready to throw in the towel at one point. Being known for taking on the issue of sexual addiction isn't a glamorous crown to wear. Some church leaders think we don't have enough faith. "Just pray for people and, if you have enough faith, they'll be delivered," they say. Others think we're into psychology: "Just preach the Word and people won't have those kinds of problems." I don't get upset by their comments; I understand that they've never really spent time with someone caught in the noose of sexual bondage. They've never really dealt with someone who loves God deeply, prays and reads the Word, understands the power of the Holy Spirit, yet is dying within.

So, again, why do it? Good question. I recently saw a news report that epitomizes America, a nation going down the drain spiritually. A little guy named Daniel had been admitted to the emergency room at the local hospital. He was beaten over every square inch of his body by his mother's live-in lover who decided to use the boy as a punching bag. ("Had a few too many beers," the man said.) The close-up of Daniel's little face left little room for doubt that Daniel's abuser was in bondage himself.

These were not people on welfare, lashing out in desperation. The mom and her lover had good jobs; apparently they were executives. But I know how Daniel feels. I've been there. *Who's going to reach his battered soul?*

- Who's going to help that mom get out of the insanity she's caught in?
- Who's going to help that man deal with his anger?
- Who's going to break this cycle of bondage, abuse and pain?

There's only one answer, and it isn't the federal or state government. The Church is the only answer.

- A Church that's a place of hope and healing.
- A group of people willing to pay the price of ministering to such a painful situation.
- A Church that believes in and has personally experienced God's power so that they can speak real hope to such hurting souls.
- A group of people who have faced the woundedness of their own souls and discovered God's amazing grace.
- A Church that doesn't see the people out there as the problem, but as prisoners of hell with a noose around their necks.

I turned off that news program and had a good time of repenting before the Lord for complaining about the cost. Then I said,

"Lord, sign me up again. And show us something we can do for Daniel."

He did.

Note

1. Larry Crabb, *Connecting* (Nashville, TN: Word Publishing, 1997), p. 150.

CHAPTER **16**

His Realities and Her Realities
A Perspective by Diane Roberts

Throughout many years of counseling, I have seen countless women fall apart in my office as they shared heart-wrenching stories of their husband's sexual betrayal. Many of those husbands had been brought up in the church, and yet they were caught in the noose of adultery, pornography, prostitution and perversion. Where could these women turn, and what were they supposed to do in light of feeling so betrayed? The experience of one woman, whom I will call Susan, typifies the struggling response of a wife whose husband finally became honest with his hidden sexual issues and all the questions that arose from that initial disclosure:

January 1995

What a year—a year I would not quickly forget. My world as I knew it was about to change; it would be shattered and blown to pieces.

I was coming face-to-face with a man I have lived with for almost 30 years. Now, you would think I would know this man, but the sexual addiction that was so hidden and closely guarded was in stark contrast to the man who shared his life with me. It was as if he were carrying on two lives.

I can remember so vividly the day my husband felt convicted to tell me his story. We were driving home from church, just coming from an FMO (For Men Only) and FWO (For Women Only) class. As Ted, the pastor and group facilitator, spoke to the men, my husband realized he had an addiction problem. As we drove into the driveway and stopped the car, the story began.

The knife of his addiction pierced my heart as I listened. I became stiff and rigid, trying not to show my hurt, anger and rage. I had a broken heart!

The weeks that followed were tough. I found myself in disbelief; my world was fuzzy, and I wanted answers. How could this have happened? I asked him a lot of questions—hard questions: How could you be like this? How could you do this to me? I wanted to understand; I was driven.

I took this situation personally; I felt humiliated and betrayed. The knife of his addiction pierced deeper and deeper into me, as I came face-to-face with decisions I had to make. I wanted to run as fast as I could. My anger boiled. I didn't know if I had the strength to cope with my husband's addiction. My personal beliefs were strong. I was appalled with men who used sex in any form to build themselves up, and I wasn't shy about verbalizing my feelings. On the other hand, I could see my husband risking everything, laying it all on the line—the incredible shame he felt and the trust he had in me—to tell his secret. Would I throw away 30 years of marriage? I was so scared!

A FAMILY PROBLEM

Susan and other women who have to face the pain of dealing with sexual addiction are impacted with realities they don't know how to cope with. As seen in figure 8, the husband has a totally different reality from the wife's. When he becomes honest for the first time in years, he feels like a load has been lifted. But the wife immediately feels like a heavy load has been dropped upon her.

HIS REALITY	HER REALITY
I'm becoming a man of integrity.	I've been betrayed.
I've never loved her more.	I've never felt less loved or worthy.
I'm beginning to see how much I value our marriage.	I've never realized until now how little the marriage meant to him.
Finally, I'm an honest man.	How could he live a lie like this?
I understand the healing process sometimes takes three to five years, but I'm pretty sure I can complete that path to freedom in a couple of years.	Five years seems like a lifetime to deal with this pain.

FIGURE 8[1]

How do we help Susan process these new realities? Women like Susan began to come to me as men from our church sought help for their sexual addictions in For Men Only groups. In this chapter, our goal is to offer some practical steps that have helped women whose husbands are struggling with sexual addiction. One of the first things we do is try to help the wife understand that in most cases this is not just his problem. It is usually a family problem. Often people with addictive behavior subconsciously are attracted to enablers. Therefore, all members of the family need to come to good health. The wife has to face the fact that God is the only One who can change her husband. But there are things she can do to create an environment for change: learning to let go, setting healthy boundaries, working on her self-esteem and learning to trust again.

In our FWO classes we spend the first few weeks helping women understand sexual addiction, as well as their husbands' realities. Addictive behaviors are usually brought into the marriage. Most addicts use sexual addiction to medicate hurt from their past and to stay one step ahead of the pain that is too difficult to face. Many of these men think that when they marry they will no longer struggle with these hidden secrets, because they will now have a legitimate way to meet their sexual needs. But unless they deal with the root of why those addictions began and choose to be accountable for their behavior, old addictive patterns will surface.

■ ■ ■ ■ ■ ■ ■ ■ ■ ■

It is important that wives understand the addictive cycle, because the first tendency a women has is to try to control her husband so he will stop his behavior. But the more she tries to control, the more he is thrown into the addictive cycle of acting in (holding down the addiction) and then acting out (reverting back to his old habits).

■ ■ ■ ■ ■ ■ ■ ■ ■ ■

Romans 7 talks about our sin nature and how we end up doing what we don't want to do. It is important that wives understand the addictive cycle, because the first tendency a women has is to try to control her husband so he will stop his behavior. But the more she tries to control, the more he is thrown into the addictive cycle of acting in (holding down the addiction) and then acting out (reverting back to his old habits).

I remember how happy Ted and I were when we got a new electric blanket. I read the instructions carefully, and we got hooked up. Then it came time to change the sheets. That night I felt cooler, and of course, turned my blanket up a notch. Nothing happened; in fact, I felt even colder. I kept turning up my blanket, but still nothing. You've already guessed what happened, haven't you? We somehow reversed the blanket when the sheets were changed, and my unit controlled Ted's side of the bed and vice versa. As I grew cooler, I kept turning up my heat; because Ted was so warm, he turned off what he assumed was his control. The results? I was a frozen ice cube, and he practically had burn marks up his legs! Just as controlling someone else's side of the bed doesn't work, trying to control someone else's life is also futile.

I discovered the futility of control early in our marriage. We were relatively new believers when God directed Ted out of the military and into seminary. Being around other military pilots who all thought they were the best (which they had to believe in order to survive Vietnam), I had never noticed Ted's pride. But once we moved into a seminary environment where everyone was "holy," that pride became only too evident. One evening when we had been with another couple, I was so embarrassed by some of Ted's statements that I was ready to confront him as soon as we got home. But before I could, the Holy Spirit urged me to remain quiet and pray.

As I did, I told God He needed to change Ted because of how embarrassed I felt. God assured me that He doesn't change people because of my embarrassment. It was then I reminded God that Ted was preparing for the pastorate, and I knew he needed to be a humble servant of the Lord. With my motives lining up with God's calling on Ted's life, my prayers were answered immediately!

Two days later Ted announced that the Holy Spirit had been dealing with him. My thought was, *Hallelujah, that was a quick answer to prayer!* Then Ted shared that God had told him to get rid of all his military gear. That is not what I wanted to hear. After all, where were we going to get money to replace that heavy flight jacket and boots now that we were in seminary? He needed them to travel to classes each day on his motorcycle in the cold Kentucky weather. How could this possibly be the answer to my prayers? But oddly enough, it was. God was actually dealing with the root of the problem that had begun when Ted was six years old and wanting to be a man's man. Ted, never having a real dad (six stepfathers), made a vow to become a pilot, and that is where the root of pride began. Second Corinthians 3:18 says that God changes us from glory to glory by the Holy Spirit—not by a nagging, controlling wife!

LET GO

There are four realities women are forced to deal with in For Women Only, and one of them is to learn to let go. So often when we see a need for our husbands to change, especially when they have a sexual addiction, we immediately want to control and try to change things ourselves; but God works from the inside out and will deal in depth with our mates if we let go and let God do His work. The following anonymous poem has been in various newspapers and recovery literature. It reinforces how healthy letting go can be:

To "Let Go" Takes Love

To "let go" does not mean to stop caring, it means that I can't do it for someone else.

To "let go" is not to cut myself off, it is to realize that I can't control another.

To "let go" is not to enable, but to allow learning from natural consequences.

To "let go" is to admit powerlessness, which means the outcome is not in my hands.

To "let go" is not to try to change or blame another, it is to make the most of myself.

To "let go" is not to care for, but to care about.

To "let go" is not to fix, but to be supportive.

To "let go" is not to judge, but to allow another to be a human being.

To "let go" is not to be in the middle arranging all the outcomes, but to allow others to effect their own destinies.

To "let go" is not to be protective, it is to permit another to face reality.

To "let go" is not to deny, but to accept.

To "let go" is not to nag, scold, or argue, but instead to search out my own shortcomings and to correct them.

To "let go" is not to adjust everything to my desires, but to take each day as it comes and to cherish myself in it.

To "let go" is not to criticize and regulate anybody, but to try to become what I dream I can be.

To "let go" is not to regret the past, but to grow and to live for the future.

To "let go" is to fear less and to love more.

When we finally let go, we can begin to see our own issues and start to work on the only person we can change—ourselves.

While in seminary, God was reminding me that instead of nagging and scolding, I should search out my own shortcomings and correct them. Matthew 7:7 says to ask, seek and knock, and it will be opened. But right before that promise, in verse 3, it says to take the beam from our own eye before we take out the speck in our brother's eye. Whenever I have prayed for change in Ted, God usually has had me deal first with my concerns over finances. God is continually working on me to trust Him. It is so much easier to focus on Ted's issues and try to "fix" him rather than to face my own shortcomings. But when I take the beam out of my own eye, it is much easier to see what God is doing with the speck in Ted's life. Not only has there been a change in me, but also in Ted. He truly has become a humble servant of the Lord.

God is committed to changing us both into His image, and that means our women in FWO have to look honestly at their own realities. What is the beam in the wife's eye that has to be removed? Many like Kathy struggled with a codependent beam.

After trying to control her marriage for many years, Kathy realized in FWO what that beam was in her own eye. She had come from a large family in which one parent was an alcoholic. Being the oldest, she mothered her younger brothers and sisters and wanted to fix her parents' pain. She thought when she left home she could start a new life, but five years into her marriage she realized her husband was sexually addicted. She immediately moved into the role she played while growing up and began to try to control his behavior and make the family "look good." But after her husband relapsed a number of times, she realized she couldn't hold things together, and she couldn't fix things by trying to control. She knew she needed help when she answered yes to all the following questions, which indicated she was trying to control out of her obsession with her husband's behavior:

Codependent behaviors:

1. Do you take responsibility for people, tasks and situations you are not responsible for?
2. Do you react to someone else's behavior instead of looking at your own motives?
3. Are you being consumed with another person and putting yourself on hold?
4. Are you obsessed with the addiction and all your spouse's feelings and behaviors, trying to fix him, keep things smooth, while neglecting your own pain, shortcomings, joy and growth?
5. Are you trying to control another person's behavior, to where your energy is drained and it draws attention away from you?[2]

Kathy realized these behaviors, as well as the following definition of codependency, described her life:

Codependency is a word used to describe life patterns commonly identified in people having relationships with alcoholics or other addicts. In essence, codependency describes a lifestyle where you focus your attention and life energy on controlling others, meeting the needs of others, and trying to change them while neglecting or avoiding aspects of your own life in the process.[3]

Let's look at a woman in the Old Testament who also could have answered yes to that definition and all five of the above statements. In 1 Samuel 25 we are told that Abigail was the intelligent and beautiful wife of a wealthy rancher named Nabal, who was harsh and evil. Nabal insulted David and refused to give food to him and his men. One of Nabal's servants warned Abigail that David and his men were ready to kill Nabal and his household:

Now think it over and see what you can do, because disaster is hanging over our master and his whole household. He is such a wicked man that no one can talk to him (v. 17).

From this quote we see the servant has apparently learned from experience that he could depend on Abigail to fix things. Sure enough, she quickly gathered food and sought out David in hopes of discouraging him from his plans. Scripture says that Abigail not only took full responsibility for Nabal's actions, but also assured David that if he had come to her first, this entire situation could have been avoided:

She fell at his feet and said: "My lord, let the blame be on me alone. Please let your servant speak to you; hear what your servant has to say. May my lord pay no attention to

that wicked man Nabal. He is just like his name—his name
is Fool, and folly goes with him. But as for me, your servant,
I did not see the men my master sent" (vv. 24-25).

Rather than allowing each person in the family to be responsible
for his or her own actions, Abigail took total responsibility for
everyone.[4]

During their marriage, it appears that Abigail never confronted
Nabal with his destructive behavior, and thus the family probably
went from crisis to crisis. Nabal was not approachable, especially
when he was drinking. Scripture says he died 10 days after finding
out about what Abigail had done.

David was persuaded by Abigail to spare their household. In
fact, he was so impressed with Abigail that he asked her to marry
him. Here is her response:

She bowed down with her face to the ground and said,
"Here is your maidservant, ready to serve you and wash the
feet of my master's servants" (v. 41).

Abigail was so codependent that she was not only willing to
take care of David but also his servants. Here again we see her going
beyond the call of duty to please others. By marrying David, she
may have thought her problems would be solved. But in reality she
married into another dysfunctional situation, since David acquired
many wives and had an adulterous relationship with Bathsheba.[5]

What can we learn from Abigail?

- If we don't let go, we, like Abigail, will be overly responsible
  and take the blame for our mates' actions. Many women
  tend to blame themselves for their husbands' sexual actions,
  thinking that if they had a better figure or looked more like
  some sex symbol or movie star, he wouldn't have this problem. The truth is that no one can compete with a fantasy.

- If we don't let go, we, like Abigail, will assume our self-esteem and survival are based on our performance (mobilizing food and washing David's servants' feet). Wives of sexual addicts begin to think that if only they had been willing to do more or to perform a particular way sexually, maybe these problems wouldn't have occurred.

- If we don't let go, we, like Abigail, will have family members (like her servants) always looking to us to fix every crisis. If we model the "I can fix it" behavior, that attitude will surely be passed on to the next generation (see Deut. 5:9,10).

- If we don't let go, we, like Abigail, will react to situations rather than confront the addict and allow him to receive the natural consequences of his actions and behavior.

- If we don't let go, we, like Abigail, can develop compulsive behavior. As you can see from the following list of behaviors, those married to sex addicts can become very obsessive and compulsive when they try to control by these actions:

    1. Listening in on a husband's phone calls
    2. Checking bank account statements and phone bills and reading his journal
    3. Feeling restless when he's not home—watching from the window
    4. Checking on him when he disappears at parties
    5. Asking for assurance all the time that he is not acting out
    6. Looking through his papers and mail
    7. Fearing to travel far from home because he might act out
    8. Driving home fast from work when he doesn't answer the phone
    9. Checking the computer for websites he has visited
    10. Driving by the home of the "lady friend" to see if he is there[6]

At this point you are probably saying, "If I have to let go and can't control, what am I supposed to do?"

Once women in our FWO classes begin to see how controlling they have been, the small group becomes a place of support and accountability. It is at this point that they can begin to deal with their other three realities: healthy boundaries, self-esteem and trust.

Establishing Healthy Boundaries

The tendency of most women who have lacked boundaries is to swing impulsively in the opposite direction and create too many unattainable boundaries. *Boundaries*, by Drs. Cloud and Townsend, helps us understand what boundaries are and are not:

> In short, boundaries are not walls. The Bible does not say that we are to be "walled off" from others; in fact, it says that we are to be one with them (John 17:11). We are to be in community with them. But in every community, all members have their own space and property. The important thing is that property lines are permeable enough to allow passing and strong enough to keep out danger. Often, when people are abused while growing up, they reverse the function of boundaries and keep the bad in and the good out.[7]

Revelation 3:20 shows us that Jesus respects our boundaries: "Behold, I stand at the door and knock; if anyone hears My voice and opens the door, I will come in to him, and will dine with him, and he with Me" (*NASB*). Maybe you have seen this concept illustrated where Jesus is knocking at a door that has no knob on the outside; the door can only be opened from the inside. God has given us control over our relationship with Him. We choose when to let Him in and how much we want to yield to Him. God has also designed us for relationship with others, but He desires that we have healthy boundaries in those relationships as well.

Some of the healthy boundaries for those whose husbands want to work through their issues and heal the marriage include:

1. If there has been sexual infidelity, both the husband and wife need to have an AIDS test and also be tested for STDs (Sexually Transmitted Diseases).

2. The husband needs to commit to a men's accountability group, and couple counseling needs to take place.

3. Usually a time of celibacy is recommended, which allows the couple to begin the process of focusing on the emotional issues and to begin to work through the repentance process.

4. If there has been a lifestyle of infidelity and an unwillingness to change, the wife may need to take steps to separate. *Affair of the Mind,* an excellent book by Laurie Hall, has helped many women understand the spiritual warfare involved with sexual addiction, and has also helped many determine what boundaries they need to set according to where their husbands are and the stand God is asking them to take.[8]

Part of setting boundaries is doing just the opposite of what we saw Abigail doing. We need to confront the issues head on. Oftentimes the addict is under the false impression that what he is doing isn't hurting anyone. A woman from our FWO group confronted that lie by writing a letter to God and then reading it to her husband:

Dear God,

I am experiencing the heartbreaking reality of learning that my husband is satisfying himself in a mental and physical affair with fantasy, substituting pictures for the warmth of my body and love.

I struggle so hard competing with an illusion to which I can't possibly compare, with an availability I can't duplicate, doing things I can't imagine. My helpless heart is being left out of his love life. The presence of the "other" woman has taken residence in his heart. I want my dwelling place alone to be there.

God, I so want to be the object of his desire. My heart longs to see the hunger in his smile for my lips, that twinkle in his eye anticipating my touch. I cry out to feel sexy simply because he delights in me!

Oh, Lord, cause my husband to see what You made me to be for him—a precious jewel without blemish, holding all my desire and all myself for him. Kindle his desire for Your very best!!! It's me, Lord.

Focusing on Healthy Self-Esteem

Not only are letting go and boundary issues important, but attention also needs to be focused on self-esteem issues. Sexually addictive behavior in the husband will throw the wife into such emotional turmoil that comparison and subjectivity begin to take over her thinking. This is the enemy's greatest tool to undermine God's healing process.

If I allow my husband's addiction or circumstances to define who I am, I can never climb out of the pit of comparison and discover who I *really* am. The negative self-esteem usually starts with these steps, and then progresses into a downward spiral:

1. Negative internal dialogue that distorts what we are saying to ourselves
2. Negative self-picturing that distorts our view of ourselves and others
3. Negative and exaggerated feelings about ourselves
4. Negative behavior

The negative behavior usually refers to my response to the other three steps in my personal life. But it can also be fueled by my perception that my husband's actions validate the negative thinking process I have already established. In other words, if I think my body is less than perfect, his addictive actions begin to validate that perception. The truth is that even Marilyn Monroe, with the "perfect body," could not compete with fantasies that have usually developed in the addict's mind from early teen years or even before.

The only way we can get out of this cycle of negative subjective thinking is to look to the Scriptures, which are very objective. Second Corinthians 10:5 reminds us to destroy and pull down speculations and imaginations. But when we pull down those speculations we need to replace them with the truth. That is why studying the character of who God is and His definition of who we are is a must. God has wonderfully created each one of us. As we begin to put off the old negative way of thinking by laying aside falsehood and putting on the new by speaking the truth (see Eph. 4:24-25), we find that a correct view of who we are can begin to emerge. Ephesians 6:13 commands us to put on the full armor of God. In this battle we need the helmet of salvation that guards our minds from wrong thinking, and the sword of the Spirit, which is right thinking and what God says to us through Scripture.

Here are a number of Scriptures we need to begin to rehearse as the truth of what God says about each one of us:

- I am a child of God (see Rom. 8:16).
- I am a new creation (see 2 Cor. 5:17).
- I am a partaker of His divine nature (see 2 Pet. 1:4).
- I am led by the Spirit of God (see Rom. 8:14).
- I am a daughter of God (see Rom. 8:14).
- I am getting all my needs met by Jesus (see Phil. 4:19).
- I am casting all my cares on Jesus (see 1 Pet. 5:7).
- I am strong in the Lord and in the power of His might (see Eph. 6:10).
- I am blessed coming in and blessed going out (see Deut. 28:6).

· I am above only and not beneath (see Deut. 28:13).

· I am not moved by what I see (see 2 Cor. 4:18).

These are but a few of the Scriptures that redefine our status and God's purpose.

The other effective tool in helping build a positive self-esteem is our small-group time that helps women realize they are not alone in their struggles, in what they have experienced and in what they are feeling. Small-group members remind each other of God's promise in Jeremiah 29:11, that they have a future and a hope and that God's plans for them are good and not evil. Many times it takes others to reflect back the truth when we are in difficult situations, because our hurt can often warp the mirrors we are looking through, and our realities can be skewed.

Learning to Trust

The final issue and probably the most difficult reality that women struggle with is trust. When a wife is deceived and betrayed, it is difficult to know when and what to believe, especially if the deception has been going on for years. Most addicts are masters of manipulation because they have had to keep the duplicity of their lives hidden. If they have made a commitment to Christ, they have literally compartmentalized their lives so they can carry on two lives at once, a public life and a secret life. They have been unable to surrender the darkness of their addiction to Christ's healing light. Paul warns in Ephesians 4:17-20:

> This I say therefore, and affirm together with the Lord, that you walk no longer just as the Gentiles also walk, in the futility of their mind, being darkened in their understanding, excluded from the life of God, because of the ignorance that is in them, because of the hardness of their heart; and they, having become callous, have given them-

selves over to sensuality, for the practice of every kind of impurity with greediness. But you did not learn Christ in this way (*NASB*).

There can develop an actual callousness toward God's ways and an openness to sensuality for those who allow darkness to control their minds. There is so much deception in their thinking that denial is a huge problem with deep roots. It usually takes a crisis—such as being found out, the possibility of facing criminal charges, or the possibility of losing their marriage—to wake them up to their need for help.

With these realities about the power of sexual addiction, how can we begin to trust again? Some women feel so violated they don't know if they even love their husbands anymore, let alone trust them. This is a normal response. There is a numbness that develops for her own self-protection. She doesn't want to be hurt again. Also, all the other hurts that have been ignored or that he has rationalized over the years now come to the surface.

For trust and reconciliation to take place, the husband has to be willing to meet the emotional needs of his wife, which in many cases have been ignored over the years because of his need to feed his own addiction. Ephesians 5:25-26 says, "Husbands, love your wives, just as Christ also loved the church and gave Himself up for her, that He might sanctify her, having cleansed her by the washing of water with the word" (*NASB*). This passage proclaims that the husband will literally need to lay his life down for his wife so that she can be cleansed. The wife defines what that is to look like. Only when a husband begins to care for his wife more than himself is there the possibility for trust to be restored. That trust goes through three stages:

1. Sincerity
2. Ability
3. Durability

For trust to begin to be established, the wife has to see a *sincere* heart. There has to be a willingness on the husband's part to be in an accountability group, to work on his issues and to seek couple counseling.

For trust to grow, the wife needs to see that he has the *ability* to follow through on what he has committed to do to meet her emotional needs and to seek the help he needs.

Finally, the wife needs to know that he is not doing these things just to placate her now, and then turn around and later go back to his old habit patterns. There has to be a *durability* to this commitment, and only time will show whether it is genuine. Dr. Patrick Carnes has followed sexual addicts through their healing process and has found it takes an average of about five years for real healing to take place. And that is when both the husband and wife are aggressively working toward that healing. So it may take awhile before in-depth trust and oneness in the relationship can be established.

As I mentioned at the beginning of this chapter, I have counseled numerous women who struggle with their husbands' betrayal. The sad reality is that not all of them make it through the healing process. Some have been afraid to confront for fear of losing their marriages. They remain in the wilderness of denial and choose to live with their husbands' duplicity. Others used their husbands' infidelity to justify their own infidelities, and wander in the wilderness away from God toward their own lusts. Others immediately divorced and remarried, only to find themselves facing a variation of the wilderness they were in before, because they never allowed time for personal healing and change.

Dealing with a husband's sexual addiction is one of the most difficult battles we ever fight in our lifetime. Like many women, we will feel like quitting many times before we work through the process. But those who are unwilling to give up, who are willing to face and fight the giants with Christ's help, will enter the Promised Land of healing and wholeness. We have seen many couples go through our FMO and FWO classes who are winning the battle and are now enjoying more intimacy and healing then they ever thought possible.

As we finish our talk on "His Realities and Her Realities," we must not forget to include the most important reality, which is God's reality for each of us, especially as expressed in Joshua 1:5. Joshua was about to enter the Promised Land when God reminded him: "Just as I have been with Moses, I will be with you; I will not fail you or forsake you" (*NASB*). I can guarantee you that just as God has been with couples at East Hill who have determined to do whatever it takes to reach the Promised Land of freedom from bondage, God will be with you as you become honest with Him and with each other and yield to His healing process.

Notes

1. Developed by Scot Oja, director of For Men Only at East Hill Church.
2. Dr. Patrick J. Carnes, *Don't Call It Love* (New York: Bantam Books, 1991), pp. 151-152.
3. C. W. Neal, *Your 30 Day Journey to Power Over Codependency* (Nashville, TN: Thomas Nelson Publishers, 1991), p. 1.
4. Earl R. Henslin, Psy.D., *The Way Out of the Wilderness* (Nashville, TN: Thomas Nelson Publishers, 1991), p. 53.
5. Ibid., p. 56.
6. Carnes, *Don't Call It Love*, pp. 152-254.
7. Dr. Henry Cloud and Dr. John Townsend, *Boundaries* (Grand Rapids, MI: Zondervan, 1992), p. 32.
8. Laurie Hall, *Affair of the Mind* (Colorado Springs, CO: Focus on the Family Publishing, 1996), n.p.

CHAPTER 17

Accept No Substitutes[1]
A Perspective by Diane Roberts

In the mood to bake my favorite cake, I opened the refrigerator only to find not a single egg in the carton. Undaunted, I remembered making an eggless cake years ago that called for vinegar and something else. I opened my cookbook to the substitution chart. Looking down the list, I spied it: "You may substitute three egg whites for two whole eggs." Great! As though I could conjure up egg whites when I was completely out of eggs.

Many of us lack essential ingredients to live life to the fullest. Some of us have become so desperate, we have been willing to substitute almost anything to find happiness and make the pain go away.

In a recent seminar where I was teaching women on sexual issues, a young woman in her early twenties pulled me aside to speak privately. She emphatically denied having any sexual problems, but in the same breath added, "But I'll do anything for love."

A UNIVERSAL NEED FOR LOVE

I have heard similar words numerous times in the counseling office from both single and married women.

All of us from cradle to grave have a built-in need for love and relationship. Many women can trace their love deficiency all the way back to childhood. When they felt deprived of love, or were in some way rejected and abandoned, their natural instinct was to try to fill that vacancy. Here is the true story of a woman I'll call Anne, who recently shared her struggles with me:

> I want to explain how the hook of love addiction came about in my life. At age seven I was told by my father that I was too old to hug or kiss him. I felt abandoned and rejected. At age ten my brother sexually abused me. It lasted for two years, and I was robbed of my childhood. In high school I became sexually promiscuous. I thought if I gave them what they wanted sexually, I would receive what I wanted emotionally. What I received was a reputation for being a slut or easy mark. I just wanted to fill the void my father and brother had created. At age 19 I married my high school sweetheart. After seven years of marriage I decided to turn to another for the emotional support that seemed to be gone from our marriage. I had an affair. Through this affair, my sexual life became perverted.
>
> In the beginning I was able to control the addiction. With each time of giving in to it, however, the hook went deeper. I felt like a toy soldier with a wind-up mechanism on its back. Whenever it was turned on, I was powerless to resist its demands.
>
> I believe God allowed me to hit bottom so I had no-where else to look but up to Him. What was bottom for me? I lost my husband and my children. I was so alone. One night I cried out to Jesus, "Please give me back my life." He said it wouldn't be easy. I decided at that point I was will-ing to try if He was. I began counseling at East Hill. Within six months God honored my prayer and my family was restored. Jesus gave me a Scripture the night I hit bottom:

"I will not forsake you nor leave you." Truly, He has been part of my life every day, encouraging, supporting, listening, and even carrying me when I thought I couldn't go on. He helps me look in the mirror and see myself through His eyes. I praise God the hook has been removed. Temptation still rears its head, but I choose not to respond.

Anne had spent her life trying to substitute various destructive ingredients to stay one step ahead of the pain. Any number of things, including sex, relationships and food, can become a means of trying to fill the black hole from past hurts.

Anne now sees herself as a woman who has chosen integrity and hope over shame and despair. No longer is she accepting hollow substitutes. How did all these changes come about?

It usually takes a crisis of experiencing the destruction and consequences of wrong choices, similar to what Anne experienced, before there is a willingness to take the appropriate steps for healing and real freedom. When our church began to deal openly with these issues without shaming people, many like Anne realized that this was a safe place to become honest with their sin and addictive behavior.

In this chapter we want to look at why women get caught up in love addiction and struggle with sexual issues. We also want to offer some practical steps for moving into freedom through Christ.

"The thief comes only to steal and kill and destroy; I have come that they may have life, and have it to the full" (John 10:10). Christ came so that we would not have to settle merely for coping or surviving. Anne tried that for years, and it didn't work. Christ came so we might conquer at every point where the enemy attacks, and that includes any addiction in all its destructive forms.

The first thing Anne had to do was to accept that she was addicted to relationships because of her neediness from childhood. This definition of love addiction helped Anne to identify the enemy she was fighting:

A person addicted to love is fully absorbed in the pursuit of love, because love is the greatest need. The desire to be loved can push women into perfectionism, sexual promiscuity and unhealthy relationships. Love is desired, demanded and pursued at all costs. The price many times turns into a compromise of moral values and devaluing of the person who pursues this addiction. Having affairs or one relationship after another to fill the emptiness can become a pattern. Fantasizing can fuel the obsession to escape from painful realities into a world where the illusion of love exists.

Ninety-nine percent of the women who have gone through our Love Addiction class have been sexually abused. Most have also come from alcoholic homes or homes that were so dysfunctional that they had many fears due to abandonment or rejection issues. Seeking love at any cost temporarily removes the pain of feeling abandoned or rejected. Childhood abandonment and rejection can mean actual physical desertion, emotional unavailability or withholding of basic human needs. Neglect is not always intentional, but still has traumatic effects on a child.

When Anne first began to face her addictive behavior and moral failure, she had no understanding of the significance of how her past abuse and feelings of abandonment affected her present choices. The hurts of the past had been buried under layers of denial. When she became a Christian, she felt that forgiveness was not an option. Anne, like many Christians, missed the fact that forgiveness is a process, and without first dealing with the impact of the hurt, we can never come to complete forgiveness.

All of us to some degree have been reared in a dysfunctional home, because we are all descendants of Adam and Eve. It was in the garden that the first denial took place. Adam and Eve took of the fruit and then Adam blamed Eve, Eve blamed the serpent, and no one wanted to take responsibility.

Most of us rarely intentionally scheme to avoid the truth, but when the pain overwhelms us, our minds rationalize in order to cope. Many times, without conscious thought, we gain skill in building walls of protection from the truth in order to shield ourselves from the pain. Mary, like Anne, lived in that denial for years:

Every holiday get-together was the same. Inevitably someone would bring up how my brother would chase me around the house with a stick in his hand yelling, "Bonsai!" Everyone would laugh, even me. It didn't bother me. Honestly, it was years ago. Just silly childhood antics. Events that happened years ago have no effect on us now, so I thought. They all laughed, just like they did when I was a little girl crying out for help. I felt like an outsider, isolated from the whole family.

We would all laugh. To some it was funny to remember a boy saying, "I can beat you up with my hands tied behind my back," then pounding his body into the little Mary crouched in a corner. What they didn't know was that when no one was around he would say, "You're fat, stupid and ugly, and no one will ever love you." Over the years I learned to laugh the loudest so no one would know how I hurt. I hid the pain from others, and from myself.

Why was I unable to tell my family how much I hurt? Why did I feel rejected when a friend didn't return my call? Why did each relationship end with my feeling abandoned? Was I such a terrible person? After giving and giving, I would be left bitterly struggling to hold on. I was always the one left with the life drained out. The hurt began to catch up with me. I just wanted the pain to stop. One day my counselor heard me say, "It doesn't matter" over a particularly hurtful situation. She quickly said, "Yes, it does matter. That person hurt you."

I cried hard over that truth. I cried because finally someone cared about my hurt. My counselor expressed God's heart to me. I now know God was there when that little Mary was being hurt and that her pain mattered to Him. Her hurt and pain still matter to Him. As I get to know that little girl, I can no longer deny her pain. I can admit now that it hurt when my brother was mean to me, and it hurt when they all laughed.

At some point, for denial to end, there has to be more than an intellectual acknowledgment. Real healing as we see in Mary's life began to come when denial began to be conquered and when she allowed her feelings to surface. There needs to be a grieving process that includes feeling the pain of the hurt and anger.

You may right now be saying to yourself, *Why bring up the past? It is over and done with; let's get on with life.* I think figure 9 (a cartoon from Mother Goose & Grimm) sums up what takes place when we have that attitude. Carrying around the burden of the past really slows us down. We may try to run from it, but every time we turn around, it's there, staring us in the face.

© Grimmy, Inc. King Features Syndicate. Reprinted with permission.

FIGURE 9

Hurts from the past are like infected wounds that cannot heal until they are lanced. The infection has to be cleansed before healing can take place. This is the way I illustrate the process in my counseling office.

Picture yourself in a chair with rollers as in figure 10. Next, picture all your hurts as books stacked under the chair. Those books will stay put as long as you don't move. But as soon as you begin to reach for something and move the chair, all the books fall out. Our hurts are like that. We push them way down, out of the way, but then something happens. We move and react (maybe with a burst of unwarranted anger), and suddenly we can't move because the stack tumbles. We quickly regroup all those hurts, shove them down again, only to watch helplessly as the stack topples the next time. God wants us to take each "book" out from under the chair and deal with it. Then He helps us place it on our personal library shelf as a point of reference.

Many times we ask God to help us forget the pain, but God will not violate us by taking out our brains and giving us new ones. We would become robots if He operated like that. When God heals us,

FIGURE 10

we will still have our past memories, just as Jesus had His scars even after the resurrection. If we yield our hurts to Him and allow Him to help us work though them, He will give us a new perspective. In fact, those very hurts can be used to help others heal, because no longer are they deeply buried and festering. They are now at our fingertips, accessible when we need the reference.

One of the reasons Anne was reluctant to deal with her hurts from childhood is that she remembered how impossible they were to deal with then. But she was looking at the situation from a child's perspective rather than an adult's. Remember, we are adults now. First Corinthians says that when we were children, we thought and reasoned as children. But God wants to help us put childish reasoning away (see 13:11). With a new adult perspective and Christ's help, Anne can now say, "I no longer have to run from the pain."

DEALING WITH DENIAL

Peter, as we saw earlier in the book, is a classic example of someone who ran from his pain before Jesus helped him deal with denial. We, as Peter, often have no idea what lies in our hearts. God loves us enough to help us not only uncover those hidden areas but also to discover His love and healing grace. And, like Peter, to be fully released into what God has called us to, we need to deal squarely with our past. God knows we cannot be fully effective if we continue to be like "Grimm" and try to fulfill our calling while dragging the past along behind us.

Not only is denial a means of keeping the pain of the past hidden, it also becomes a coping mechanism that adults use to avoid dealing with their addictions. Anne made all kinds of excuses to herself to rationalize her involvement in the affair, one of the most destructive being that her emotional void had temporarily been met through someone other than her mate. The guilt, shame and possibility of losing her family helped her break through the rationalization and denial.

In the story of David and Bathsheba, which we also saw earlier in the book, David is always the person we focus on. But let's think about what might have been happening with Bathsheba. She too is responsible for the sin.

Having an authority figure initiating the affair must have put Bathsheba in a compromising position. I have known women who felt their jobs were on the line or who have been seduced by a therapist or religious leader, and to some extent were manipulated by the power or authority that individual had over them. That could have been the case with Bathsheba. However, a person who uses his power to seduce someone usually senses a need and vulnerability in his victim and feeds off those susceptibilities and hurts.

Was Bathsheba entirely innocent? Was she not aware that the king's roof (see 2 Sam. 11:2) overlooked her bathing area? Bathsheba may have been very lonely. We know her husband, Uriah, was a military man who put his loyalties to God, king and fellow warriors above the needs of his wife. When David tried to cover his sin by having Uriah sleep with his wife, this was Uriah's response: "The ark and Israel and Judah are staying in tents, and my master Joab and my lord's men are camped in the open fields. How could I go to my house to eat and drink and lie with my wife? As surely as you live, I will not do such a thing!" (see v. 11). Uriah was a man of integrity, but in Bathsheba's loneliness this kind of loyalty may have made her feel he was not sensitive to her needs. She may have felt rejected, and David's interest in her may have caused her to rationalize and compromise her values. Some of that rationalization may have sounded like this:

- My husband always puts his work before my needs.

- He never cares about my feelings; why should I care about how he feels?

- He's gone more than he's here; I need to find some way to fill this emptiness.

Loneliness and the need for love can lead us to rationalize and even trick ourselves into thinking we aren't really doing anything worse than what someone or something has done to us. When conscious or unconscious denial continues over a sustained period, delusions follow, and we begin to lose someone very close to us—ourselves. We lose sight of the great price we pay for this type of decision:

- A broken marriage commitment
- A broken relationship with God
- A compromise of our values

In Bathsheba's case, the loss was even greater:

- The death of her husband
- The death of her child

Denial tricks us into practicing deception to deal with the pain. This deception will travel right through a family system. Not only are there immediate consequences, but we see King Solomon, David and Bathsheba's son, who started out so wise, end up acting like a fool. Solomon, after seeking pleasure without worrying about the consequences, wrote in Ecclesiastes 2:10-11:

> And all that my eyes desired I did not refuse them. I did not withhold my heart from any pleasure.... Thus I considered all my activities which my hands had done...and behold all was vanity and striving after wind and there was no profit under the sun (*NASB*).

Anne could begin the healing process by admitting her struggle as David did in Psalm 32:3,5:

> When I kept silent, my bones wasted away through my groaning all day long.... Then I acknowledged my sin to

you and did not cover up my iniquity. I said, "I will confess my transgressions to the Lord"— and you forgave the guilt of my sin.

As David received forgiveness, the Lord began to instruct him:

I will instruct you and teach you in the way you should go; I will counsel you and watch over you. Do not be like the horse or the mule, which have no understanding but must be controlled by bit and bridle or they will not come to you. Many are the woes of the wicked, but the LORD'S unfailing love surrounds the man who trusts in him (Ps. 32:8-10).

FACING THE CORE ISSUE

Once we begin to see our denial and face the fear of our past, we can start to work with the core issue of addiction, which is shame. Anne for years assumed there was something wrong with her; why else would her dad no longer want hugs and kisses? The trauma of the sexual abuse by her brother also added to her feelings of shame and victimization. Although this abuse was not her fault, the lack of family support and the deep need for love led her into a lifestyle of sexual behavior that created more shame.

Anne came from a shame-based home where she had to live by the "don't feel, don't talk, don't trust" mentality. With this mentality comes the following type of thinking:

- I cannot make mistakes.
- I cannot do things right; I am failure prone.
- Performance will make me okay and acceptable; therefore, I must try harder.
- I can't rely on anyone but myself.
- I have to be in control at all times.

Anne and other women who are caught in the shame trap will have a lot of negative self-talk that has come from being or feeling devalued. Some of that self-talk may sound a lot like the following statements:

1. I was born the wrong gender. (Dad really wanted a boy and then even gave me a boy's name.)
2. I will never amount to anything; my parents say I'll end up just like...
3. I can never do anything right.
4. Physical things that I have been teased about tell me there is something wrong with me.
5. I'm stupid because my grades aren't as good as my siblings, and my parents remind me of that.
6. If I had tried harder, my parents wouldn't have gotten a divorce.
7. When things go wrong, it is my fault.
8. If I blow it, people won't accept me.
9. People will leave me because I am unlovable.
10. If people really knew about me, they would leave me.

Recently I saw a bumper sticker that read, "Question Reality." God wants us to question what we *perceive* as reality if it gives us a view of ourselves that is less than the beauty of who He created us to be.

The best way to question our reality is to begin to understand the difference between guilt and shame. Guilt declares we did something wrong and we need to repent. Because of the Cross, we can ask for forgiveness to deal with the guilt of what we have done wrong. Hebrews 9:22 says, "All things are cleansed with blood, and without shedding of blood there is no forgiveness" (*NASB*). Shame declares there is something wrong with us as people, that we are defective. The following chart delineates the differences between guilt and shame:[2]

GUILT	SHAME
1. Is about behavior (what I have done).	1. Is about me (who I am).
2. The fault is in what I did.	2. The fault is in who I am.
3. Involves a choice I made.	3. Something I had no choice about.
4. Deals with internal judgment (I have a choice to change behavior).	4. Deals with external judgments made by others (I give others power to make judgment against me).
5. Is proportionate to the act.	5. Is disproportionate to the act.
6. Focuses on specifics: "You told a lie."	6. Focuses on personhood: "You're a liar."

How do we get rid of shame in our lives? We have to receive the truth from God's Word and allow Him to reprogram our minds. Romans 10:11 says, "Anyone who trusts in him will never be put to shame."

During Christ's time, crucifixion was the most shameful means to punish a criminal. It was an open display intended to ridicule, disgrace and dishonor. Christ hung naked and was openly shamed by many. The soldiers and others mocked Him, demanding that He save Himself if He was the Christ. Yet, in Hebrews 12:2, Scripture describes Jesus as the One "who for the joy set before him endured the cross, scorning its shame." Other translations say He despised the shame. In other words, He refused to accept that shame. He refused to allow others to define who He was. Only His Heavenly Father who said, "This is my Son, whom I love; with him I am well pleased" (Matt. 3:17), could accurately define Christ. For real healing to come, we have to despise the shame and refuse to carry it. We also have to hear what Father God says and accept that as our new reality.

Jesus did just that for the woman at the well (see John 4). The Samaritan woman was caught in the grip of a sinful lifestyle, having had five husbands and now living with a man that wasn't her husband. Jesus neither shamed her nor condemned her. Instead, He offered her rivers of living water. He also gave her a new perspective when she expressed her concern about which mountain was the correct place to worship:

> Woman, believe Me, an hour is coming when neither in this mountain, nor in Jerusalem, shall you worship the Father.... But an hour is coming, and now is, when the true worshipers shall worship the Father in spirit and truth (vv. 21,23, *NASB*).

Jesus was offering this woman a new way to experience God—not on a mountain, but inside her very being. Stephen Covey, in his book *The 7 Habits of Highly Effective People*, helps us understand what Jesus was up to in this woman's life. He talks about how our present thinking, which contains perceptions, assumptions or a frame of reference, is known as a paradigm. He further explains that paradigms are life maps; we use them for direction in our lives. The map itself is not the territory; it's a picture of our understanding of the territory.

If we have the wrong map of the territory (such as an addiction with all its shame messages), we will be lost. For instance, if I have a map of Portland but am trying to find my way around Los Angeles, no matter how hard I try, it is not going to work. I could change my behavior and look for my destination faster or slower and still not get there. I could change my attitude and try to be more positive and have more patience and pray more and still not get there. Covey goes on to say that there needs to be a paradigm shift. We essentially need a new map. Once we have the correct map, diligence in our behavior and attitude become important in finding our destination.

Jesus was communicating to the woman at the well that she had the wrong map. Rather than going to a place of holiness (a certain mountain for worship), God wanted to make her life into a temple of holiness where the Holy Spirit dwells. As she chose to yield to the Holy Spirit, He could lead her into all truth.

Anne had to make a choice to change her map. She asked Jesus to show her who she really was. He then began to let her see herself in light of her destiny and the calling He has on her life. Because Anne sought help from God and others and made herself accountable to the healing process, she no longer defines herself according to her past but according to where she is going. She has learned to put off the old and put on the new (see Eph. 4:23-25). What does her new map look like? Jeremiah 29 says that we are to seek and search for God with all our hearts, and He will restore our fortunes; He will give us those things that have been taken away:

"For I know the plans I have for you," declares the LORD, "plans to prosper you and not to harm you, plans to give you hope and a future" (v. 11).

If you are struggling with some of the issues in this chapter and are willing to work through the healing process, God will be as faithful to you as He has been to Anne and to the woman at the well.

Notes

1. Diane Roberts, *Accept No Substitutes, The Journey to Healthy Love and Sexuality* (Gresham, OR: East Hill Church, 1995), n.p.
2. Merie A. Forson and Marilyn J. Mason, *Facing Shame* (New York: W. W. Norton & Co., 1986), pp. 5-6.

APPENDIX **A**

Testimonies

DANE

A couple of years ago I drove past a drive-in restaurant that has been in its same location for well over 30 years. For whatever reason, I hadn't driven by there for a while, or maybe just hadn't taken notice, but on this day I did. Immediately there was an ache in my gut. No, I never had bad food from there. Actually I remember a rather tasty hamburger and milkshake combo. Unfortunately, the painful memory of this restaurant was that it became a substitute for meals at home when my father's drinking got out of hand.

Dinnertime became particularly painful as I approached my teen years. If Dad wasn't home by dinner, we didn't know when he was coming home. Often, amid the chaos of our home life, my two brothers and I were taken to this drive-in for hamburgers and milkshakes. Thirty-five years later, I was getting emotionally blindsided by the pain of the past as I drove by this drive-in once again.

As a 12- or 13-year-old, I wasn't telling myself I needed something to dull the pain of a family affected by alcoholism; but, like many boys of that age, I stumbled onto something that turned out to be an excellent analgesic. It's called masturbation, and I liked it—a lot! As my involvement with masturbation progressed, it seemed to me that I had an intense interest in sex that others my age did not. And if they did, no one was talking about it. I therefore assumed I was the only one involved in this behavior, which had now become a daily occurrence. As a result, I next discovered shame: What was wrong with me? By the time I was 14, sex and shame had melded together.

Around the age of 18, after a four-year diet of soft porn magazines, I saw my first X-rated video at an adult bookstore. What a new rush! By this time my "drug of choice" was the high from sexual arousal. In the next seven years, I put myself through college, had a number of girlfriends I was sexual with, and also returned again and again to the adult bookstores to watch videos and masturbate. No one knew, and I couldn't seem to stop.

Shame, secrecy and sexuality: I had an area of my life that was secret, and filled with shame. The shame bred more secrecy: *You can't tell anyone.* The secrecy reinforced the shame: *If anyone found out, what would they think of you?*

I decided my problem was that I needed marriage and guilt-free sex. At the age of 25 I married, and soon rededicated my life to Christ, having originally given my life to Christ when I was 16. To my amazement (and shame), my secret sexual behavior didn't subside with marriage; in fact, it escalated! With 20/20 hindsight, I now know that marriage brings conflict—the tension of two people coming together. Conflict and tension at best is uncomfortable, at other times downright painful. I had been unknowingly training myself since the age of 12 or 13 that pain was to be avoided; if it couldn't be, the solution was sex. Pornography had taught me that illicit sex was even better.

All the while, how could I ever tell anyone at church what was truly going on? Certainly my shame wouldn't let me. And then to hear from the pulpit on Sunday morning that marital conflict went as deep as fighting over who squeezed the toothpaste tube from the bottom rather than the top only reinforced my belief that something was terribly wrong with me!

I was in bondage, deeply caught in sexual addiction. For all the reasons someone might use a drug, I used sex—to numb out. I did it for the rush and sheer sensation of exhilaration it gave me, similar to cocaine or amphetamines or the pull of a fantasy world, akin to LSD or marijuana. This continued for the next 13 years of my marriage. There were prostitutes, but I renounced them. There were "massage" parlors, and I renounced them. (Or maybe they all just eventually went out of business.) There would be confession (partial) and heartfelt repentance. Yet what haunted me was a carnal appetite, fed for the last 25 years, lurking deep within me—sometimes quieted, but always restless, just the same.

At the age of 38 some critical things happened. I was in a church where I was beginning to be more open and honest, and was starting to experience some freedom. Then another opportunity for an affair presented itself. The woman lived out of town, and the day I left to see her for the first time, the Lord provided a way of escape. Two of my closest friends (both pastors) were meeting together that day, and invited me to be with them. But I chose the lady out of town—I chose not to take the Lord's way of escape.

I remember vividly the last full day I spent with my children. We went inner tubing in the snow. What sickens me is that I was heartsick that day about the adulterous affair, to the point of trying to convince myself that it was over. But instead of relishing in the delight of being with my kids, I spent my time with them obsessing on the relationship. At the end of the day, when my wife asked for a separation, rather than choosing to fight to save my marriage, I chose to leave and go to this woman's home. A divorce followed nine months later.

So there I was, 38 years old, divorced, and finally beginning to see that sex might be a problem for me. I started attending East Hill Church, where Ted Roberts is the senior pastor. Over and over I heard him speak of how committed Jesus Christ is to me and how much He loves me. I always thought Jesus was disappointed in me. I was scared. I felt like I was being asked to leave a best friend; but

Christ called me away from what I thought of as my faithful, dependable friend. What would life be like without that friend? Who would comfort me if my old friend of 25 years wasn't there? How could I ever walk away from the faithful, dependable, *destructive* relationship that I had found in my sexual addiction?

But I made the choice. I walked away—but not alone. I joined a handful of men and became part of a small group. I determined not to have a secret life. These men heard everything. Perhaps even more revealing than just admitting my behavior, I actually confessed my desires. I admitted that a part of me had an appetite for sin. As I began to practice the *discipline of transparency,* the shame and secrecy of 25 years came face-to-face with the tangible grace of God displayed in these men, and the adventure of a surrendered life began.

> That I may know Him and the power of His resurrection, and the fellowship of His sufferings, being conformed to His death (Phil. 3:10, *NKJV*).

RICHARD

I'm 52 years old and was involved in sexual, compulsive, addictive behavior for 40 years. My wife and daughter know about my sin, so the reason I can talk about it is because I no longer have a secret life. Satan no longer controls me as his puppet.

My secret started when I was eight. I was molested by a teenage boy, who introduced me to masturbation. I had my first sexual intercourse at the age of 13, and by the time I hit high school, I was involved in sexual activity on a constant basis.

After high school graduation, I entered the military and became an alcoholic. Wanting to help me find employment after I was out of the service, my parents got me a job in the pornography industry. I remember my mom in her naïveté saying that it didn't hurt anybody, and I was just on the other side of the counter taking the money. But that job showed me the magnitude of the problem: Countless men struggled just as I did.

Pornography taught me to take but never to give love. When I got married, I had no clue how to love my wife. My self-centered lifestyle soon digressed to prostitution.

I maintained my secret life for 10 years, with my wife none the wiser. Then she accepted Jesus. She wouldn't fight with me anymore. She had this peaceful smile on her face. She'd come home on Sundays and tell me all about church, and I'd tell her all about the football game. I finally figured out that if she was happy with Jesus and I was still miserable without Him, then one of us was stupid— me! My wife led me to Christ; but without someone in my life to counsel and disciple me, I soon went back to my secret obsessions.

Finally, at the height of my addiction, I asked for a divorce. My wife said, "You tell your daughter you're leaving us for another woman."

"Sure," I said. I figured it would be easy—after all, I had just told *her*. As my seven-year-old daughter and I both cried, she looked at me and said, "I know all about divorce. Lots of kids at school have two moms and two dads, but *you're my dad!*" She said it like I was some kind of god or something.

I decided to stay and try to work things out. My wife and I went through counseling, but we fought constantly, while I pretended to work on my problems. Then the counselor said to me, "If you can't make it with this woman, you can't make it with any woman." That made me mad!

But he was right. When I was involved in compulsive behavior, I couldn't stop. I didn't know how to stop! It was like I was the producer, director and star of my own self-absorbed, self-destructive disaster movie.

Five years ago, For Men Only started here at East Hill. I had been tempted more than once to give up on even trying to save my marriage, but I joined the group and stuck with it. I started to release my will, and God's grace started working in my life. I don't know where I would be now without For Men Only. I believe what impacted my struggle the most, and what I thought would be impossible to do, was to tell my wife and daughter about my sinful, secret life. Instead it has led to the greatest blessing and strengthened our family, because the truth and forgiveness has finally set us free.

My daughter is now 22. When she was 19, she came to me after the Christmas Eve service and said three words to me: "I forgive you." It had taken 12 years to release the pain I caused her. Last October 6, at exactly 8:30 P.M., my pager went off. It read: "You are a great man of character and love. Your daughter."

Healing continues with my wife, too. Recently, about four hours after a time of physical intimacy, my wife said, "Thanks for loving me." She didn't say thanks for sex; she thanked me for loving her. Once I actually told my wife how much *she* had changed. She replied, "No, you don't get it. You're the one who's changed. I just submitted to your love."

The Sexual Addiction Screening Test (SAST)

Note: With appreciation to Dr. Carnes. This is not for general use, but for clinicians, which is why the scoring is not included.

The Sexual Addiction Screening Test (SAST) is designed to assist in the assessment of sexually compulsive or addictive behavior. Developed in cooperation with hospitals, treatment programs, private therapists and community groups, the SAST provides a profile of responses that helps to discriminate between addictive and nonaddictive behavior. To complete the test, answer each question by placing a check in the appropriate yes/no column.

Yes   No

____ ____   1. Were you sexually abused as a child or adolescent?

____ ____   2. Have you subscribed to or regularly purchased sexually explicit magazines or frequently browsed the adult sites on the Internet?

____ ____   3. Did your parents have trouble with sexual behavior?

Yes   No

___ ___ 4. Do you often find yourself preoccupied with sexual thoughts?

___ ___ 5. Do you feel that your sexual behavior is not normal?

___ ___ 6. Does your spouse (or significant other[s]) ever worry or complain about your sexual behavior?

___ ___ 7. Do you have trouble stopping your sexual behavior when you know it is inappropriate?

___ ___ 8. Do you ever feel bad about your sexual behavior?

___ ___ 9. Has your sexual behavior ever created problems for you and your family?

___ ___ 10. Have you ever sought help for sexual behavior you did not like?

___ ___ 11. Have you ever worried about people finding out about your sexual activities?

___ ___ 12. Has anyone been hurt emotionally because of your sexual behavior?

___ ___ 13. Are any of your sexual activities against the law?

___ ___ 14. Have you made promises to yourself to quit some aspect of your sexual behavior?

___ ___ 15. Have you made efforts to quit a type of sexual activity and failed?

Yes No

___ ___ 16. Do you hide some of your sexual behavior from others?

___ ___ 17. Have you attempted to stop some parts of your sexual activity?

___ ___ 18. Have you ever felt degraded by your sexual behavior?

___ ___ 19. Has sex been a way for you to escape your problems?

___ ___ 20. When you have sex, do you feel depressed afterwards?

___ ___ 21. Have you felt the need to discontinue a certain form of sexual activity?

___ ___ 22. Has your sexual activity interfered with your family life?

___ ___ 23. Have you been sexual with minors?

___ ___ 24. Do you feel controlled by your sexual desire?

___ ___ 25. Do you ever think your sexual desire is stronger than you are?

Count up your "Yes" answers and record here: _____

Note

Reprinted from *Contrary to Love: Helping the Sexual Addict*, by Patrick J. Carnes, Ph.D., CompCare Publishers, 1989. All rights reserved. Used with permission.

Suggested Resources

The following publications are suggestions for your further study and growth. There is so much to learn if we are ever going to be effective as a group of believers called "the Church" in a lost and hurting world. These resources can give you tremendous insights into the depth of hurts in our world today and practical answers on how to help. (An * indicates non-Christian or secular resources.)

Arterburn, Stephen. *Addicted to Love: Recovering from Unhealthy Dependence in Romance, Relationship and Sex.* Ann Arbor, MI: Servant Publications, 1991.

Arterburn, Stephen. "Freeing the Sex Addict: The Process Requires More Than Forgiveness." *Leadership,* vol. 16, no. 3, summer 1995, pp. 72-75.

Blanchard, Gerald T. "Sexually Abusive Clergymen; Framework for Intervention and Recovery." *Pastoral Psychology,* vol. 39, no. 4, 1991, pp. 237-245.

Brock, R. T.; Lukens, H. C. Jr. "Affair Prevention in the Ministry." *Journal of Psychology and Christianity,* vol. 8, no. 4, 1989, pp. 44, 45.

*Carnes, Patrick J. *Contrary to Love.* Minneapolis, MN: CompCare, 1989.

Craddock, Jim; McCleshey, Dale W.; McGee, Robert S.; Springle, Pat. *Breaking the Cycle of Hurtful Family Experiences.* Houston, TX: Rapha Publishing, 1990.

Dalbey, Gordon. *Healing the Masculine Soul*. Dallas, TX: Word Publishers: 1988.

Davies, Bob; Renzel, Lori. *Coming Out of Homosexuality*. Downer's Grove, IL: Intervarsity Press, 1993.

*Editors. *What Everyone Needs to Know About Sex Addiction*. Minneapolis, MN: CompCare, 1987.

Kubetin, Cynthia; Mallory, James; Truitt, Jacqualine C. *Shelter From the Storm: Hope for Survivors of Sexual Abuse*. Houston, TX: Rapha Publishing, 1992.

Laazer, Mark. *Faithful and True: Sexual Integrity in a Fallen World*. Grand Rapids, MI: Zondervan, 1996.

Muck, Terry. *Sins of the Body: Ministry in a Sexual Society*. Dallas, TX: Word Publishers, 1989.

Schaumburg, Harry. *False Intimacy: Understanding the Struggle of Sexual Addictions*. Colorado Springs, CO: Navpress, 1992.

White, John. *Eros Redeemed: Breaking the Stronghold of Sexual Sin*. Downer's Grove, IL: Intervarsity Press, 1993.

For information about having Dr. Roberts
speak at your church, to share your comments or
suggestions about this book, or to sign up
for Dr. Robert's free newsletter, visit his website
at www.puredesire.org.

For other resources by
Ted Roberts, please contact:

East Hill Church
P.O. Box 650
Gresham, OR 97030-0203
Phone: (503) 661-4444
Toll Free: (800) 234-0072
www.easthill.org